12 ^{50}

W9-DHN-938

12 $\frac{50}{}$

PERGAMON CHESS OPENINGS

PLAY THE
KING'S GAMBIT

Volume 1

King's Gambit Accepted

PERGAMON CHESS OPENINGS

Executive Editor
MARTIN J. RICHARDSON
General Editor
CRAIG PRITCHETT

Other Titles in the Series

ESTRIN, Y. B. & GLASKOV, I. B.
Play the King's Gambit
Volume 1 — King's Gambit Accepted

ESTRIN, Y. B. & GLASKOV, I. B.
Play the King's Gambit
Volume 2 — King's Gambit Declined

VARNUSZ, E.
Play the Caro-Kann

PLAY THE KING'S GAMBIT

Volume 1

King's Gambit Accepted

By

Y. B. ESTRIN and I. B. GLASKOV

Translated by
KENNETH P. NEAT

PERGAMON PRESS

OXFORD · NEW YORK · TORONTO · SYDNEY · PARIS · FRANKFURT

U.K.	Pergamon Press Ltd., Headington Hill Hall, Oxford OX3 0BW, England
U.S.A.	Pergamon Press Inc., Maxwell House, Fairview Park, Elmsford, New York 10523, U.S.A.
CANADA	Pergamon Press Canada Ltd., Suite 104, 150 Consumers Rd., Willowdale, Ontario M2J 1P9, Canada
AUSTRALIA	Pergamon Press (Aust.) Pty. Ltd., P.O. Box 544, Potts Point, N.S.W. 2011, Australia
FRANCE	Pergamon Press SARL, 24 rue des Ecoles, 75240 Paris, Cedex 05, France
FEDERAL REPUBLIC OF GERMANY	Pergamon Press GmbH, 6242 Kronberg-Taunus, Hammerweg 6, Federal Republic of Germany

English translation copyright © 1982 K. P. Neat

All Rights Reserved. No part of this publication may be reproduced, stored in a retrieval system or transmitted in any form or by any means: electronic, electrostatic, magnetic tape, mechanical, photocopying, recording or otherwise, without permission in writing from the publishers.

First English edition 1982

This is a translation of the Russian book "Korolevskii Gambit" published by Fizkultura i Sport (1982).

Library of Congress Cataloging in Publication Data

Estrin, IA. (IAkov)
Play the king's gambit.
(Pergamon chess openings)
Translation of Korolevskii gambit.
Includes bibliographies and indexes.
Contents: v. 1. King's gambit accepted — v. 2. King's gambit declined.
1. Chess—Openings—Collected works.
I. Glazkov, I. B. (Igor B.) II. Title. III. Series.
GV1450.2.E8713   1982   794.1'22   81-23469

British Library Cataloguing in Publication Data

Estrin, Y.B.
Play the King's Gambit.—(Pergamon chess openings)
Vol.1: King's Gambit accepted
1. Chess—Openings
I. Title II. Glaskov, I.B. III. Korolevskii gambit. *English*
794.1'22   GV1450.2.K/
ISBN 0-08-026873-0 (Hardcover)
ISBN 0-08-026872-2 (Flexicover)

Printed in Great Britain by A. Wheaton & Co. Ltd., Exeter

Contents

Foreword

In modern-day chess an enormous rôle is played by opening information. And it has to be said that today there are more than adequate means for communicating this information. One only has to think of such publications as *Encyclopaedia of Chess Openings*, *Informator*, *The Chess Player*, *Shakhmatny Bulletin*, etc.

The enormous number of events, both large and small, taking place all over the world, provides chess enthusiasts with extensive material both for use in practice, and for independent analysis.

Chess theory literature is constantly being supplied with new monographs, articles, opening reviews, and analyses of critical positions. The Sicilian and King's Indian Defences, currently the most popular openings, have been especially deeply analysed. But nevertheless, even in these openings there is still much unexplored territory. Such is chess!

This lends added interest to the book which you now have before you. A book devoted to an opening which has not only historical, but also great instructional value.

The King's Gambit! How many odes have been composed in its honour! How many tournaments have been devoted to this splendid opening, in which the organizers have set the rigid condition that all the players should begin their games with the moves 1 e4 e5 2 f4.

Already on his second move White sacrifices a pawn, and opens up his K-side. He is prepared if necessary to allow the enemy queen into his position, just so as to open the f-file, seize the centre, and later, with a bit of luck...

What a fascinating battle develops when the gambit idea is fulfilled! The sacrifice of the bishop at f7, the rook at a1... The evocative names of Polerio, Muzio, Salvio...

Although with time it has grown slightly tarnished, even to this day the King's Gambit is surrounded by a halo of original, attractive romanticism.

This book is not only an invitation into a wonderful, if slightly forgotten world. The authors have tried to show that even today, in the age of the technological revolution, the ancient King's Gambit still has every right to exist.

It would be difficult to state that the authors' analysis is perfectly correct. In certain variations specialists and even enthusiasts will undoubtedly be able to find improvements for one side or the other. But I will venture to assert that the authors have achieved their aim, and that, with the appearance of such a monograph, the ranks of the King's Gambit's supporters will be swelled.

It should also be recalled that this opening has been successfully employed by such great players as Chigorin, Alekhine, Keres, Bronstein and Spassky.

Now the time has come to introduce the authors of this book. One of them is the well known chess theorist, World Correspondence Champion, ICCF International Grandmaster and FIDE International Master Yakov Estrin, who has always been interested in the analysis of all sorts of variations, surrounded by the halo of romanticism. Chess enthusiasts will be well acquainted with his researches in the Two Knights' Defence and the Italian Game.

But times change, and quite recently Estrin was one of the authors of a book devoted to a popular modern opening, the Grünfeld Defence.

His co-author in the present work is a lesser known player, but one who has long shown his prowess as a researcher into the unexplored — candidate master Igor Glazkov, who back in the fifties and sixties devoted to the ageing King's Gambit a number of interesting analyses. And I, an experienced practical player, am bound to say that his analyses in this monograph have made on me a great impression.

I repeat: by no means everything that is stated in this book, by no means every variation, should be taken on trust. But what is here is a wealth of ideas, and the adoption of the King's Gambit in tournaments, and a critical study of the authors' conclusions, will undoubtedly assist the development of the reader's combinational vision. And this is one of the components of practical success.

Introduction

1	e4	e5
2	f4	

Every chess opening has its own unique character and appearance, but on no opening have chess masters expressed such conflicting opinions, as on the King's Gambit.

"In general, very fine attacks result from all gambits; the chief of these is the King's Gambit, which comprises one of the most interesting sections of opening theory" (Chigorin).

"If the Spanish Game is like a Bach symphony, the King's Gambit is like dance music for a wind orchestra" (Tarrasch). Alas, Dr. Tarrasch did not live till the age of modern popular music...

"If a chess novice plays 2 f4, and knows what consequences it can lead to, this means that he is beginning to understand the game of chess" (Blackburne).

"I play the King's Gambit only when I am in a bad mood" (Rubinstein).

"This opening has practically disappeared from the practice of modern masters, which is explained mainly by the almost complete lack of literature on it. There can be no doubt that the King's Gambit will once again be taken up in serious play" (Keres).

"To play the King's Gambit means to escape from ideas of progress in chess, and to attempt, by confusing matters, to gain a superficial win for purely competitive aims".

"With its rich content of ideas, the King's Gambit has the right to aspire to join the family of modern openings, and to regain its former glory..."

These last two opinions belong to Romanovsky. The first was expressed in 1931, and the second in 1949. A very interesting change of view.

"I will venture to predict that, in the not-too-distant future, when chess players have had a surfeit of currently fashionable openings, they will return more and more often to the heritage of the old masters. But not so as to copy forgotten ideas, but with the aim of finding new positional ideas, and of instilling them with new content. The positional treatment of gambits and the old open games is a characteristic feature of the present stage of chess development. It is sufficient to recall the brilliant victories of Spassky and Bronstein in the 'grey-haired' and 'long since refuted' King's Gambit" (Petrosian).

A brief historical review

In 1559 the Spanish priest Ruy Lopez de Segura visited Rome, and defeated the best players in Italy. On returning to Madrid, he published his treatise on the game, *Libro de la Invencion Liberal y Arte del Juego del Axedrez* (1561). In it we find the first variations of the King's Gambit. The concern of future researchers did not worry Lopez, otherwise he would probably have indicated whether he had discovered this opening in Italy, or whether he had invented it himself; it is nevertheless obvious that the idea was Lopez's.

In his theoretical discussions, the first in the history of chess, Lopez drew attention to the importance of the pawn centre (pawns at e4 and d4), and, after all, it is with the aim of creating such a centre that White plays the King's Gambit, by trying to eliminate the opponent's e-pawn.

In 1574 the strongest Italian masters Leonardo and Polerio made a return visit to Madrid. They played in the purely Italian manner, aiming for the rapid development of the pieces, and were not afraid to make material sacrifices. From Polerio's manuscripts it is apparent that, although by that time the repertoire of openings had expanded considerably, the leading place, both in practice and in theoretical analyses, was occupied by the King's Gambit. This same proportion was maintained in subsequent centuries.

In the mid-18th century the strongest French player André Danican Philidor cast doubts on the brilliant Italian combinations, and put forward a new slogan: the pawn is the soul of chess. But it was by virtue of this conception that after 1 e4 e5 he himself recommended that the f-pawn be first advanced, and only then the king's knight developed.

In 1851 the first international tournament was held in London. The winner Adolf Anderssen, a mathematics teacher from Breslau, possessed an exceptional talent for combinations. The celebrated 'immortal' game Anderssen-Kieseritzky, played with the King's Gambit, for a long time became a standard for what is beautiful in chess.

The victory of the great Paul Morphy over Anderssen in 1858 did not essentially change anything, but merely consolidated the position of the romantics. Morphy's contemporaries carefully studied the great dynamism of his set-ups, and were captivated by the beauty of his wonderful combinations, especially since the King's Gambit occupied a leading place in his repertoire. The romantic trend became widespread, and began to entice many of the leading players of the world. No one could then have thought that, within a few years, gambits would be struck a crippling blow...

Early in the 1870s the Austrian maestro Wilhelm Steinitz subjected the games of his contemporaries to a mercilessly critical analysis, and made a surprising discovery: in the majority of cases the brilliant combinational attacks should have led to a directly opposite result.

As a result of this painstaking research work there was born the famous 'Steinitz theory', which sharply changed the philosophy of chess. In place of impetuous combinational play came the logical accumulation of small positional advantages, and an intensive analysis of the Queen's Gambit and the semi-open games began. In the open games the Spanish Game became a formidable weapon. In such a situation it was irrational to employ the double-edged King's Gambit, although, of course, no one had refuted it. In the Spanish Game (which, incidentally, was also first suggested by Lopez)

White, while avoiding any risks, would obtain the better chances.

From the mid-1870s, the King's Gambit gradually faded in popularity, and only Chigorin remained as a principal supporter of it until the end of his days in 1908.

But interest in the King's Gambit did not die. In 1903 a tournament was organised in Vienna where all the games began with the King's Gambit Accepted. As expected, first place in it was taken by the greatest specialist in gambit play, Chigorin.

After Chigorin's death, similar thematic gambit tournaments were held in Abbazia (1912) and in Baden-Baden (1914). In these events victory went to the brilliant master of attack Rudolf Spielmann, but only a few years passed, and under the influence of a series of crippling defeats at the hands of Tarrasch and Bogoljubow in the early 1920s, Spielmann published his well-known article 'From the sick-bed of the King's Gambit', in which, in particular, he stated the following: "God knows, I have battled honourably and have suffered for the King's Gambit over my entire chess career. I am very sad that the age of Morphy and Anderssen cannot be repeated again". It could have been thought that the King's Gambit was finished for ever.

But subsequently this romantic opening again emerged into the arena. In the 1930s the young Paul Keres began to adopt the King's Gambit, and in 1945 he was joined by the resourceful David Bronstein. In the 1960s the star of Boris Spassky appeared on the gambit horizon. Contributions to the revived opening were also made by the sparkling Mikhail Tal, and by the enigmatic Robert Fischer, and after them — by a whole group of young masters and grandmasters.

We are living in a time of unprecedented chess expansion. Every year, in different parts of the world, all kinds of international tournaments are held. Even from the numerous periodicals it is difficult to follow the appearance of all opening innovations. Over its long years of adoption, the Spanish Game has been transformed into a complete branch of chess science.

But the ancient King's Gambit has still not lost its romantic freshness, and it cannot fail to attract genuine lovers of chess! We are fully justified in speaking of a renaissance of the King's Gambit, which in our time is enjoying its second youth.

Experience with the King's Gambit over the last twenty years has shown that, if Black attempts to simplify the game in the hope of equalizing, the slight initiative remaining with White assures him of a small, but persistent advantage. Therefore, in order to achieve a fully equal game, Black is forced to go in for a sharp uncompromising struggle, leaving both sides with broad scope for creative searching.

Over the past few years, in various countries, several monographs devoted to the King's Gambit have been published. And although many variations of this ancient opening have been very deeply studied, the modern status of the King's Gambit is inadequately reflected in the new theoretical guides. They are incomplete, and do not generalize to a sufficient extent the experience of the recent events.

The present monograph, which consists of two volumes, is intended to fill this gap, and to draw new admirers to that reliable weapon of chess romantics — the King's Gambit.

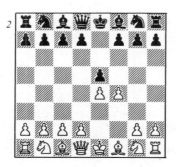

With his last move White has offered a pawn sacrifice.

In this first volume we analyse all variations involving the acceptance of this sacrifice by 2 ... exf4 — the **King's Gambit Accepted**.

In the second volume we examine all variations where Black avoids, or at least delays, the acceptance of the pawn sacrifice — the **King's Gambit Declined**.

King's Gambit Accepted

1	e4	e5
2	f4	exf4

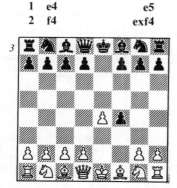

The acceptance of the pawn sacrifice is the most important reply. Subsequently Black aims either to hold on to his pawn, in the hope of parrying the attack, or else to return the material acquired, with the aim of gaining time for harmonious development.

The material on the King's Gambit Accepted, which includes references up to 1st January 1980, is divided into two main parts:

Chapters 1-5 — Rare Gambit Systems.

Chapters 6-15 — King's Knight's Gambit.

RARE GAMBIT SYSTEMS

Under this heading we include all reasonable continuations for White on his third move, with the exception of 3 Nf3, to which the second part of the book is devoted.

Speaking of the rare gambit systems as a whole, we should point out that, since they are objectively not the strongest, against these continuations it is significantly easier for Black to defend. It should be borne in mind, however, that even the slightest omission can quickly lead to serious difficulties for Black.

Here we will consider the following five sections:

Chapter 1 — 3 Qf3 (Breyer Gambit)
Chapter 2 — 3 d4 (Central Gambit)
Chapter 3 — 3 Nc3 (Mason Gambit)
Chapter 4 — 3 Be2 (Petroff Gambit)
Chapter 5 — 3 Bc4 (Bishop's Gambit)

1　Breyer Gambit

1	e4		e5
2	f4		exf4
3	Qf3		

4

An original idea of the Hungarian maestro Breyer. If Black now plays **3 ... Qh4+**, then after *4 g3 fxg3 5 hxg3 Qf6 6 Nc3! Qxf3 7 Nxf3*, despite the exchange of queens White gains perfectly adequate compensation for the pawn. For example: *7 ... Bc5 8 Nd5 Bb6 9 b3*, or *7 ... Be7 8 Nd5 Bd8 9 b3 Nf6 (if 9 ... c6, then 10 Ne3; the variation 9 ... Ne7 10 Bb2 0-0 11 Ne3! also leaves White with the initiative) 10*

Bb2 Nxd5 11 exd5 0-0 12 d6!, with a promising position for White.

Even so, the advanced position of the white queen affords Black good counter-attacking chances.

3	...		d5

Until recently it was thought that by continuing **3 ... Nc6** 4 c3 (weak is *4 Qxf4 d5 5 exd5 Nb4 6 Qe4+ Be7!*) 4 ... Nf6 5 d4 d5 6 e5 Ne4 7 Bxf4 Be7 Black gains good chances. This opinion was based on the game Spielmann-Grünfeld (Baden-Baden 1925), in which after 8 Nd2 f5 9 exf6 Nxf6 10 Bd3 0-0 Black firmly seized the initiative. White, however, could have played more strongly: 8 Bd3!, and if 8 ... f5, then 9 exf6 Nxf6 10 Ne2, with equal chances. Instead of 7 ... Be7, 7 ... f6 has also been recommended, but after the obvious reply 8 exf6! Nxf6 9 Bd3 White again achieves a perfectly acceptable position.

4	exd5		

There is nothing better. On 4 Nc3

dxe4 5 Qxe4+ there follows 5 ...
Be7!

4 ... Nf6

The usual continuation, although 4
... c6!? is also fairly strong. Since
the variations 5 d4 Nf6 6 Bxf4 Qb6,
or 6 Qxf4 Nxd5 favour Black, White
has to continue 5 dxc6 Nxc6 6 Bb5,
but here too Black has an excellent
game. For example: 6 ... Qb6! (*6 ...
Nf6 7 d4 Qb6!* is also good) 7 Nc3
Nf6 8 Nge2 Bd6 9 Bxc6+ bxc6 10
Ne4 Nxe4 11 Qxe4+ Kd8, with a
virtually irresistible attack (Issler-
Basagic, 1973).

5 Bb5+

Formerly it was thought that in this
way White could obtain slightly the
better game, but this is not so.

Other continuations also fail to
give White equality. For example:
a) 5 Nc3 Bg4 (*5 ... c6* should also be
considered) 6 Qxf4 Bd6 7 Qe3+ Be7
(*7 ... Kd7!?* is an interesting try) 8
Bc4 0-0 9 Nf3 (Planinc-Gligorić,
1968), and now by 9 ... c6! Black
could have obtained the better
game.
b) 5 Bc4 Bd6 6 Nc3 (here *6 Ne2 Bg4
7 Qb3* has also been suggested, but
after the obvious *7 ... Nh5! 8 0-0
Qh4* Black has a clear advantage) 6
... 0-0 (*6 ... c6*, which is examined
in chapter 5, also leads to an
advantage for Black) 7 Nge2 Bg4 8
Qf2 Nbd7! 9 h3 Bh5 10 d3 f3! 11
gxf3 Ne5, and Black has a clear

advantage (Ree-Gligorić, Teesside
1972).

5 ... c6

In the well known game Reti-
Rubinstein (1919) there followed 5
... Bd7 6 Nc3 Bb4 7 Nge2 0-0 8 Bxd7
Nbxd7 9 0-0 Nb6 10 Nxf4, and
White gained the advantage.

6 dxc6

Here **6 ... Nxc6** followed by 7 ...
Qb6 is good, since it is extremely
risky for White to play 7 Bxc6+
bxc6 8 Qxc6+ Bd7, when Black has
a significant lead in development.
6 ... bxc6 also deserves consideration. If then the white bishop
retreats to c4, there follows 7 ... Bg4
or 7 ... Bd6. In Dementiev-
Pugachevsky (Voronezh 1973)
White chose 7 Ne2, but after 7 ...
Qb6 8 Bc4 Bd6 9 d4 0-0 10 0-0 Bg4
Black had clearly the better chances.

Thus the manoeuvre 3 ... d5
followed by ... c6 casts doubts on
Breyer's opening idea.

2 Centre Gambit

1	e4		e5
2	f4		exf4
3	d4		

This continuation would be fine, were it not for the strong counter-blow available to Black.

3 ... Qh4+

This is the point! Other continuations fail to cause White any difficulty, for example:

a) 3 ... **Nf6** 4 Bd3 d5 5 e5 Ne4 6 Bxf4, or

b) 3 ... **d5** 4 exd5 Nf6 (*4 ... Qh4+* leads to the main variation) 5 c4 (also possible is *5 Nc3 Bb4 6 Qe2+*, with a good game for White) 5 ... c6 6 Qb3 cxd5 7 Nc3, and according to Bilguer, in both variations White has a good game.

4 Ke2

White's king is forced to occupy a clearly unfavourable position.

The continuation recommended by Tartakover, **4 Kd2**, is weaker: 4 ... d5 5 exd5 Bd6 (on *5 ... Qg5* Tartakover recommends *6 Qf3 Nf6 7 c4! Bg4 8 Nh3 Bxh3 9 Qxh3 f3+ 10 Kc2*, with a roughly equal game) 6 Qe1+ (after *6 Qe2+ Ne7 7 c4 c5 8 Nf3 Qh6 9 dxc5 Bxc5* Black gained the advantage in Terpugov-Brazilsky, Moscow 1959) 6 ... Qxe1+ 7 Kxe1 c6, and Black is ahead in development.

According to Polerio, 400 years ago this variation of the King's Gambit was highly popular in Spain. Then White used to continue: **4 g3** fxg3 5 Kg2!!? (A jump by the king! At that time castling was not yet in existence.) 5

... Qxe4+ 6 Nf3 gxh2 7 Rxh2 d5 8 Nc3 Qf5 9 Bd3, with great complications. In our time, all this is, alas, impossible...

4 ...   d5

According to Keres, good here is **4 ... f5** 5 Nf3 Qh5 6 e5 g5 7 h4 Nc6!, with the better chances for Black. Here White should choose 6 exf5!, and if 6 ... Qxf5, then 7 Qd3, with an acceptable game.

Also favourable for White is the continuation **4 ... d6** 5 Nf3 Bg4 6 Kd3, and if 6 ... Bxf3 7 Qxf3 g5, then 8 g3 Qh6 9 gxf4 gxf4 10 Bxf4, with a clear advantage (Steinitz-N.N., 1884).

In a correspondence game Keres-Toldsepp (1932) Black tried **4 ... b6** (the variation *4 ... g5 5 Nf3 Qh5 6 h4* also cannot be recommended) 5 c4 g5 6 Nf3 Qh6, but after 7 g3 Nf6 8 Nc3 Ba6 9 Kf2 fxg3+ 10 Kg2! he came under a crushing attack, and lost.

5 Nf3

5 exd5 can lead to a repetition of moves after 5 ... Qe7+ 6 Kf2 Qh4+, but 5 ... Bg4+ 6 Nf3 leads to the main variation.

5 ...   Bg4

Black achieves nothing by 5 ... Qe7, in view of 6 e5 g5 (*6 ... f6* is well met by *7 Kf2! fxe5 8 Nxe5 Qh4+ 9 g3 fxg3+ 10 hxg3!*) 7 g3 g4 8 Nh4 f3+ 9 Kf2, and in view of the threat of 10 h3, White gains a good

position.

6 exd5   Nf6

6 ... Ne7 7 Nc3 Bxf3+ 8 Kxf3! Qh5+ is weaker, in view of 9 Kxf4! Nxd5+ 10 Nxd5 Qxd5 11 Qe2+ Kd8 12 Qe4, when White gains a slight advantage (Krause-Ritzen, Corr. 1911).

6 ... Bd6 7 c4 c5 is also insufficiently convincing, in view of 8 Nc3, for example:

a) 8 ... Nf6 9 dxc5 Bxc5 10 Kd2 Be3+ 11 Kc2 Bf5+ 12 Bd3 Qf2+ 13 Qe2 Qxe2+ 14 Nxe2 Bxd3+ 15 Kxd3 Ng4 16 Nxf4 Bxf4 17 Re1+, with a clear advantage to White (Mason-Kurschner, Nuremberg 1882).

b) 8 ... Na6 9 Ne4 Qe7 10 Kf2! Qxe4 11 Bd3 Bxf3 (*11 ... Qxd4+ 12 Nxd4 Bxd1* is also bad, because of *13 Nb5!*) 12 Qa4+ Kf8 13 Bxe4 Bxe4, and now in a certain consultation game, by 14 Qd7! Bc7 15 dxc5 Rd8 16 Qb5 White could have gained a won position.

After 6 ... Nf6 the following position is reached.

Diagram 7

There can follow **7 Qe1** Qxe1+ (but not *7 ... Bxf3+?*, in view of *8 Kxf3+! Qxe1 9 Bb5+*) 8 Kxe1 Bxf3 9 gxf3 Nxd5 10 c4 Nb4 11 Kd1, when, according to Tartakover, White has sufficient compensation for the sacrificed pawn. However, by playing 10 ... Ne3! (instead of *10 ... Nb4*) Black gains the advantage.

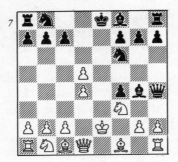

3 Mason Gambit

1	e4	e5
2	f4	exf4
3	Nc3	

This interesting continuation first occcured in the game Mason-Rosenthal (Paris 1878). the idea of it is basically similar to that of the Steinitz Gambit: 3 ... Nc6 4 d4 Qh4+ 5 Ke2, which is examined in Volume II. The temptation to try to exploit immediately the advanced position of the white king is very great, and incautious play can lead Black into great difficulties. However, by playing sufficiently carefully, Black has every hope of achieving an equal game.

3	...	Qh4+

3 ... Nc6 leads by transposition to positions examined in Volume II.

4	Ke2	

see diagram 8

4	...	d5!

Only after this energetic counter-blow can Black hope for success.

Other continuations afford White good chances:

a) 4 ... Ne7 (*4 ... Qe7* is well answered by *5 d3*) 5 Nf3 Qh5 6 Kf2 g5 7 g4!?, with complications favourable for White (Willemson-Shanyavsky, Corr. 1932).

b) 4 ... Bb4 5 Nd5 Bd6 6 Nf3 Qg4 7 d4 Ne7 8 Nc3, and White has the better prospects. A correspondence game Keres-Toldstepp (1932) continued 8 ... b6 9 Kf2 Ng6 10 Be2 Be7 11 g3, with advantage to White. In the correspondence game Keres-Menke (1933) Black chose a different path: 8 ... c6 9 Kf2 0-0 10 e5 Bc7, but after 11 g3 he again encountered serious difficulties.

c) 4 ... d6 5 Nf3 Bg4 6 Nd5 Bxf3+ (if *6 ... Na6*, then *7 Qe1!*) 7 gxf3 Kd8 8 d3! g5 9 Bd2 Bg7 10 Be1 Qh5 11 h4 h6 12 Bh3, with a won position for White (Keres-Kunerth, Corr. 1936).

5 Nxd5   Bg4

6 Nf3   Nc6

Unfavourable for Black is **6 ... Na6**, when there can follow 7 d4 Nf6 (or *7 ... g5 8 Qe1*) 8 Nxf6+ Qxf6 9 Kf2! 0-0-0 10 e5, with advantage to White (Willemson-Eckel, Corr. 1931).

An alternative is **6 ... Bd6** 7 d4, and now:

a) 7 ... Ne7 8 Nxf4! (*E.C.O.* gives only *8 Nxe7 Qxe7*, with the better chances for Black) 8 ... Bxf3+ 9 Kxf3, and if 9 ... f5, then after 10 exf5 Nxf5 11 Bc4 Nc6 12 Qe1+ White gains an obvious advantage (Solovyev-Varezhkin, Moscow 1979).

b) 7 ... Nf6 8 Nxf6+ gxf6 9 c3, with the better chances for White (Bronstein-Alatortsev, Moscow 1945).

c) 7 ... Nc6 (this is best) 8 c3! (it is risky to play *8 e5 0-0-0! 9 Bxf4 Nge7 10 c4*, Spassky-Furman, Tallinn 1959, since by *10 ... Bb4! 11 Bg3 Qh5 12 Nxe7+ Bxe7* Black can gain a clear advantage) 8 ... 0-0-0 9 Kd3 Qh6 10 Kc2 (Keres-Menke, Corr. 1933), with a sharp and roughly

equal game.

Here two possibilities for White should be considered: **7 Nxc7+ (3.1)** and **7 c3 (3.2)**.

3.1

7 Nxc7+

In choosing this continuation, it should be borne in mind that Black can, if he wishes, force a quick draw.

7 ...   Kd8

It would be a blunder to move to the king to d7, in view of 8 Nxa8 Ne5 9 d4 Nxf3 10 gxf3 Bxf3+ 11 Kxf3 Qh5+ 12 Kf2 Qxd1 13 Bb5+, when White wins immediately.

8 Nxa8

In Lein-Terentiev (Orel 1965) White did not risk taking the rook, but chose 8 Nd5. However, after 8 ... f5! 9 e5 Nxe5 10 Nc3 Bb4 Black developed a very strong attack. The game continued 11 d4 Nxf3 12 gxf3 Bxc3 13 Bg2 Nf6 14 Kd3 Ne4! 15 Qf1 Qf6!, and Black won quickly.

8 ...   Ne5

An interesting attempt at refuting White's opening play was made in the correspondence game Jago-J.Littlewood (1964-65), which proceeded in the style of the masters of the last century: **8 ... Nd4+** 9 Kd3 Qf6 10 c3 Qa6+ 11 c4 (if *11 Kxd4, then 11 ... Qd6+ 12 Kc4 Be6+ 13 Kb5 Qa6 mate*) 11 ... Bc5! 12 b4! Nf6 13 bxc5 Nxe4! 14 Qe1 Re8 15 Qxe4! (if *15 Qh4+*, then by *15 ... g5 16 Nxg5 Nxc5+ 17 Kxd4 Qf6+ 18 Kxc5 Qe7+! 19 Kd4 Qf6+* Black forces a draw by perpetual check) 15 ... Rxe4 16 Kxe4 Nxf3 17 gxf3? Qc6+, and Black won. But by playing instead 17 Nb6!, White would have had every hope of beating off the opponent's attack.

9 h3

9 Qe1 Nxf3 10 Qxh4 Nxh4+ 11 Ke1, recommended by K.Torre, leads after 11 ... f3! 12 Kf2 Nf6 13 Kg3 Bd6+ to a decisive advantage for Black (Rosit-Neishtadt, Moscow 1952).

9 ...   Bxf3+

In another correspondence game Keres-Menke (1933) Black continued **9 ... Bh5**, and after the erroneous 10 Rg1? Qg3 he won. On the basis of this, White's opening set-up was considered refuted. However, in the resulting situation White can boldly part with his queen: 10 d4! Nxf3 11 gxf3 Bxf3+ 12 Kxf3 Qh5+ 13 Kg2 Qxd1 14 Bd3! Qh5 15 Bxf4, with quite sufficient

compensation for it (cf. Game No. 1, Jago-Thomas).

10 gxf3   Qg3

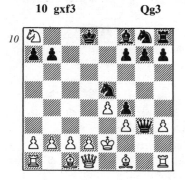

After **11 d4** Black is obliged to force a draw: 11 ... Qxf3+ 12 Ke1 Qg3+ 13 Ke2 Qf2+. If instead White plays **11 d3**, then along with the drawing variation 11 ... Qxf3+ 12 Ke1 (*12 Kd2??* loses to *12 ... Nc4+!*) 12 ... Qg3+ 13 Ke2 Qf3+, also possible is 12 ... Qxh1 13 Bxf4 Nf3+ (Kuindzhi-Gusev, Moscow 1970). In this case White should reply 14 Ke2! Bc5 15 c3 Nf6 16 Qa4, with a complicated, double-edged game. Thus the position in the diagram can be considered equal.

3.2

7 c3

After this move the advantage passes to Black. No better is **7 d4** in view of the reply 7 ... 0-0-0! (but not *7 ... f5 8 Nxc7+*, and if *8 ... Kd8*, then *9 Ne6+!*) 8 c3 f5!, and now:

In a correspondence game Keres-Kunerth (1935-36) after **9 Qd3** Nf6

10 Nxf6 gxf6 11 Bxf4 fxe4 12 Qxe4 Bh6 Black gained a won position.

If instead White chooses **9 Qe1**, then by 9 ... Qxe1+ 10 Kxe1 fxe4 11 Ng5 Rxd5 12 Nf7 Nh6 13 Nxh8 Rf5! Black again retains the advantage.

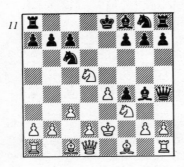

7 ...   0-0-0

Instead, Black can play 7 ... **Bd6** (*7 ... Ne5 is weak in view of 8 d4, and if 8 ... Nxf3 9 gxf3 Bxf3+ 10 Kxf3 Qh5+, then 11 Kf2 Qxd1 12 Bb5+, when White wins*) 8 d4 0-0-0 9 Kd3 etc., transposing into the double-edged position reached in the note to Black's sixth move.

Also good is 7 ... **f5**, which after 8 Qe1 Qxe1+ 9 Kxe1 0-0-0 leads to the main variation.

8 Qe1

8 d4 is also weak, in view of 8 ... f5!, as already mentioned.

8 ...   Qxe1+

Also to be considered is 8 ... **Qh6** 9 d4 f5 10 Kf2 (*weak is 10 Bxf4? g5 11 Bxc7 fxe4 12 Bxd8 Qe6!, with advantage to Black*) 10 ... g5 11 h4 fxe4 12 Qxe4 Qe6 13 Qxe6+ Bxe6 14

c4, with roughly equal chances.

9 Kxe1   f5!
10 Ng5

On **10 d3** there can follow 10 ... fxe4 11 dxe4 Nf6 12 Nxf6 gxf6 13 Bxf4 Bc5!, with an excellent position for the sacrificed pawn, while after **10 h3** fxe4 11 hxg4 Rxd5 12 Bc4 Rc5 13 Be6+ Kb8! 14 b4 exf3 15 bxc5 fxg2 16 Rg1 Bxc5 17 Rxg2 Nf6 18 g5 f3 19 Rg3 f2+ 20 Kf1 Nh5 Black has the advantage.

10 ...   fxe4
11 Nxf4

Of course, not 11 Nf7 Rxd5 12 Nxh8 Nh6, when Black has an obvious advantage.

11 ...   Bd6

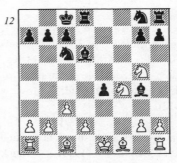

Black has a clear advantage. On **12 Be2**, for example, he continues 12 ... Bxe2 13 Nxe2 Ne5!, while in the event of **12 d4** exd3 13 Nf7 there follows 13 ... Nf6! (*but not 13 ... Re8+ 14 Kf2 Rf8, in view of 15 Nxd6+ cxd6 16 Kg3*) 14 Nxd8 Re8+!, when White is in serious difficulties (Estrin).

Game No. 1
Jago-Thomas
Correspondence 1954
**1 e4 e5 2 f4 exf4 3 Nc3 Qh4+ 4 Ke2
d5 5 Nxd5 Bg4+ 6 Nf3 Nc6 7 Nxc7+**
The soundest continuation. For 7
c3 or 7 d4, cf. the theoretical section
3.1.
7 ... Kd8 8 Nxa8 Ne5 9 h3!
Until the present game was played,
this variation was considered
favourable for Black. But Jago
succeeds in demonstrating that by
the following tactical manoeuvre
White can seize the initiative.
**9 ... Bh5 10 d4 Nxf3 11 gxf3 Bxf3+
12 Kxf3 Qh5+ 13 Kg2 Qxd1 14 Bd3**
It should be mentioned that if on
his seventh move Black had played 7
... Kd7, White would have won
immediately here by 14 Bb5+.
14 ... Qh5 15 Bxf4

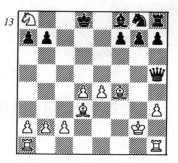

13

see diagram 13
seriously behind in development, his
king is exposed, and it is not easy
for him to find a satisfactory plan.
15 ... Ne7 16 Rhf1 f5?
As a result of Jago's manoeuvre,
White has obtained rook, bishop
and pawn for his queen, plus an
active position, which is more than
adequate compensation. Black is

Opening the game can only be
playing into the hands of White,
who already has all his forces in
play. Black should have continued
16 ... Ng6, and if 17 Bg3, then 17 ...
Nh4+! 18 Bxh4 Qxh4, exchanging
the important enemy bishop, while
after 17 Bc7+ Kc8 18 e5 Nh4+ he
gains counter-play.
**17 Rae1 Kd7 18 Rf2 fxe4 19 Rxe4
Qd5 20 Bg3 g6 21 Nc7**
White's one badly-placed piece
comes into play with gain of tempo,
and Black's position becomes hopeless. There followed:
**21 ... Qxa2 22 d5! a6 23 Rf7 Rg8 24
b3 Rg7 25 Rexe7+ Bxe7 26 Rxg7
Qa5 27 d6** and **Black resigned**, since
further loss of material is inevitable.

4 Petroff Gambit

1	e4	e5
2	f4	exf4
3	Be2	

This continuation was first suggested by the well known Russian player Petroff in the 1840s. For all its apparent inoffensiveness, it is not without a certain amount of venom.

3	...	d5

Although on general grounds this reply cannot be bad, it is not clear that it is the strongest.

3 ... Qh4+ 4 Kf1, as shown by Petroff, is favourable for White,

while 3 ... Ne7 leads after 4 Nf3 to the main variation. Apart from the text move, the following continuations have also occurred in practice:

a) 3 ... h6 4 d4 g5 5 h4 Bg7 6 g3 fxg3 7 hxg5 hxg5 8 Rxh8 Bxh8 9 Be3, and now instead of 9 ... d5!, which leads to a double-edged position, in N.Littlewood-Zwaig (Tel Aviv 1964) there followed 9 ... d6 10 Nc3 Nc6, and after 11 Qd2 g4 12 0-0-0 Bd7 13 Nd5 White gained the advantage.

b) 3 ... Be7 4 d4 d5 5 exd5 Qxd5 6 Nf3 g5 (if *6 ... Qd6*, then *7 Nc3*) 7 c4 Qd6 8 Nc3 Bf5 9 h4! with advantage to White (Heuer-Ijm, Viljandi 1972).

c) 3 ... f5. This counter-blow was recommended by Zukertort.

On 4 exf5 Black can favourably continue 4 ... Qh4+ 5 Kf1 Qf6, so White does best to reply 4 e5 d6 5 d4! dxe5 (*5 ... Qh4+ 6 Kf1 Nc6* is less promising because of *7 Nf3 Qh6 8 Nc3*) 6 dxe5 Qh4+ 7 Kf1 Bc5 8

Qe1 Qxe1+ 9 Kxe1 Be3, and, according to Keres, after 10 Nc3 White gains sufficient compensation for the pawn.

Instead of 8 Qe1, White can also consider 8 Nh3!? Be3 9 Nc3 Be6, as in Mieses-Maroczy (Vienna 1903). By continuing 10 Bxe3! fxe3 11 Bb5+ White could have gained a dangerous initiative.

4 exd5 Nf6

On 4 ... g5 (4 ... *Qxd5* is weak in view of *5 Nf3* followed by *6 Nc3*) 5 h4 Qxd5 Petroff gives the following romantic variation: 6 Nc3!? Qxg2 7 Bf3 Qg3+ 8 Kf1 gxh4 9 Ne4, with a dangerous attack for White.

If instead **4 ... Ne7**, then 5 c4 (*5 Nf3* is also good) 5 ... c6 6 d4 Ng6 7 Nc3 Bb4 8 Bf3, with a sharp game, but roughly equal chances (*E.C.O.*).

15

5 Nf3!

Undoubtedly the most promising continuation.

Tartakover-Capablanca (New York 1924) went instead 5 c4 c6 6 d4 (according to Keres, *6 Nc3! cxd5 7*

cxd5 is better) 6 ... Bb4+! 7 Kf1 cxd5 8 Bxf4 (On *8 c5* Black replies *8 ... Ne4*) 8 ... dxc4 9 Bxb8 (if *9 Bxc4*, then *9 ... 0-0*) 9 ... Nd5!, with a manifest advantage for Black.

Tartakover recommended **5 Nc3** Nxd5 6 Bf3 Be6 7 Nge2, with roughly equal chances.

It should be mentioned that, instead of 5 ... Nxd5, stronger is 5 ... Bd6! 6 d4 0-0 7 Nf3 Nbd7. After 8 0-0 a position is reached which Keres considers equal. However, in Aurbach-Duras (Abbazia 1912), by continuing 8 ... Nb6 9 Ne5 Nbxd5 10 Nxd5 Nxd5 11 Bxf4 Nxf4 12 Rxf4 Qg5 Black gained an advantage.

5 ... Be7

5 ... Bd6 6 c4 c6 7 d4 cxd5 8 c5 Bc7 9 b4 gave White the advantage in Ignatiev-Freidin (Moscow 1972). On 5 ... Nxd5 there follows 6 c4 and 7 d4, with adequate compensation for the sacrificed pawn.

6 0-0!

E.C.O. considers only **6 Nc3** Nxd5 7 Nxd5 Qxd5 8 d4 g5 9 0-0, with some compensation for the pawn. The text move is much stronger, and sets Black difficult problems. The immediate **6 c4** also deserves consideration.

6 ... 0-0
7 c4

see diagram 16

In this critical position the undermining 7 ... c6 is not dangerous for

16

White. There can follow 8 dxc6 Nxc6 9 d4 Bg4 10 d5 Bxf3 11 Bxf3 Ne5 12 Bxf4 Nxc4 13 Nc3, when White has the better game.

In Heuer-Nei (1959) Black chose **7 ... b5**, but after 8 cxb5 Nxd5 9 Nc3 Bb7 10 d4 c5 11 Nxd5 Qxd5 12 Bxf4 White again gained an advantage.

Thus the resulting position can be assessed as favourable for White.

Transpositions following

    1. e4 e5 2. f4 ef 3. Bc4 <u>Nc6</u> 4. Nf3 g5

    other 4th moves should give a good version
    of Bishops Gambit 4...g5 yields knigts Gambit

5. 0-0   (most flexible)

A1) 5 ... g4 6. d4 gf 7. Nc3   Pierce

A2) 5 ... g4 6. Nc3 gf 7. d4 Pierce

                  7. Qf3 !? $\pm$ Polerio variation
                        a) page 54 Estrin

B) 5 ... Bg7 6. d4 h6 7. c3 d6

    8. g3 Hanstein Gambit p74 Estrin

    8. h4 Greco p 69 Estrin

5 Bishop's Gambit

1 e4	e5
2 f4	exf4
3 Bc4	

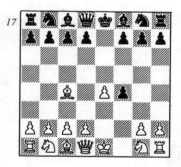

17

Over a period of several centuries the Bishop's Gambit used to delight chess enthusiasts. The first variations of it are given in the book by Ruy López, who analysed three replies: 3 ... Qh4+, 3 ... f5 and 3 ... Nf6. There have been numerous very fine games played with the Bishop's Gambit, including the 'Immortal' Game Anderssen-Kieseritzky (cf. Game No.2).

For a long time no one was able to disclose the fundamental defects of White's set-up. It was only in the middle of the last century that the Russian theorist Jaenisch hit upon the correct plan of defence — ... c7-c6 followed by the counter-blow ... d7-d5. In the 1920s this plan enabled Bogoljubov to inflict a series of crushing defeats on the knight of the King's Gambit, Rudolf Spielmann, which forced him (for a certain time!) to give up the King's Gambit altogether. Subsequently it was found that White can after all maintain the balance, but it is unlikely that he can achieve anything more.

For this reason the Bishop's Gambit has almost entirely disappeared from practice — after all, Black's defence in it is considerably simpler than in the Knight's Gambit.

From the diagram position the following main continuations will be considered:

3 ... Qh4+ (5.1), 3 ... f5(5.2), 3 ... d5(5.3) and 3 ... Nf6!(5.4).

We should also mention certain rarely used defences for Black.

3 ... g5 appears clearly unsatisfactory on account of 4 h4 h6 5 hxg5 Qxg5 6 Nf3 (Chigorin). If 3 ... b5 4 Bxb5 c6 (*4 ... Qh4+* leads to variation 5.13) then, according to Bilguer after 5 Bc4 d5 6 exd5 Qh4+ 7 Kf1 f3 8 d4 fxg2+ 9 Kxg2 Bd6 10 Nc3 Nf6 11 Qe2+ Kd8 12 Qf2 White gains the advantage.

After 3 ... Nc6, the continuation 4 Nf3! g5 leads to the Knight's Gambit, while 4 d4 Nf6 is considered in Volume II.

In the event of 3 ... Ne7, which was recommended by Steinitz, White advantageously continues 4 Nc3 (also possible is *4 Qf3 Ng6 5 d4 Qe7 6 Nc3*, Shabelsky-Antushev, 1902) 4 ... c6 5 Qe2! (*5 Qh5 Ng6 6 Nf3 Be7 7 d4* also deserves consideration, *Deutsche Schachzeitung* 1898) 5 ... Ng6, with the following possibilities:

6 Nf3 b5 7 Bb3 b4 8 Nd1 Ba6 9 d3 Bc5 10 h4 (Janowski-Steinitz, Vienna 1898), or
6 h4 h5 (if *6 ... Nxh4*, then *7 Qh5 Ng6 8 Nf3*) 7 Nf3 Be7 8 d4 d6 9 g3! Bg4 10 Bxf4 Nxf4 11 gxf4 Bxh4+ 12 Rxh4! Bxf3 13 Qh2 (Halprin-Steinitz, Vienna 1898), in both cases with a clear advantage for White.

5.1

3 ...   Qh4+
The so-called 'classical' defence.
4 Kf1

A crucial variation: White has lost the right to castle, but the black queen is badly placed. In whose favour is this position?

Practice has shown that White has good chances of gaining an advantage, while Black can only hope for equality. He now has several possibilities:
4 ... g5(5.11), 4 ... Nf6(5.12), 4 ... b5(5.13) and 4 ... d5 (5.14).

Of the other rarely-adopted defences we can mention the following:

a) 4 ... Qf6 (*4... f5* is well answered by *5 Nf3 Qh5 6 e5*) 5 Nc3 Ne7 6 d4 d6 7 Nf3 g5 8 h4 h6 9 e5 Qg7 10 hxg5 hxg5 11 Rxh8 Qxh8 12 Ne4!, with advantage to White (Jaenisch).

b) 4 ... d6 (the continuations *4 ... Nc6 5 d4! g5 6 Nc3*, and *4 ... c6 5 Qf3 g5 6 Nc3* both transpose into variation 5.11, considered below) 5 d4! Be6 (a game McDonnell-La Bourdonnais, 1837, went *5 ... Bg4 6 Qd3 Nc6*, and now, as shown by Bilguer, by *7 Bb5! Bd7 8 Nf3 Qh6 9 Nc3 g5 10 d5 Nd8 11 Bxd7+ Kxd7 12 h4 Be7 13 e5* White could have gained a clear advantage) 6 Qd3 Bxc4 (if *5 ... Nf6*, then *7 Bxe6 fxe6 8 Ng3 Qg4 9 Qb5+*) 7 Qxc4 c6 8 Qb3, and in the game Hanstein-Bilguer, 1838, White gained a clear advantage.

5.11

| 4 ... | g5 |

This move securely defends Black's extra pawn, but significantly weakens his position, which, together with the poor position of the black queen, gives White more than sufficient compensation for the sacrificed material.

5 Nc3!

The most accurate reply. Less convincing is 5 Nf3 Qh5 6 h4 Bg7! 7 d4 h6! 8 Nc3 Ne7 9 Kg1 (variation by Polerio) 9 ... Qg6 10 e5 Nc6! 11 Bd3 f5, when, according to Berger, Black maintains the balance.

Black has three main defensive possibilities: 5 ... Nc6(5.111), 5 ... Ne7(5.112) and 5 ... Bg7(5.113).

The game Lange-Dufresne (1852) went 5 ... c6 6 Qf3 (*6 g3! fxg3 7 Kg2* is also good) 6 ... d6 7 g3 Qg4 8 gxf4 gxf4 9 d4 Bh6 10 Nce2, and White gained the advantage. If **5 ... d6**, then, according to Bilguer, White should play 6 Nd5! Kd8 7 Qf3 Bg7 (the threat was *8 Qc3*) 8 g3 Bh3+ 9 Kf2, again obtaining an advantage.

5.111

| 5 ... | Nc6 |
| 6 d4 | |

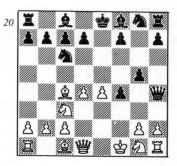

This position is rightly judged to be favourable for White. For example: **a) 6 ... d6** 7 Nf3 Qh5 (or *7 ... Qh6 8 h4*) 8 Nd5 Kd8 9 h4 f6 (if *9 ... h6*, then *10 Kf2*) 10 Kg1 Qg6 11 e5! Bg4 12 exf6 Nxf6 13 hxg5 (Cambridge-Newcastle, Corr. 1850).
b) 6 ... Nge7 7 g3! fxg3 (*7 ... Qh6* is bad because of *8 h4!*) 8 Kg2 g4 9 Qf1 Qh5 10 Nb5 (analysis by Lange).

c) 6 ... Bg7 7 Nf3 Qh5 8 Nd5! Kd8 9 Be2 Qg6 10 Nxg5! Qxg5 11 Bxf4, with a winning attack for White (I.Berger, 1874).

5.112

5 ...	Ne7
6 d4	

The usual continuation. However, back in 1766(!) Kozio pointed out that the immediate **6 g3!?** fxg3 7 Kg2 is also good.

6 ...	Bg7

A game Lange-Mayet (1852) went 6 ... f5 (*6 ... d6 can be met by 7 Nf3 and 8 h4*) 7 Nf3 Qh5 8 exf5 Nxf5 9 Ne4 Be7 10 Qe2 Kd8 11 Nfxg5, with advantage to White.

7 g3	fxg3

After 7 ... Qh6 the standard manoeuvre 8 h4 Qf6 9 hxg5 gains White the advantage.

8 Kg2	Qh6

According to Nenarokov, 8 ... g4 also favours White after 9 hxg3 Qf6 10 Be3! d6 (or *10 ... Nc6 11 Qd2*) 11 Qd2 Be6 12 Rf1 Qg6 13 Bd3.

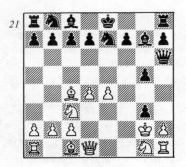

In this critical position, opening guides recommend **9 hxg3** Qg6 10 Nf3 h6 11 Nd5 (first suggested by Neumann), but after Chigorin's 11 ... Kd8 there is nothing decisive apparent for White. Consideration should therefore be given to two other possibilities:

9 h4 Qf6 (or *9 ... Qg6 10 hxg5 h6 11 Be3 followed by Qd2*) 10 Be3 h6 (*10 ... g4 or 10 ... gxh4 is well met by 11 Qd2 and 12 Rf1*) 11 hxg5 hxg5 12 Rxh8+ Bxh8 13 Qh5 Ng6 14 Rf1, with a clear advantage for White (Lange).

9 Nf3! gxh2 10 Nxg5 Rf8 11 Rxh2 Qg6 12 Kh1 h6 13 Nh3, with a very strong attack for White (Suhle-Kroneberg, Bonn 1859).

5.113

5 ...	Bg7
6 d4	

McDonnell recommended 6 g3! fxg3 7 Qf3.

6 ...	d6
7 Nf3	

According to Stanley, 7 e5!? dxe5 8 Nd5 Kd8 9 dxe5 Bd7 10 Nf3 Qh5 11 Bd2 is also good.

7 ...	Qh5
8 h4	h6

After 8 ... Bg4, according to Lange, White should continue 9 Nd5! Kd8 10 Kf2 Bxf3 11 gxf3 h6 12 hxg5 Bxd4+ 13 Qxd4 Qxh1 14 Bxf4!, with a decisive advantage.

9 e5!

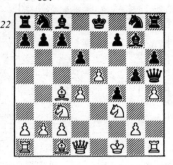

22

In this position Black appears to have no satisfactory defence against the numerous threats. For example:

a) 9 ... dxe5 (on *9 ... Qg6* Jaenisch recommends *10 Qe2*) 10 Kg1! Qg6 (or *10 ... g4 11 Nxe5 Bxe5 12 dxe5 Qxe5 13 Nd5*) 11 Nxe5 Bxe5 12 dxe5 Qb6+ 13 Kf1, when White, according to Bilguer, has a decisive advantage.

b) 9 ... g4 (if *9 ... Bg4*, then *10 Nd5 Kd8 11 Kf2*) 10 Ne1 dxe5 (or *10 ... Qf5 11 exd6 cxd6 12 Nd5*) 11 Nd5 Kd8 12 dxe5 Bd7 13 e6! fxe6 14 Nxf4, with a winning attack (Szen-Budzinsky, 1846).

It can be concluded that the old defence 4 ... g5 does not give Black equality in this variation.

5.12

| 4 ... | Nf6 |

This defence was recommended by Jaenisch, but it has not stood the test of time.

| 5 Nf3 | Qh5 |

No better is 5 ... Qh6 6 Nc3 Be7 7 d4 0-0 8 e5 Nh5, when in Malutin-Levitsky (1906) White gained a won position by the original manoeuvre 9 Rg1! g5 10 g4 fxg3 11 Nd5 Bd8 12 h4 Qc6 13 Qd3.

6 Qe1!

White gains no advantage by 6 d3 (if *6 e5*, then *6 ... Ne4*), in view of 6 ... d5! 7 exd5 Bd6, but 6 Nc3!? deserves consideration.

23

White has a clear advantage.

Bilguer gives the following variations:

a) 6 ... h6 7 d4 g5 8 Ne5.

b) 6 ... Nc6 7 e5 Ng8 8 Nc3 g5 9 Nd5 Kd8 10 d4.

c) 6 ... d6 7 e5 dxe5 8 Nxe5 Be6 9 Nxf7! Qxf7 10 Bxe6 Qe7 11 Bc8!

Thus the 4 ... Nf6 defence must be deemed inadequate for equality.

5.13

| 4 ... | b5 |
see diagram 24

In the middle of the last century the Pole Lionel Kieseritzky gained a series of spectacular victories using this interesting counter-

gambit. However, Black's counter-sacrifice also has its drawback, which is incorrectly reflected in modern opening guides.

5 Bxb5 **Nf6**

Here Black can also play differently, but without achieving any better results. For example:

a) **5 ... g5** 6 Nc3 Bb7 7 Nf3 Qh5 8 d4 Bg7 9 d5 Ne7 10 h4 h6 11 Be2 Qg6 12 Nb5 Na6 13 d6, with advantage to White (Bardeleben and Mieses).

b) **5 ... Bb7** 6 Nc3 Nf6 7 Nf3, and so on as in the main line.

c) **5 ... f5** 6 Nc3 c6 7 Ba4 fxe4 8 Nxe4 Nf6 9 Nf3 Qh6 10 Qe1 Nxe4 11 Qxe4+ Kd8 12 d3 Bd6 13 Bd2, with a clear advantage to White (Swiderski-Maroczy, Vienna 1903).

6 Nf3 **Qh6**

6 ... Qh5 7 Nc3 Bb7 is refuted by 8 Bc4! Nxe4 (or *8 ... Bb4 9 d3 Bxc3 10 bxc3 g5 11 h4*) 9 Nxe4! d5 10 Bb5+ c6 11 Nc3!

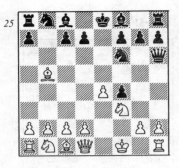

7 Nc3!

Opening guides state that at this point White should play **7 d3**. But Black can reply 7 ... Bc5! (regarding *7 ... Nh5,* cf. Game No.2), and after 8 d4 Bb6 9 Nc3 Bb7 10 Bd3 by transposition of moves we reach a position from Anderssen-Pollmacher (1852), in which, by playing 10 ... g5! 11 h4 Rg8!, Black could have gained good counter-play. On **7 Bc4** Black should again reply 7 ... Bc5 8 d4 Bb6.

But after the strong text move Black already appears to have no satisfactory continuation.

7 ... **Bb7**

Raphael-Morphy (New York 1957) went 7 ... g5 8 d4 Bg7, when White should have continued 9 h4! Nh5 10 Rh2 g4 11 Ng5 Ng3+ 12 Ke1!, with advantage.

8 d4

There can follow **8 ... Nxe4** (also inadequate is *8 ... Bb4 9 e5 Nh5 10 Kf2,* or *8 ... Be7 9 Bd3*) 9 Qe2, when both 9 ... f5 10 d5, and 9 ... Qe6 10

Nxe4 Qxe4 11 Bxf4! give White the better game.

On the basis of this the Kieseritzy Counter-Gambit must be considered insufficient for equality.

5.14

4 ...   d5!

Only in combination with this counter-blow in the centre can the early sortie of the queen to h4 be justified. Black returns his extra pawn, and aims for the rapid development of his pieces.

5 Bxd5

After 5 exd5 Black has no difficulties. For example: 5 ... Bd6 6 Nf3 Qh5 7 Nc3 Ne7 8 d4 0-0, with an equal game (Blackburne-Schlechter, Vienna 1898).

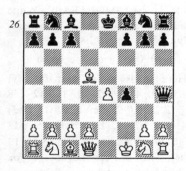

In this position Black has two possible replies: 5 ... g5 (5.141) and 5 ... Bd6 (5.142)

Less promising is 5 ... Nf6, on which Nenarokov recommended 6 Nf3 Qh5 7 Bb3, with good chances of obtaining the advantage. Also

possible is the normal 6 Nc3, after which Black has a wide choice of continuations:

a) 6 ... Bb4 7 Nf3 Qh5 8 Bb3 Nc6 9 e5 Bxc3 10 dxc3! (*E.C.O.*).

b) 6 ... Bd6 7 Nf3 Qh5 8 Bc4 (Euwe).

c) 6 ... c6 7 Bb3 Be7 8 Nf3 Qh5 9 d3 g5 10 h4.

d) 6 ... Nxd5 7 Nxd5 Bd6 8 d4! c6 (*8 ... f6 9 e5!*) 9 e5! cxd5 10 exd6, with the threat of Qf3 (A.Rabinovich).

e) 6 ... g5 7 d4 c6 8 Bb3 Bg7 9 Nf3 Qh5 10 h4 Bg4 (or *10 ... h6 11 Kg1 Qg6 12 Ne5*) 11 e5, as in Spielmann-Levenfish, Moscow 1925 (see below p.36), in all cases with the better chances for White.

5.141

5 ...   g5

In the given situation this advance is better than on the 4th move.

6 Nc3

Keres points out that **6 Qf3** Nf6 7 Qc3 Nbd7!, or **6 d4** Bg7 7 c3 Nf6! leads to a roughly equal game. White also achieves nothing by **6 Nf3** Qh5 7 h4 h6! 8 Bxf7+ Qxf7 9 Ne5 because of 9 ... Qf6 10 Qh5+ Kd8 (Chigorin-Arnous de Riviere, Paris 1883).

6 g3!, introduced into tournament practice by Chigorin, deserves serious consideration. There can follow 6 ... fxg3 (if *6 ... Qh6, then 7 d4! Nf6 8 Qf3! Nxd5 exd5 Bd6 10 c4 b6 11 h4*, with a good game for

White, Duras-Spielmann, Abbazia 1912) 7 Qf3 g2+ 8 Kxg2 Nh6 9 Qg3 Bd6 10 Qxh4 gxh4 11 d4 Rg8+ 12 Kf1 Rg6 13 e5 Be7 14 Be4! Nf5 (Chigorin-Maroczy, Vienna 1903), and now by 15 c3! White could have consolidated his advantage.

　　6 ...　　　　　　Bg7

Weak is **6 ... Ne7** 7 Nf3 Qh5 8 h4 h6, in view of 9 Bxf7+! followed by 10 Ne5 (Sanders). On Fritz's move **6 ... Nc6** there can follow 7 Nb5.

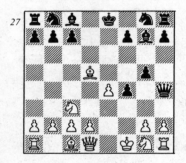

27

　　　　7 Nf3!

Opening guides assert that the move order in this variation is of no great significance. But this is not so! If in the diagram position White first plays **7 d4 Ne7**, and then 8 Nf3 Qh5 9 h4, then instead of 9 ... h6 Black can reply 9 ... Nbc6!, when the *E.C.O.* recommendation of 10 Nb5 is erroneous in view of 10 ... 0-0! 11 Nxc7 Nxd5 12 exd5 Nxd4 13 Nxa8 Bg4, with a very strong attack for Black (Glazkov). Better, instead of 10 Nb5?, is 10 Nxg5, which after

10 ... Qxd1+ 11 Nxd1 Nxd5 12 exd5 Nxd4 13 Bxf4 Nxc2 14 Rc1 Bf5 leads to an equal game (Tarrasch-Pillsbury, consultation game 1903).

　　7 ...　　　　　　Qh5
　　8 h4　　　　　　h6

Practice has shown that **8 ... c6** 9 Bc4 Bg4 10 d4 favours White. For example:
10 ... Nd7 11 Kf2 Bxf3 12 gxf3 0-0 13 hxg5! Qxg5 14 Ne2 Qe7 15 c3 Ne5 16 Qa4 Nxc4 17 Qxc4 Nf6 18 Bxf4 (Charousek-Lasker, Nuremberg 1896), or
10 ... Nf6 11 e5 Bxf3 12 Qxf3 Qxf3+ 13 gxf3 Nh5 14 Ne4 h6 15 hxg5 hxg5 16 Kf2 (Spielmann-Levenfish, Moscow 1925).

　　9 d4　　　　　　Ne7

After **9 ... c6** 10 Bc4 Bg4 11 Qd3 Nd7 12 Ne2 0-0-0 13 Qb3 White had the advantage in Maroczy-Gunsberg (Vienna 1903).

　　10 Qd3　　　　　Nbc6

Here too **10 ... c6** is unsatisfactory: 11 Bc4 Bg4 12 Ne2 Nd7 13 Kf2 Rd8 (if *13 ... 0-0-0*, then again *14 Qa3*) 14 Qa3 Nf6 15 Bd3 Bxf3 16 gxf3 Ng6 17 e5 Nxh4 18 Bf5 Nd5 19 Be4, with a clear advantage for White in Teichmann-Schlechter (Vienna 1903).

see diagram 28

The critical position of this variation. **11 Nb5** is well met by 11 ... 0-0!, and if 12 Nxc7, then 12 ... Nb4! 13 Qd2 Nxd5 14 Nxd5 Nxd5

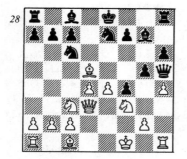

15 exd5 Re8, with a very strong attack for Black (Charousek-Chigorin, Budapest 1896).

Best for White is **11 Bxc6+!** bxc6 (or *11 ... Nxc6 12 Nb5*) 12 Na4, with a slight advantage (Teichmann-Pillsbury, Vienna 1903).

5.142

    5 ...   **Bd6!**

This move gives Black the best chances of equalizing.

    6 Nc3

The tempting 6 e5? Bxe5 7 Nf3 Qh5 8 Qe2 is incorrect because of 8 ... Nd7! 9 d4 Ne7, with advantage to Black (Duras-Leonhardt, Abbazia 1912).

    6 ...   **Ne7**

On 6 ... Nf6 Euwe recommends 7 Nf3 Qh5 8 Bc4 etc.

    7 d4   **f6!**

But not 7 ... Nxd5? 8 Nxd5, which leads to the 6 ... Nxd5 variation in section 5.14. *(d) p 35*

    8 Nf3

8 Nb5!? deserves consideration.

    8 ...   **Qh5**

    9 Bc4

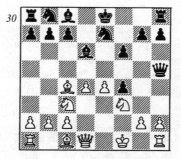

This position was reached in Szekely-Nyholm (Abbazia 1912) which continued **9 ... c6** 10 Ne2 g5 11 e5 fxe5 12 dxe5 Bc7, and Black gained the advantage. Instead of 10 Ne2 White should have played immediately 10 e5! fxe5 11 Ne4 Nf5 (or *11 ... Bc7 12 dxe5*) 12 dxe5 Bxe5 13 Qe1! Nd7 14 Bxf4!, when he gains a clear advantage (Glazkov-Malyuzhinets, Moscow 1965).

More promising for Black is **9 ... Bg4!** and then 10 ... g5, which gives him a fully equal game.

As we see, the 'classical' defence to the Bishop's Gambit consists of a large number of diverse variations, in which, with the exception of the last one, White obtains the better chances.

We will now consider continuations in which Black avoids the committing move 3 ... Qh4+, and endeavours to solve the problems of defence by other means.

5.2

     3 ...   f5

This counter-gambit, which was mentioned by Ruy Lopez, was until recently considered sufficient for complete equality. Only the latest investigations have cast doubts on this evaluation.

     4 Qe2!

Only this move gives White chances of obtaining an advantage. Other replies allow Black to obtain the better game. For example:

a) 4 Qh5+ (if *4 Bxg8*, then *4 ... Qh4+*) 4 ... g6 5 Qe2 fxe4 6 Qxe4+ Be7 7 Qd5 Nh6 8 Qe5 Rf8 9 Qg7

Bh4+ (Schulten-Suhle, Berlin 1864).

b) 4 Nc3 (or *4 e5 d5 5 exd6 Bxd6 6 Nf3 Qf6*) 4 ... Qh4+ 5 Kf1 fxe4 6 Nxe4 Be7 7 d4 Nh6 8 Nf3 Qh5 9 Bxf4 d5 10 Ng3 Qf7 11 Bb5+ c6 12 Bxh6 cxb5 (Maroczy-Marco, Vienna 1903).

     4 ...   Qh4+

The rook sacrifice **4 ... fxe4** 5 Qh5+ g6 6 Qe5+ Qe7 7 Qxh8 Nf6 (Pillsbury-Marshall, Vienna 1903) is incorrect on account of the continuation suggested by Neumann: 8 b3! d5 9 Ba3 c5 10 Bxc5 Qxc5 11 Qxf6 dxc4 12 Qxf4, with a clear advantage for White.

Also unsatisfactory is **4 ... Nf6** 5 e5 Ne4 6 Nf3 Be7 (Rosenthal-From, Paris 1867), in view of 7 d3! Bh4+ 8 Kf1.

     5 Kd1   fxe4

No better is **5 ... Qe7** (*5 ... Kd8 6 e5!* and *5 ... Nf6 6 Nf3 Qh5 7 Nc3!* are also in White's favour) 6 Nc3 c6 7 d3 fxe4 8 dxe4 d6 9 Bxf4, with a good game for White (Swiderski-Gunsberg, Vienna 1903).

     6 Qxe4+

6 Nc3 is well met by 6 ... Kd8!, when there can follow 7 Bxg8 Rxg8 8 Qxe4 g5 9 Nf3 Qh5 10 Nd5 Qg6! (Zukertort), or 7 Nxe4 c6 8 Nf3 Qe7 9 Bxg8 Rxg8 10 d3 d5 11 Bxf4 h6 (Dekker-Svitsar, 1875), in both cases with an equal game.

6 ...	Be7
7 Nf3	Qh5
8 Re1	

Also good is **8 Bxg8!**, immediately eliminating the enemy knight, when there can follow: 8 ... Rxg8 9 Nc3 Nc6 10 Nd5 (*10 Re1* leads to the main line) 10 ... Kd8 11 Nxf4 Qf7 12 Qxh7 d5 13 d3! Bf5 14 Qh5 g6 15 Ng5 Qf6 16 Qf3, with a clear advantage for White in Cordel-Neumann (Paris 1867).

8 ...	Nc6
9 Bxg8	Rxg8
10 Nc3	d6

10 ... Kd8 is also met by 11 Nd5.

11 Nd5!

Opening guides suggest only 11 d3, with an equal game. The move played is significantly stronger.

11 ...	Bf5
12 Qc4	Bxc2+
13 Ke2!	

Capturing the bishop with either queen or king is answered by 13 ... Qxd5!

The critical position of the Lopez Counter-Gambit, in which it is not easy for Black to defend against the numerous threats. In Hoffer-Grischfeld (London 1882) Black chose **13 ... Qg6**, on which White should have replied 14 Kf2!, and if 14 ... Kd7, then 15 Rxe7+!, winning. **13 ... Ne5** is also unsatisfactory, in view of 14 Qxc7 Qf7 (*14 ... Bf6 15 Kf2 Bd3 16 Qxd6*, or *14 ... Bd3+ 15 Kd1* is also inadequate) 15 Qxb7 Rd8 (or *15 ... Bd3+ 16 Kd1 Rd8 17 Nxe5*) 16 Kf1! Bd3+ 17 Kg1 Kf8 18 Nd4, with a clear advantage for White (analysis by Glazkov).

5.3

3 ...	d5

This counter-sacrifice, which first occurred in Bilguer-Bledow (1841), is sufficient to maintain the balance for Black.

4 Bxd5	Nf6

4 ... Qh4+ transposes into variation 5.14.

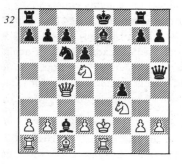

5 Nc3

Also to be considered is **5 Nf3** Nxd5 6 exd5 Qxd5 7 Nc3, with the following alternatives:

a) 7 ... **Qh5** 8 d4 (*8 Qe2+* is also good) 8 ... Bd6 9 Qe2+ Kd8 10 Ne5, with advantage to White (Leonhardt-Szekely, Abbazia 1912).

b) 7 ... **Qf5** 8 Qe2+ Be7 (*8 ... Be6 9 d4 Be7* transposes) 9 d4 c6 10 0-0 Be6 11 Ne4 h6 (on *11 ... 0-0* there follows *12 Ne5*, with the threat of g2-g4), and now, by continuing 12 Bxf4 Qxf4 13 Ne5 Qh4 14 g3 Qh3 15 Nf2 Qf5 16 Ne4, White can force a draw by repetition of moves.

c) 7 ... **Qd8** 8 0-0 Be7 9 d4 0-0 10 Bxf4 Nc6 with a roughly equal game (*E.C.O.*) Instead of 8 0-0, it would be interesting to test 8 Qe2+ Be7 9 d4 0-0 10 Bxf4, since 10 ... Bh4+ 11 Nxh4 Re8 (or *11 ... Qxh4+ 12 Qf2 Re8+ 13 Be5*) 12 Be5! Qxh4+ 13 Qf2 leaves White with the better prospects.

5 ...   Bb4

Other replies give White the better chances. For example:

a) 5 ... **Bg4** 6 Nf3 Nxd5 7 Nxd5 Bxf3 8 Qxf3 (Cordel-Leitzman, 1863).

b) 5 ... **c6** 6 Bb3 Bb4 (also inadequate is *6 ... Bg4 7 Nf3 Bd6 8 0-0 0-0 9 d4,* as in Mongredien — Blackburne, London 1862) 7 Nge2 (also good is *7 d3 Bg4 8 Nf3 0-0 9 Bxf4,* Riki-Minckwitz, 1866) 7 ... Bg4 8 0-0!, and if 8 ... Bxc3 9 bxc3 Nxe4 10 Rxf4 Qb6+ 11 Kf1 Nf6,

there can follow 12 Qe1! 0-0 13 Rxf6 Bxe2+ 14 Qxe2 gxf6 15 d3, with a very strong attack for White (A.Rabinovich).

c) 5 ... **Be7** 6 Nf3 Nxd5 7 Nxd5 g5 (if *7 ... Bh4+,* then *8 Kf1! 0-0 9 Nxf4 f5 10 e5 Be7 11 h4!,* with advantage to White) 8 d3 c6, and after 9 Nxe7 Qxe7 10 Qe2 White has the advantage (Tringov-Pedersen, Bulgaria 1965).

6 Nf3

On **6 Nge2** Black equalizes by 6 ... Bxc3! 7 bxc3 (but not *7 Nxc3 Bg4*) 7 ... Nxd5 8 exd5 Qh4+ 9 Kf1 Bg4 10 Qe1 Qxe1+ 11 Kxe1 f3 (Cordel).

Less promising for White is **6 Qf3** 0-0 7 Nge2, on which which there can follow 7 ... Re8 8 0-0 Bg4 9 Qxf4 Bxe2 10 Nxe2 Nxd5 11 exd5 Rxe2 12 Qxb4 Qg5, with the better prospects for Black (Flamberg — Spielmann, Abbazia 1912). Better, instead of 9 Qxf4, is 9 Qf2 Bxe2! 10 Nxe2, and after 10 ... Nxd5 11 exd5 Qxd5 12 Nxf4 Qd7 the two sides' chances are roughly equal.

In the event of 7 ... Bg4 (*7 ... Nbd7 8 0-0 g5* is also good) 8 Qxf4 Bxe2 9 Nxe2 Nxd5 10 exd5 Na6 Black again has an active position, with sufficient compensation for the pawn (Cherepkov-Polyak, Moscow 1949).

6 ...   Bxc3!

The only way. Less good is 6 ... c6 7 Bb3 Bxc3 8 bxc3 Nxe4, when there can follow 9 Ba3 Ng5 10 0-0 Nxf3+ 11 Qxf3, with a clear advantage to White (Anderssen-Journod, Paris 1860).

White also has the better prospects after 6 ... 0-0 7 0-0 c6 (or *7... Bxc3 8 dxc3 c6 9 Bc4 Qxd1 10 Rxd1 Nxe4 11 Bxf4* with the better game, Chigorin-Khardin, 1877) 8 Bc4 Qb6+ 9 d4 Bxc3 10 bxc3 Nxe4 11 Bxf4 (Pillsbury-Swiderski, Vienna 1903).

7 dxc3

By now continuing 7 ... c6 8 Bc4 Qxd1+ 9 Kxd1 0-0 10 Bxf4 Nxe4 Black achieves an equal game.

5.4

3 ...   Nf6!

This simple defence was known back in the time of Lopez, but it acquired genuine significance only after analyses by Jaenisch and refinements by Bogoljubov. To avoid ending up in an inferior positon, White must play very exactly.

Two main possibilities should be considered for White: **4 Qe2 (5.41)** and **4 Nc3 (5.42)**

Other continuations give White nothing. For example:

a) 4 e5 d5 5 Bb5 Ne4 6 Nf3 Bg4 7 0-0 Nc6, and Black advantageously retains his extra pawn (Anderssen-Morphy, Paris 1858).

b) 4 Qf3 Nc6 5 Qxf4 d5 6 exd5 Nxd5 7 Qe4+ Be6 8 Nc3 Nf6 9 Qe3 Ng4 10 Qe4 Qd4!

c) 4 d3 Nc6! (*4 ... d5* or *4 ... c6 5 Bxf4 d5* also gives Black a good game, but the text move is stronger) 5 Bxf4 d5 6 exd5 Nxd5 7 Bd2 (on *7 Bxd5 Qxd5 8 Nf3* there follows *8 ... Bg4 9 0-0 0-0-0* with the better prospects for Black, Alapin-Chigorin, St Petersburg 1881) 7 ... Bc5 8 Qf3 Qe7+! 9 Ne2 Nd4 10 Qe4 Nxc2+ 11 Kd1 Nde3+, with a winning position for Black (Spielmann-Chigorin, Nuremberg 1906).

5.41

4 Qe2

Lopez's move, which in recent years has again occurred in tournament practice.

4 ...   Bc5!

Only this little-known move leads to an advantage for Black.

The continuation 4 ... d5 5 exd5+ Be7 6 Nf3 has been met in recent tournaments, after which it is considered that Black gains the advantage by 6 ... 0-0! (but not *6 ... Nxd5 7 Bxd5!*, transposing into the note to White's 5th move in section 5.3) 7 0-0 c6! 8 dxc6 Nxc6 9 c3 Bd6 10 d4 Bg4, as in Gheorghiu-Portisch (Amsterdam 1969).

But in fact **4 ... d5** gives Black nothing, in view of the simple reply 5 Bxd5! Nxd5 6 exd5+ Be7, and now, along with 7 Nf3, which leads to the afore-mentioned variation from section 5.3, White can follow the recommendation in Bilguer: 7 Qf3 Bh4+ 8 g3 fxg3 9 hxg3 Bg5 10 Nc3, with roughly equal chances.

5 Nf3

Unsatisfactory is 5 e5 0-0 6 Nf3 d5 7 Bb3 Nc6 8 c3 d4!, with advantage to Black, while on 5 c3 he does best to choose 5 ... Bxg1 6 Rxg1 0-0.

5 ...   Nc6

In this position Black's chances are better. For example:

6 Nc3 0-0 7 d3 (Harrwitz-Löwenthal 1854), and now, by continuing 7 ... Nd4! 8 Nxd4 Bxd4 9 Bxf4 d5! Black would have gained the advantage.

6 c3 0-0 7 d4 (on *7 e5* Black advantageously replies *7 ... d5! 8 Bb5 d4!*) 7 ... d5! with advantage to Black (Lange-Hanneken, 1862).

5.42

4 Nc3!

This natural move is the only acceptable one.

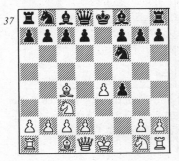

Three continuations occur in this position: **4 ... Nc6 (5.421)** 4 ... Bb4 **(5.422)** and **4 ... c6! (5.423)**.

5.421

4 ...   Nc6

According to modern assessments, this defence does not give equality.

5 Nf3   Bb4

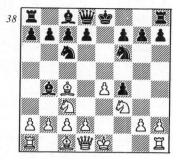

6 Nd5

This is considered the strongest, although **6 0-0** d6 7 d4 is also perfectly possible. Alapin-Chigorin (St Petersburg 1877) continued 7 ... Bg4 8 Bb5 0-0 9 Bxc6 bxc6 10 Qd3 Nh5 11 Ne2 g5 12 Qc4 Rb8!, and Black gained the advantage. But instead of 8 Bb5 White should have played 8 Kh1!, with excellent prospects (Estrin).

6 ...   0-0

The resulting position is analogous to that reached in the Schliemann Defence to the Ruy Lopez, with colours reversed and an extra tempo for White. This latter factor is clearly in his favour. Here **6 ... d6** 7 0-0 has also occurred, with the following alternatives:

a) 7 ... Bg4 (if *7 ... Ba5*, then *8 d4!*) 8 c3 Ba5 9 Qb3 Nxd5 10 Bxd5 Bb6+ 11 d4 Na5 12 Bxf7+ Kf8 13 Qd5 Qf6 14 b4!, with advantage to White (Chigorin-Zibin, corr. 1899).

b) 7 ... Nxd5 8 exd5 Ne5 9 Nxe5 dxe5 10 d4 Qe7 (after *10 ... Qd6 11 c3 Bc5 12 Qe2! 0-0 13 dxc5 Qxc5+*

14 Kh1 White remains a piece up, Charlick-Mann, USA 1881) 11 Bb5+! c6 12 dxc6 0-0 13 c4 exd4 14 a3 Bd6 15 Bxf4, with advantage to White (Chigorin-Grabbe, corr. 1899).

7 0-0   Nxe4

7 ... Nxd5 8 exd5 Ne7 9 Ng5 h6 10 Ne4 Ng6 11 c3 Ba5 12 d4 is also to White's advantage.

8 d4   Nf6

In Spielmann-Grünfeld (Innsbruck 1922) Black played **8 ... Be7** 9 Bxf4 d6 10 Qd3 Nf6 (if *10 ... Bf5*, then *11 Rfe1!*), but after 11 Ng5 g6 12 Nxe7+ Nxe7 13 Nxf7! Rxf7 14 Bxf7+ Kxf7 15 Bg5 Neg8 16 Rxf6+ Nxf6 17 Rf1 he suffered defeat.

Against Nyholm at the tournament in Abbazia (1912), Cohn chose **8 ... Ba5** 9 Bxf4 d6 10 c3 Be6? 11 Qc2 f5, but after 12 b4! he came out a piece down.

Here White has a pleasant choice. He can either play **9 Nxb4**, as in Spielmann-Bogoljubov (Triberg 1921), wich continued 9 ... Nxb4 10

Bxf4 d5 11 Bb3 Ne4 12 Nd2 Ng5 13 Qh5 Ne6 14 Be3 Nc6 15 c3 Ne7 16 g4, with a dangerous attack for White, or he can follow Bogoljubov's recommendation of **9 Ng5 Nxd5 10 Nxf7 Rxf7 11 Bxd5**, with a strong attacking position.

In Khlusevich-Verkhovtsev (Izhevsk 1973), instead of 9 ... Nxd5 Black played 9 ... h6, which was again met by the sacrifice of the knight: 10 Nxf7! Rxf7 11 Nxf6+ gxf6 12 Qh5 Qe7 13 Qg6+ Kf8 14 Bxf4, with a decisive attack for White.

From the given examples it is evident that in this variation White obtains quite sufficient compensation for the sacrificed pawn.

5.422

4 ...	Bb4
5 e5	

The position resulting after **5 Nf3 Nc6** is considered in section 5.421.

The continuation **5 Nge2 d5** (on *5 ... Nxe4* there follows *6 0-0*) 6 exd5 f3 7 gxf3 0-0 occurred in Alekhine-Levitsky (Moscow 1913), and, now, according to Alekhine, White should have continued 8 0-0 c6 9 dxc6 Nxc6 10 d4 Bh3 11 Rf2, with good chances of gaining an advantage.

5 ...	d5!
6 Bb5+	c6
7 exf6	cxb5
8 Qe2+	

Not 8 fxg7? Rg8 9 Qe2+ Be6 10 Qxb5+ Nc6 11 Qxb7, as in Castro-Karpov (Stockholm 1969). By continuing 11 ... Rc8 12 Nf3 Rxg7 13 0-0 Bh3 Black gained the advantage.

8 ...	Be6
9 Qxb5+	Nc6
10 Nf3	Bxc3

Less promising is 10 ... Qxf6 11 Qxb7 Rc8, in view of 12 Nxd5!, with advantage to White (Paulsen-Kolisch, Paris 1862).

11 bxc3!	Qc7

According to Nenarokov, 11 ... Qxf6 12 Qxb7 Rc8 13 Ba3! favours White.

12 fxg7	Rg8

In this double-edged position the chances are roughly equal. There can follow **13 c4 0-0-0 14 Bb2 d4**, with a complicated game.

5.423

4 ...	c6!

see diagram 41

It is on account of this defence, suggested by the Russian theorist

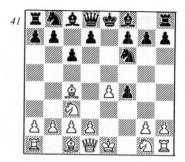

41

Jaenisch in the middle of the last century, that the Bishop's Gambit has practically disappeared from tournament practice.

Strangely enough, it is not Black, but White who must now think in terms of equalizing.

5 Bb3!

Only this move gives White a fully equal game. After other continuations Black's chances are better:

a) 5 Nf3 b5 6 Bb3 b4, followed by 7 ... Nxe4.

b) 5 Qe2 d5 (*5 ... Bb4 6 e5 0-0!* is also good) 6 exd5+ Be7 7 dxc6 Nxc6 8 Nf3 0-0 9 0-0 Bc5+ 10 Kh1 Bg4 11 d3 Re8, with a clear advantage to Black (Bogoljubov).

c) 5 Qf3 d5 6 exd5 Bd6 7 d3 (Winkelman-Horowitz, Philadelphia 1936, went *7 d4 0-0 8 Bxf4 Bg4 9 Qg3 Re8+ 10 Kf1 Bxf4 11 Qxf4 cxd5 12 Bd3 Nc6*, again with advantage to Black) 7 ... Bg4 8 Qf2 0-0 9 Bxf4 Re8+! 10 Kf1 b5! 11 Bb3 b4 12 Nce2 Nxd5 13 Bxd5 cxd5, and now both 14 Qg3 Bxe2+! 15 Nxe2 Qf6,

and 14 Bxd6 Qxd6 15 Qf4 Bxe2+ 16 Nxe2 Qc5, lead to an advantage for Black.

d) 5 d4. After 5 ... Bb4 6 e5 (Spielmann-Bogoljubov, Carlsbad 1932, went *6 Qf3 d5 7 exd5 0-0 8 Nge2 cxd5 9 Bd3 Bg4 10 Qxf4 Bxe2 11 Kxe2 Nc6 12 Be3 Re8*, with a clear advantage to Black) 6 ... Ne4 7 Qf3 (Glazkov's recommendation of *7 Kf1!? Nxc3 8 bxc3 Bxc3 9 Ba3* deserves consideration, and if *9 ... Bxa1?*, then *10 Bd6!* with a very strong attack) 7 ... d5! 8 exd6 0-0 9 Nge2 Qh4+ 10 g3 fxg3 11 hxg3 Qg4 Black retains his extra pawn with a good position (Keres).

Less promising for Black, instead of 5 ... Bb4, is 5 ... d5 6 exd5 cxd5 7 Bb5+ Nc6 8 Bxf4 Bd6 9 Nge2 0-0 10 0-0 Bg4. Lepeshkin-Yudovich (Moscow 1971) continued 11 Qd2 a6 12 Bd3 Qc7 13 Rae1, with slightly the better chances for White.

Against Nogueiras at Yurmala, 1978, Bronstein chose 11 Bg5 (instead of *11 Qd2*) 11 ... Be7 12 Ba4 Rc8 13 Kh1 Rfe8 14 Bxf6 Bxf6 15 Qd3, and after 15 ... Bh5 16 Nf4 Bg6 17 Qd1 a6 18 Ncxd5 Bxd4 19 c3 Ba7 20 Nxg6 hxg6 he offered a spectacular, but incorrect rook sacrifice — 21 Rxf7?! By continuing 21 ... Kxf7 22 Bb3 Re5! 23 Nf4+ Ke8 24 Qg4 Ne7 25 Rd1 Qxd1+! 26 Qxd1 Rd8 27 Qf1 Rd2 Black gained a clear advantage.

5 . . .	**d5**
6 exd5	**cxd5**

6 ... Nxd5 7 Nxd5 cxd5 8 d4 Qh4+
9 Kf1 Be6 10 Nf3 Qh5 11 Qe2,
according to analyses by
Tartakover, is advantageous to
White.

7 d4	**Bd6**
8 Nge2	**0-0**
9 0-0!	

White has no time to regain the
gambit pawn. On **9 Nxf4** there
follows 9 ... Re8+ 10 Nfe2 Ng4,
while after **9 Bxf4** Black continues 9
... Bxf4 10 Nxf4 Re8+ 11 Nfe2 Ng4.
In this latter variation Fisher
recommended that White should
play 12 Nxd5 Be6 13 h3 Bxd5 14
hxg4 Bxg2 15 Rh2, with
approximate equality, but instead of
13 ... Bxd5 Black should play 13 ...
Nh6!, retaining dangerous threats.

9 . . .	**g5**
10 Nxd5	**Nc6**
11 h4!	

An essential move. The quiet
continuation 11 c3 Nxd5 12 Bxd5
Ne7 13 Be4 f5 14 Bd3 b6 15 Bd2
Ng6 16 Qb3+ Kg7 lead to a
clear advantage for Black in
Spielmann-Bogoljubov (Marisch-
Ostrau 1932).

11 . . .	**h6**
12 hxg5	**hxg5**
13 Nec3!	

see diagram 42

According to Tartakover, the
chances of the two sides should be

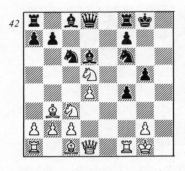

considered approximately equal.

With this we conclude our analysis
of the rare gambit systems. It should
be mentioned that the widely-held
opinion that they are ineffective is
insufficiently justified. With the
exception of, perhaps, the Breyer
Gambit, they are all perfectly
suitable for serious tournament
practice.

Game No. 2
Anderssen-Kieseritzky
London 1851

**1 e4 e5 2 f4 exf4 3 Bc4 Qh4+ 4 Kf1
b5**

The point of this move is to divert
the enemy bishop away from the
vulnerable f7 square.

5 Bxb5 Nf6

Other replies for Black are
analysed in the theoretical section
5.13.

6 Nf3 Qh6

Kieseritzky leaves h5 free for his
knight. On 6 ... Qh5 there would
have followed 7 Nc3.

7 d3

Raphael-Morphy (New York 1857) went 7 Nc3, and after 7 ... g5 8 d4 Bg7 9 e5 Nh5 10 Kg1 Bb7 Black gained the initiative.

After 7 ... Bb7 8 d4 Nxe4? 9 Qe2 f5 10 d5! White obtains a clear advantage.

7 ... Nh5

As shown in the analysis, stronger is 7 ... Bc5, which after 8 d4 Bb6 9 Nc3 Bb7 10 Bd3 g5! 11 h4 Rg8! gives Black the advantage.

8 Nh4

8 Rg1 was stronger, parrying the prosaic threat of 8 ... Ng3+, and, in turn, threatening 9 g4.

8 ... Qg5

Subsequently Kieseritzky himself showed in the magazine *La Regens* that, instead of this move, Black should have played 8 ... g6!, when after 9 g3 Be7 or 9 g4 Nf6 10 Ng2 Qh3 11 Bxf4 Nxg4 he would have gained the better chances.

But now the advantage passes to White.

9 Nf5 c6 10 g4 Nf6

Clearly, after 10 ... cxb5 11 gxh5 White has a positional advantage.

see diagram 43

11 Rg1!

Anderssen has subtly weighed up the situation. By the sacrifice of a piece he gains a clear advantage.

11 ... cxb5 12 h4 Qg6 13 h5 Qg5 14 Qf3

Now White threatens 15 Bxf4, winning the queen. In vacating a retreat for his queen, Black loses several tempi, and comes under a very strong attack.

14 ... Ng8 15 Bxf4 Qf6 16 Nc3

White has a colossal lead in development, which is more than sufficient compensation for the sacrificed piece.

16 ... Bc5

On 16 ... Bb7 White can advantageously continue either 17 Nxb5, or 17 Qg3!

17 Nd5 Qxb2 18 Bd6!

A spectacular move, allowing the opponent to capture either rook. However, 18 Be3 or 18 Re1 was good enough to win.

18 ... Bxg1

As was shown by Steinitz, 18 ... Qxa1+ 19 Ke2 Qb2! would have given Black hopes of saving the game. It would appear that Anderssen's brilliant combination was not the best continuation of the attack, but this in no way diminishes its charm.

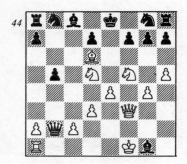

44

19 e5!!

A 'quiet' move, after which White threatens mate in two. A rook and a minor piece down,

Anderssen allows the opponent to capture a second rook with check.

19 ... Qxa1+ 20 Ke2 Na6

As shown by Falkbeer, on 20 ... Ba6 White would have won by 21 Nc7+ Kd8 22 Nxa6!

21 Nxg7+ Kd8 22 Qf6+! Nxf6 23 Be7 mate.

In the final position White is a queen, two rooks and a bishop down. Falkbeer, who in 1855 published a detailed analysis of this game in the magazine *Wiener Schachzeitung*, called it 'The Immortal Game'.

King's Knight's Gambit

1	e4	e5
2	f4	exf4
3	Nf3	

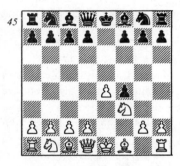

45

The King's Knight's Gambit is the main and most extensive section of the King's Gambit. When one talks of the King's Gambit, one normally has in mind the King's Knight's Gambit, with its boundless, double-edged variations.

By playing 3 Nf3, White prevents the early attack by the black queen at h4, and plans by 4 d4 to seize the centre.

The four hundred years during which the King's Gambit has been employed have revealed for Black a large number of defences, of widely differing content.

We will first consider the most natural continuation 3 ... g5, with the idea of driving away the white knight by 4 ... g4, and then launching a counter-attack with 5 ... Qh4+ (the so-called 'Classical Defence').

The Classical Defence features in Chapters 6-11, where we analyse: the Polerio Gambit, Greco-Philidor Gambit, Hanstein Gambit, Rosentreter Gambit, Allgaier Gambit and Kieseritzky Gambit.

Subsequent chapters will examine other defences for Black:

Defence).

Chapter 16 — 3 ... d5 (Modern Defence).

The following continuations have also been played:

a) 3 ... f5 4 e5!, and now:

4 ... g5 5 d4 g4 (on *5 ... d5* there can follow *6 c4! Be6 7 Nc3 Bb4 8 h4* with advantage to White, Glazkov-Yaroshevsky, Moscow 1971) 6 Bxf4! gxf3 7 Qxf3 Qh4+ 8 g3 Qg4 9 Qe3 Nc6 10 Be2 Qg6 11 Nc3 Bb4 12 d5 Nd8 13 0-0-0, and in Schlechter-Teichmann (Vienna 1903) White gained an excellent attacking position (cf. Game No.3).

4 ... d5 (*4 ... d6* is well met by *5 Qe2 dxe5 6 Nxe5 Qe7 7 d4*) 5 h4 Be7 6 d4 Nh6 7 Bxf4 Ng4 8 Nc3 0-0 9 Qd2 c6 (Gunsberg-Swiderski, Vienna 1903), and now by continuing 10 0-0-0! White could have consolidated his advantage.

b) 3 ... Ne7 4 d4 d5 (if *4 ... Ng6*, then *5 h4! Be7 6 h5*, with the better game for White) 5 Nc3 dxe4 6 Nxe4 Ng6 7 h4! Be7 (in the event of *7 ... h5 8 Bc4 Be6 9 Bxe6 fxe6 10 Qd3* White has excellent prospects) 8 h5 Nh4 9 Bxf Bg4 10 h6!, with advantage to White (Kuznetsov-Bonch-Osmolovsky, Moscow 1964).

c) 3 ... c6, when there can follow 4 Nc3 d5 5 d4 dxe4 6 Nxe4 Nf6 7 Qe2 Nxe4 8 Qxe4+ Qe7 9 Qxe7+ Bxe7 10 Bxf4, with a slight advantage to White (Bronstein-Bikhovsky, Tallinn 1965).

Game No. 3
Schlechter-Teichmann
Vienna 1903

1 e4 e5 2 f4 exf4 3 Nf3 f5

A dubious continuation, which after the following move of Alapin gives White good attacking chances.
4 e5!

The point. After 4 exf5 d5 Black gains sufficient counter-play.
4 ... g5

Regarding 4 ... d5, cf. the theoretical section.
5 d4 g4 6 Bxf4!

A perfectly correct piece sacrifice, which gives White a very strong attack.
6 ... gxf3 7 Qxf3 Qh4+ 8 g3 Qg4 9 Qe3 Nc6 10 Be2 Qg6 11 Nc3

White has a considerable lead in development, and his initiative develops unchecked.
11 ... Bb4 12 d5! Nd8 13 0-0-0 h6

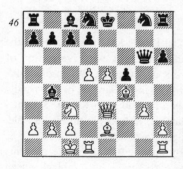

46

14 g4!

After this move all White's pieces come decisively into play.
14 ... Ne7 15 d6 Ne6

Black is forced to return the piece, but this does not get him out of his difficulties. 15 ... Nec6 would have been met by the simple 16 gxf5, with a decisive opening of files and diagonals, along which the white pieces would have approached without difficulty the enemy king caught in the centre.

16 dxe7 Bc5 17 Qg3 Bxe7 18 gxf5 Qxf5 19 Be3 Bg5 20 Nd5! Bxe3+ 21 Qxe3 Kd8

Black's position is hopeless, but he fails to display sufficient tenacity in defence. He should have played 21 ... Qg5, so as to weaken the opponent's attack by the exchange of queens. It is true that, although after 22 Qxg5 hxg5 23 Bg4 Rb8 24 Bxe6 dxe6 25 Nxc7+ Ke7 Teichmann would 'only' have been a pawn down, things would have been very difficult for him after 26 Rhg1.

22 Rhg1 Qf8 23 Rdf1 Qc5 24 Qf3 Rf8 25 Rg8! Resigns

On 25 ... Rxg8 there follows 26 Qf6+ Ke8 27 Qf7+ .

6 Polerio Gambit

1 e4	e5
2 f4	exf4
3 Nf3	g5

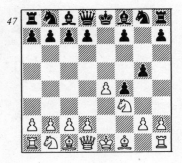

47

4 Bc4

The immediate undermining of Black's pawn chain by 4 h4 is considered in chapters 10 and 11.

4 ... g4

The alternative 4 ... Bg7 is analysed in chapters 7 and 8.

5 0-0!

The strongest continuation, incorrectly called the Muzio Gambit. This Gambit was made popular by Verdoni (around 1800) and his pupil Sarratt. Against his opponent's swift counter-attack, White answers with a piece sacrifice. But before rushing into the labyrinth of this highly interesting continuation, which was recorded in Polerio's manuscripts of more than 400 years ago, let us consider other, less energetic replies for White:

a) 5 Ne5? (the Salvio Gambit) 5 ... Qh4+ 6 Kf1 Nc6! (the most convincing refutation of White's plan; *6 ... f3 or 6 ... Nh6 is also good*).

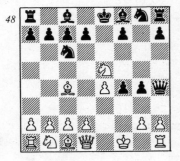

48

In this position Black has a definite advantage. For example:

7 Bxf7+ (on *7 Qxg4* there follows *7 ... Qxg4 8 Nxg4 d5 9 exd5 Nd4!*) 7 ... Ke7 8 Nxc6+ dxc6 9 Bb3 (*9 Bxg8 Rxg8 10 Qe1* is even worse, in view of *10 ... g3 11 d4 f3 12 h3 Bg4! 13 Qe3 Rg6*, and Black wins, Dublin-Cambridge, Corr. 1892) 9 ... Nf6 10 d3 Nh5 11 Qe1 g3! 12 Nd2 Bg4! 13 h3 Bh6 14 Kg1 Bg7! 15 c3 f3 16 Nxf3 Bxf3 17 gxf3 Raf8 18 Kg2 Rxf3, and Black wins (*E.C.O.*).

On **7 Nxf7** (if *7 d4*, then *7 ... Nxe5 8 dxe5 Bc5 9 Bxf7+ Kf8 10 Qe2 f3 11 gxf3 Qh3+ 12 Ke1 gxf3*, and wins, Bilguer) Black does best to continue 7 ... Bc5 (*7 ... f3, 7 ... Nh6* or *7 ... Nf6* is also good) 8 Qe1 (on *8 d4 Bxd4 9 Qe1* there follows *9 ... Qxe1+ 10 Kxe1 Ne5*) 8 ... g3! 9 Nxh8 Bf2 10 Qd1 Nf6 11 d4 d5 12 exd5 Bg4 13 Be2 Nxd4, with a winning position for Black.

b) 5 Bxf7+. This piece sacrifice was studied in detail by Lolli back in 1763. After 5 ... Kxf7 6 Ne5+ Ke8! 7 Qxg4 Nf6! 8 Qxf4 d6! 9 Nf3 (Polerio recommended *9 0-0* here, but then there follows *9 ... dxe5 10 Qxe5+ Kf7 11 Qh5+ Kg8*, when White's attack reaches an impasse) 9 ... Rg8! 10 0-0 Rg4 11 Qe3 Rxe4 Black has a winning position.

c) 5 d4. This move leads to the gambit named after the Indian Ghulam Kassim, 1826. By continuing 5 ... gxf3 6 Qxf3 d5 7 Bxd5 Nf6!

8 0-0 c6 9 Bxf7+ (or *9 Nc3 cxd5 10 exd5 Bg7*) 9 ... Kxf7 10 Qxf4 Bg7 11 e5 Rf8 12 exf6 Kg8 Black gains a decisive advantage.

d) 5 Nc3 (The MacDonnell Gambit) 5 ... gxf3 6 Qxf3 d6! 7 d4 (on *7 0-0* there follows *7 ... Be6 8 Bxe6 fxe6 9 Qh5+ Kd7 10 d4 Qe7! 11 Qb5+ Kc8 12 Bxf4 Bg7 13 Rad1 a6 14 Qb3 Nd7*, with advantage to Black) 7 ... Be6 8 Nd5 (*8 d5* is strongly met by *8 ... Qh4+!*) 8 ... c6 9 0-0 cxd5 10 exd5 Bf5 11 Bxf4 Bg6 12 Bb5+ Nd7 13 Rael+ Be7 14 Bxd6.

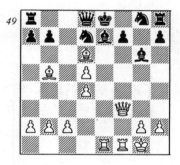

This position was reached in Maroczy-Chigorin (Vienna 1903), in which Black replied **14 ... Kf8**, but after 15 Rxe7! Nxe7 16 Re1 Kg7 17 Bxe7 found himself in a lost position. Much stronger is **14 ... Qb6!** 15 Qa3 (on *15 Rxe7+ Nxe7 16 Qf6* there follows *16 ... 0-0-0!*) 15 ... Qxd4+ 16 Rf2 Be4 17 Bxe7 Nxe7 18 d6 Rg8 19 Rxe4 Qxe4 20 Re2 Qxe2 21 Bxe2 Nc6, with advantage to Black (Barth-Lentz, corr. 1913).

The strongest move **5 0-0!**, which we now consider. gives White sufficient of an attack.

5 ...   gxf3

The counter-blow **5 ... d5** does nothing to weaken White's attack. There can follow 6 Bxd5 c6 (6 ... *gxf3* leads to the main variation) 7 Bxf7+! Kxf7 8 Ne5+ Ke8 9 d4 f3 10 gxf3 Bg7 11 f4 Ne7 12 c3 Ng6 13 Nxg4 Qh4 14 f5, with advantage to White.

6 Qxf3

The sacrifice of a second piece by **6 Bxf7+** Kxf7 7 Qxf3 gives White nothing after the strong reply **7 ... d6!**

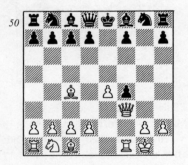

50

Here the following replies have been employed for Black: **6 ... d5 (6.1)**, **6 ... Qe7 (6.2)** and **6 ... Qf6 (6.3)**.

Of the rarely adopted continuations we should mention **6 ... Nc6** (6

... *Bh6 7 d4 Qf6* is weak, in view of *8 e5 Qf5 9 Nc3 Ne7 10 Ne4*), when White's attack can develop in two ways:

a) 7 Nc3 Ne5 (acording to analysis by Schiffers, *7 ... Qf6 8 Nd5 Qd4+ 9 Ne3! Bh6 10 c3 Qf6 11 Nd5* favours White) 8 Qxf4 Qf6 (or *8 ... Qe7 9 Nd5 Qc5+ 10 d4 Qxd4+ 11 Be3*) 9 Qg3 Qb6+ 10 Kh1 d6 11 Nd5 Qc5 12 Be2 Be6 13 d4 Qxd4 14 Nxc7+, with advantage to White (Khardin, *Shakmatnoe Obozrenye* 1909).

b) 7 Qxf4 Qe7 (*7 ... f6 8 Nc3 Qe7* is even worse, because of *9 Bxg8! Rxg8 10 Nd5 Qc5+ 11 Kh1 Bd6 12 Qh4 Be5 13 c3*, with a dangerous initiative for White) 8 Bxf7+ Kd8 9 Nc3 Qe5 (after *9 ... Bg7 10 Nd5 Qe5 11 Qh4+ Nge7 12 d4 Nxd4 13 Bg5* White gains a strong attack) 13 10 Qxe5 Nxe5 11 d4! Nxf7 12 Rxf7 Ke8 (after *12 ... Be7 13 Nd5* followed by *14 Nxe7* and *15 Bg5* White maintains a dangerous attack) 13 Rxf8+! Kxf8 14 Nd5, and, in spite of his extra rook, Black has serious difficulties. For example: **14 ... d6** 15 Nxc7 Rb8 16 Bf4 Ke7 17 Nb5, or **14 ... c6** 15 Nc7 Rb8 16 Bf4 Nf6 17 Rf1 Ke7 18 Bg5 Rf8 19 e5 Kd8 20 Rxf6 Rxf6 21 exf6, and White wins (analysis by Schallopp and Suhle).

6.1 6 ... d5

7. exd5

or 7. Bxd5! Nf6 (7...c6

8 Qxf4 Nf6 9 Nc3! Be7 leads to a transposition of moves) 8 Qxf4 Be7 9 Nc3! 0-0 (9 ... c6 is well met by *10 Bb3*, or *10 d3*) 10 d3 c6 11 Bb3 Be6 12 Bd2 Bxb3 13 axb3 Nbd7 14 Rf3 and 15 Raf1, with a strong attacking position for White (Aurbach-Spielmann, Abbazia 1912).

      7 ...   **Bd6**

7 ... Nf6 8 Qxf4 Be7 is weak in view of 9 b3! (Keres).

      8 d3

At the tournament in Abbazia (1912) Reti successfully adopted **8 d4.**

After **8 ... Qf6** 9 Qe4+ Qe7 (if *9 ... Ne7*, then *10 Bxf4 Bf5 11 Bxd6*) 10 Nc3 Nd7 11 Bxf4 Qxe4 12 Nxe4, despite the exchange of queens, White retains a strong attack for the sacrificed piece (Reti-Flamberg).

In the event of **8 ... Ne7** 9 Bxf4 Bxf4 10 Qxf4 0-0 11 Nc3 Ng6 12 Qe3 Kg7 13 Rae1 Nd7 14 Ne4 f5 15 Ng3 White has a splendid attacking position (Reti-Freymann).

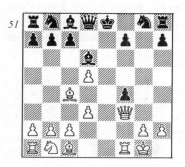

51

In the resulting position White undoubtedly has sufficient compensation for the sacrificed

piece. For example:

a) 8 ... Bf5 9 Bxf4 Bg6 10 Nc3 Ne7 11 Rae1 Bxf4 12 Qxf4 0-0 13 Ne4 Nd7 14 d6!, with a dangerous initiative for White.

b) 8 ... Qg5 9 Nc3 Bg4 10 Qe4+, and, according to Bilguer, after 10 ... Qe7 11 Bxf4 Qxe4 12 Nxe4 Bxf4 13 Rxf4 Bh5 14 Re1, or 10 ...Kd8 11 Bxf4 Bxf4 12 Rxf4 f5 13 Qe5 Qf6 14 Qxf6+ Nxf6 15 h3, or, finally, 10 ... Ne7 11 Bxf4 Bxf4 12 Rxf4 f5 13 Qe5 White has a clear advantage.

c) 8 ... Ne7. Schlechter-Marco (Vienna 1903) continued 9 Bxf4 Bxf4 10 Qxf4 0-0 11 Nc3! Ng6 12 Qg3 Nd7, and now by 13 Rae1! White could have gained a strong attack. After **13 ... Kg7** 14 Nb5 c6 15 Nc7 Rb8 16 dxc6 bxc6 17 Rxf7+!, or **13 ... Nb6** 14 Bb3 Qd6 15 Qxd6 cxd6 16 Nb5 Rd8 17 Nc7 Rb8 18 Re8+ he has an undisputed advantage.

6.2

      6 ...   **Qe7**

This continuation, which was highly popular in former times, affords White good chances of developing his initiative.

see diagram 52

      7 d4!

White can also consider **7 b3** Bg7 8 Nc3, or **7 d3** followed by 8 Nc3 and Nd5, which gives him good attacking chances.

White gains no advantage by **7 Qxf4** Qc5+ (weaker is *7 ... Nh6 8*

Nc3 c6 9 d4 d6 10 Bd2 Rg8 11 Rae1,
with a strong attack for White) **8 d4
Qxd4+** (after *8 ... Qxc4 9 Qe5+ Ne7
10 Qxh8 Ng6 11 Qf6 Be7 12 Qf2*
White has the advantage) **9 Be3
Qxc4 10 Qe5+ Qe6** (*10 ... Ne7 11
Qxh8 Qxe4 12 Bh6 Ng6 13 Qg8 Qe7
14 Nc3 d5 15 Rae1* leads to an
advantage for White — *E.C.O.*) **11
Qxh8 Qg6 12 Qe5+ Be7!** **13 Qxc7
Nc6 14 Qf4**, when, according to
Keres, the chances are roughly
equal.

7 ...   Nc6
8 Nc3!

This timely pawn sacrifice affords
White the better chances, whereas **8
Bxf4** (no better is *8 Qxf4 Bh6*, or *8
c3 Ne5!*) **8 ... Nxd4 9 Qh5 Ne6 10
Be5 Bg7 11 Bxg7** (*11 Bxe6 is not
good, on account of 11 ... Qc5+*
and 12 ... Qxe5) **11 ... Nxg7 12**

Bxf7+ Kd8 gives Black the
advantage.

8 ...   Nxd4
8 ... Ne5 9 dxe5 Qc5+ 10 Kh1 Qxc4
is not good in view of 11 Nd5!

9 Qd3   Ne6
10 Nd5
10 Bxf4 also derserves consideration.

10 ...   Qc5+
11 Kh1   Bh6
Steinitz-Anderssen (1862) went
instead 11 ... b5 12 Bb3 Bh6 13 Bd2
Qf8, and now 14 Qc3! would have
given White a manifest advantage.

12 Bd2   Qf8
13 Rad1!
A strong move, confronting Black
with numerous threats.

13 ...   d6
After **13 ... c6** 14 Bb4 c5 15 Bc3
Bg7 White has the decisive 16 Nxf4,
while on **13 ... Ne7** there follows 14
Nf6+ Kd8 15 Bb4.

14 Bc3   f6
On 14 ... Bg7 there follows 15 Bxg7
Qxg7 16 Nxc7+!, with a rapid win.

15 e5!
A strong move, which demolishes
Black's position.

see diagram 53

White's attack is now irresistible.
On **15 ... Nc5** (if *15 ... dxe5?*, then
16 Nxc7+) 16 Nxc7+ Kd8 he wins
by 17 Qd5!. In a correspondence
game Efrenov-Podsipanin (1949)
Black replied **15 ... fxe5**, but after

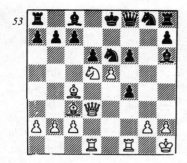

53

16 Bxe5 dxe5 17 Nxc7+ Kf7 18 Qf5+! was soon forced to capitulate.

It can be concluded that 7 d4 Nc6 8 Nc3! casts doubts on the entire variation with 6 ... Qe7.

6.3

    6 ...   Qf6

At the present time this move is considered the strongest.

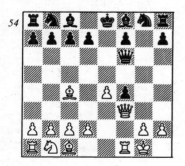

54

7 e5!

Only this additional pawn sacrifice gives White chances of obtaining an advantage. Other continuations

cause Black considerably less trouble. For example:

a) 7 Nc3? This sacrifice of a second piece, suggested by Bell, is too risky. After 7 ... Qd4+ 8 Kh1 Qxc4 9 d3 Qe6 10 Bxf4 both 10 ... Ne7! and 10 ... d6 11 e5 (*11 Nb5 Kd8*) 11 ... Qg4 12 Qe3 Be6 (A.Rabinovich) allow Black successfully to beat off the attack.

b) 7 c3 d6! (*7 ... Nc6 8 d4 Nxd4* is weaker, in view of *9 Bxf7+*, with an unclear position) 8 d4 Bh6 9 g3 Bh3 10 Re1. Rabinovich now gives the variation **10 ... fxg3** 11 Qxf6 gxh2+ 12 Kxh2 Nxf6 13 Bxh6 Ng4+ 14 Kxh3 Nxh6, assuming it to be in favour of Black.

But by continuing now 15 e5! White gets out of all his difficulties. Stronger, instead of 10 ... fxg3, is **10 ... Ne7!**, and if 11 e5 (on *11 gxf4* there follows *11 ... Rg8+* and ... *Bg2*), then 11 ... dxe5 12 dxe5 (not *12 Qxb7? fxg3!*) 12 ... Qb6+! 13 Kh1 Qc6, when Black retains a clear advantage (Glazkov).

c) 7 d3. This modest move gives White roughly equal chances. After 7 ... Bh6! 8 Nc3 Ne7 9 Bxf4 (it is better to transpose into one of the lines of the main variation by *9 e5! Qxe5 10 Bd2*, although in reply to *9 e5* Black can consider *9 ... Qf5!?*) 9 ... Bxf4 10 Qxf4 Qxf4 11 Rxf4 f5! 12 exf5 c6 13 Re1 Kd8 14 Bf7 d5 15 f6 Ng6 16 Bxg6 hxg6 17 Re7 Nd7 18

Rg7 a position is reached, in which, in Chigorin's opinion, White has sufficient compensation for the sacrificed material. However, Rabinovich's suggestion of 18 ... Nf8! gives Black clearly the better chances. On 19 g4, for example, there follows 19 ... Bd7! and 20 ... Ne6, while if 19 Ne2 (no better is *19 b6*, or *19 f7 Ke7*), then 19 ... Bd7! 20 Nd4 Kc7, in all cases with advantage to Black.

    7 ...   **Qxe5**

Forced, since after 7 ... **Qb6+** 8 Kh1 Bh6 9 Nc3 Qc5 10 d3, or 7 ... **Qf5** 8 d4 Bh6 9 Nc3 White gains the advantage.

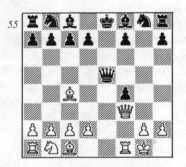

55

Here two main continuations for White should be considered: **8 Bxf7+ (6.31)** and **8 d3 (6.32)**.

8 Nc3 is less promising, allowing Black to beat off the attack after 8 ... Qd4+ 9 Kh1 Qxc4 10 d3 Qc6! 11 Qxf4 f6.

After **8 b3** Qxa1 (the rook can be taken without great risk, but also good is *8 ... d5 9 Bxd5 Ne7 10 Bc4 Nbc6 11 c3 Bf5*, with advantage to Black, as in Tartakover-Leonhardt, Vienna 1908) 9 Nc3 Bc5+ 10 Kh1 Ne7 11 d4 (if *11 Qxf4*, then *11 ... Rf8*) 11 ... Bxd4 12 Bxf7+ (on *12 Qxf4* Black should reply *12 ... Qxc1! 13 Qxd4 Qxf1+ 14 Bxf1 Rf8*, with a clear advantage) 12 ... Kd8! 13 Bd2 Qxf1+ 14 Qxf1 Rf8 15 Qxf4 Nbc6! 16 Nb5 Be5 17 Qf1 Bg7! Black repels his opponent's attack, retaining a material advantage.

6.31
    8 Bxf7+!?

It is possible that this bold sacrifice of a second piece may have decisive significance for the evaluation of the Polerio Gambit as a whole. For the moment, however, the theory of this variation has not been developed, and all that is known is that practice has been decidedly in favour of White.

    8 ...   **Kxf7**
    9 d4   **Qxd4+**

9 ... Qf6 10 Bxf4 Bh6 is considerably weaker, in view of 11 Qh5+ Qg6 12 Bxh6+ Nf6 13 Rxf6+! Kxf6 14 Qe5+ Kf7 15 Nc3, and White wins (Gotz-Merklein, 1888). In Ashikhin-Ivanov (1961) **9 ... Qf5** was played, when there followed 10 g4! Qg6 11 Bxf4 Nf6 12 Be5, with a very strong attack for White.

    10 Be3   **Qf6**

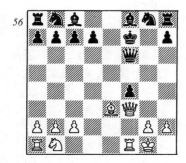

11 Bxf4!

The strongest continuation of the attack. Shumov-Beskorny (St Petersburg, 1869) went instead **11 Qh5+ Qg6 12 Rxf4+ Nf6 13 Rxf6+ Kxf6 14 Bd4+ Kf7 15 Qd5+ Qe6 16 Qf3+**, and now, by continuing 16 ... Ke8!, Black could have beaten off the attack, retaining a material advantage.

Similarly after **11 Qd5+ Qe6 12 Rxf4+ Nf6 13 Nc3 Bh6 14 Rxf6+ Kxf6 15 Rf1+ Ke7 16 Bg5+**, as in Charlick-Fagan (Adelaide 1882), Black, by continuing 16 ... Ke8! 17 Bxh6 Qxd5! 18 Nxd5 Na6, could have gained a decisive advantage.

It is curious that, if the knight at b1 is removed from the board, by **11 Qh5+ Qg6 12 Rxf4+ Nf6 13 Rxf6+ Kxf6 14 Bd4+ Ke7 15 Re1+ Kf7 16 Qd5+ Qe6 17 Qf3+ Ke8 18 Qh5+ Kd8 19 Rxe6 dxe6 20 Bxh8** White gains a winning position (Morphy-N.N., New York 1857, White gave the odds of queen's knight). A similar game against an amateur

was also won by Steinitz. In view of this, along with the move in the text, Keres' recommendation of **11 Nc3!?** also deserves consideration.

11 ...   Ne7

This move is considered best, although even it does not get Black out of serious difficulties. Other continuations adopted in practice have quickly led to a clear advantage for White, for example:
a) 11 ... Bg7 12 Nc3 Ne7 13 Nd5 Nxd5 14 Qxd5+ Qe6 15 Bd2+ (Rosenthal's recommendation in 1885 of *15 Bh6+ Kg8 16 Rae1!* is also immediately decisive) 15 ... Kg8 16 Rae1 Qxd5 17 Re8+ Bf8 18 Bh6!! and Black resigned (Smirnov-Tikhonov, 1954).
b) 11 ... Bc5+ 12 Kh1 d6 13 Nc3 Ne7 14 Ne4 Qf5 15 Nxc5 dxc5 16 Qc3! Nd5 17 Qxh8 Nxf4 18 Rf3, with a clear advantage for White (Glazkov-Naglis, Moscow 1974).

12 Nc3

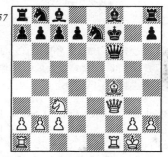

In this critical position White has a very strong attack for the two sacrificed pieces. Here are two examples from practice:

a) 12 ... Qf5 13 Qe2 Ke8 14 Be5 Qe6 15 Rf6 Qg8 16 Qh5+ **Kd8** 17 Raf1 Bg7 18 Rf7 Bxe5 19 Qxe5 Nbc6 20 Qxh8!, and Black resigned (Glazkov-Muratov, Moscow 1973). Instead of 16 ... Kd8, **16 ... Ng6** fails to save Black, since there follows 17 Rxf8+! Kxf8 (if *17 ... Qxf8, then 18 Re1!*) 18 Rf1+ Ke8 19 Bxh8 Qxh8 20 Nd5 Na6 21 Re1+ Kf8 22 Qf5+ Kg7 23 Re7+!, with a quick win.

b) 12 ... Nf5 13 Ne4 Qg6 14 g4!? Be7 15 Kh1 Nh4 (Schussler-Akvist, Sweden 1976), and now by 16 Qe3! White could have gained a clear advantage, since on 16 ... Kg8 there follows 17 Be5!, while after Berglund's recommendation of 16 ... Qc6 17 Bg5+ (*17 Be5+ Kg8 18 Bxh8 Kxh8 19 Rf7* is also good) 17 ... Ke8 18 Bxe7 Kxe7 19 Qg5+ Ke8 20 Qe5+ White again wins quickly.

6.32

8 d3

A sound, thoroughly studied continuation, which promises White at least equal chances.

8 ...   Bh6

Black must defend his f4 pawn. In the event of **8 ... Nc6** 9 Bxf4 Qf6 10 Nc3 Nge7 11 Rae1, or **8 ... Bc5+** 9 Kh1 Be3 10 Bxe3 Qxe3 11 Qh5 Qe7 12 Nc3, White has the advantage.

9 Nc3   Ne7
10 Bd2

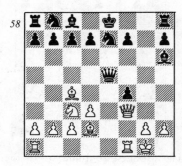

58

White has a big lead in development, and his attack appears very menacing.

10 ...   Nbc6

The most natural reply. Weaker is **10 ... c6** 11 Rae1 Qc5+ (but not *11 ... Qf5? 12 Qe2!*) 12 Kh1 (Staunton recommended *12 Rf2*) 12 ... d5 (*12 ... 0-0 leads to a decisive advantage for White after 13 Ne4 Qf5 14 Bc3 Bg7 15 Nd6 Qg5 16 Bxg7 Kxg7 17 Rxe7!*) 13 Qh5 Qd6 14 Bxd5! cxd5 15 Nb5! Qb6 16 Bb4 Nc6 17 Nd6+ Kd7 18 Ba3! Bg7 19 Qg4+ Kc7 20 Qxf4, with a clear advantage for White (Sämisch-Gunter, Hannover 1926).

Black also comes under a strong attack after **10 ... 0-0** 11 Rae1 Qc5+ 12 Kh1, for example:

a) 12 ... Ng6 13 Ne4 Qc6 (if *13 ... Qf5, then 14 g4*) 14 Qh5 Kg7 (or *14 ... Bg7 15 Ng5 h6 16 Nxf7*, with a

[handwritten margin note:] a) 17...b6 △ 18... Bb7+ ECO

winning position for White) 15
Bc3+ f6 16 Nxf6 Rxf6 17 Re7+! Kf8
and now, according to analysis by
Keres, after 18 Qxh6+! Kxe7 19
Qg7+ Ke8 20 Bxf6 White wins.
b) In the event of **12 ... Nbc6** 13
Bxf4 Bg7 14 Be3 Nd4 (the *E.C.O.*
recommendation of *14 ... Qa5* is
well met by *15 Bd2! Qc5 16 Ne4*)
White, as pointed out in Collijn's
handbook, gains a clear advantage
by continuing 15 Bxf7+ Kh8 16
Qe4! Nec6 17 Nd5 Qa5 18 c3 Ne6 19
Rf5.

11 Rae1   Qf5
Less promising for Black is the
formerly popular **11 ... Qc5+ 12
Kh1.**
Now **12 ... 0-0** 13 Bxf4 leads to
positions examined in the notes to
Black's 10th move, while after **12 ...
d6** 13 Nd5 Ne5 White gains the
advantage by 14 Rxe5! dxe5 15 Bb4.
In a consultation game Maroczy-
Tartakover (1920) Black chose **12 ...
Kd8,** but after 13 Bxf4 Nd4 14 Qf2
Bxf4 15 Qxf4 White again
developed a dangerous attack.
On the immediate **12 ... Nd4** there
can follow either **13 Rxe7+!** Kxe7
(*13 ... Qxe7* also loses, to *14 Qh5 d5
15 Nxd5 Qd6 16 Bb4,* Sjernsen-
Moller, 1871) 14 Nd5+ Kd8 15 Qh5
Qf8 16 Bxf4 Bxf4 17 Rxf4 Ne6 18
Qh4+ Ke8 19 Nf6+! Kd8 20 Bxe6,
when White wins, or **13 Qh3** Bg5 (or
13 ... d5 14 Qxh6 dxc4 15 Qg7 Rf8

16 Ne4) 14 Qh5 Qf5 15 Ne4 h6 16
Bc3 Nxc2 17 Nf6+, with a clear
advantage to White (analysis by
Mozor).

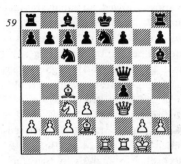

12 Nd5
The most natural continuation of
the attack. White achieves nothing
by **12 Re4** (*12 g4?* is also bad, on
account of *12 ... Rg8 13 h3 d6*) 12 ...
0-0! 13 Bxf4 Bg7! 14 Qe2 (if *14 Qg3*
or *14 g4,* then *14 ... Qg6*) 14 ... d5!,
with a clear advantage to Black
(Dukje-Schwede, 1873).

12 ...   Kd8
13 Qe2
The Maclean Attack, which was
studied in detail by Chigorin in the
last years of his life. A special
brochure by Znosko-Borovsky
(Leipzig 1911) was devoted to this
interesting continuation.
13 Bc3 was recommended in its
time, but this continuation is significantly weaker, and allows Black to
obtain the advantage in two ways:
a) 13 ... Rf8! 14 g4 (in the event of

*14 Nxe7 Nxe7 15 Re5 Qg6 16 Rfe1
Nc6 17 Qe2 Nxe5 18 Qxe5 Bg5 19
Bxf7 d6!* Black wins) 14 ... Qg6 15
h4 Nxd5 16 Bxd5 f6 17 Qe2.

Panov showed in analysis that
after 17 ... d6 18 Bxc6 Qxg4+ 19
Qxg4 Bxg4 20 Bxb7 White has a
good game. But by continuing 17 ...
Ne5! 18 g5 Bxg5! 19 hxg5 Qxg5+
Black gains a clear advantage (Zak).
b) 13 ... Re8 14 Bf6 (*14 Nf6 Rf8 15
g4 Qg6 16 h4 d5! 17 Bxd5 Bxg4* is
also in Black's favour, Anderssen-
Zukertort, 1865) 14 ... Bg5 15 g4
(according to analysis by Schiffers,
*15 Bxg5 Qxg5 16 Nxf4 d6! 17 Bxf7
Ne5 18 Rxe5 dxe5 19 Bxe8 exf4 20
Ba4 c6* leads to a clear advantage for
Black) 15 ... Qg6 16 Bxg5 Qxg5 17
h4 Qxh4 18 Qxf4 d6 19 Nf6
(Chigorin-Davidov, St Petersburg
1874), and now analysis by A.
Rabinovich shows that Black could
have gained the advantage by 19 ...
Rf8! 20 Re2 Bf5! (cf. Game No. 4).

After 13 Qe2 the following
position is reached:

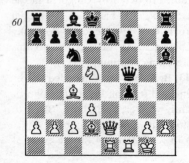

13 ...   Qe6

Here other possibilities for Black
should also be considered:
a) 13 ... Re8 (bad is *13 ... Bg5? 14
h4!*) 14 Bxf4 Bxf4 15 Rxf4 Qg5 16
Rxf7 d6. After 17 Nf6 Ne5 18 Nxe8
Nxf7 19 Bxf7 White has the
advantage (Chigorin).
b) 13 ... Nxd5 14 Bxd5 Qxd5 (after
*14 ... Bg5 15 Bxc6 dxc6 16 Rxf4!
Qc5+ 17 d4 Qd6 18 Re4* White wins)
15 Bc3 Bg5 16 Bxh8 Qe6! 17 Qh5 (*17
Qf2 Qg6 18 h4 Be7! 19 Qxf4 d6 20
Qxf7 Qxf7 21 Rxf7 Bxh4 22 g3 Bg5*
also leads to equality) 17 ... Qg6.

According to analysis by
Mirotvorsky, after 18 Qxf6 fxg6! 19
Rxf4 Bxf4 (*19 ... Be7 20 Rfe4 d5* is
weaker, in view of *21 Rxe7 Nxe7 22
Bf6*, with advantage to White) 20
Bf6+ Ne7 21 Bxe7+ Ke8 22 Bg5+
Kf7 23 Rf1 d6 Black equalises.
c) 13 ... b5. This continuation of
Berger is also sufficient for equality.
There can follow 14 Nxe7 Qc5+ 15
Rf2 **Qxe7** 16 Qh5 Qg5 17 Qxf7 Qg6
(*17 ... bxc4? 18 Bc3 Rf8* is unsatis-
factory, on account of *19 Rfe2! Ne5
20 Bxe5! Rxf7 21 Bf6+ Re7 22
Bxe7+ Qxe7 23 Rxe7* and then *24
Rxh7*, with winning chances for
White, E.C.O.*) 18 Bc3 Rf8 19
Bf6+! Qxf6 20 Re8+ Rxe8 21
Qxf6+ Re7 22 Qh8+, with a draw
by repetition of moves.

Instead of 15 ... Qxe7, E.C.O.
recommends 15 ... **Nxe7**, and

considers Black's position to be decidedly preferable. But there can follow 16 Bc3 Re8 17 Bxf7 Rf8 18 Bd4!, with advantage to White, since 18 ... Qg5 is very strongly met by 19 Rxf4, with the threat of 20 Bf6, while after 18 ... Qd6 19 Be5 Qb6 20 Bxf4 Rxf7 21 Bxh6 Qxf2+ 22 Qxf2 Rxf2 23 Kxf2 Ke8 24 Bg5 White has clearly the better chances in the ending (Glazkov).

After 13 ... Qe6 the following position is reached:

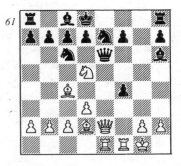

At the start of the present century, this position was the object of thorough investigation. After Chigorin's death, analyses were discovered in his archives, devoted to the given theme, which were then published in the literary supplement of the periodical *Niva*. Chigorin persistently sought a decisive strengthening of White's attack, but failed to find one. Subsequently Znosko-Borovsky devoted to this position a special monograph, published in Leipzig in 1910.

In the diagram position two basic possibilities for White should be considered: **14 Bc3 (6.321)** and **14 Nxe7 (6.322)**.

14 Qf3 Qf5 15 Qe2 Qe6 allows White to force a draw immediately.

6.321

14 Bc3   Qxe2

The exchange of queens is forced, since in the event of 14 ... Re8 15 Bf6! Qxe2 16 Rxe2 d6 17 Nxe7 Rxe7 (Galkin-Mirotvorsky, corr. 1909) White gains winning chances by continuing 18 Rfe1! Bf8 19 Bxf7.

15 Rxe2   Rg8

16 Nxf4

16 Bf6 Bg5 17 Bxg5 Rxg5 18 Rfe1 loses to 18 ... f3!

16 ...   d6

The best reply. 16 ... Bxf4 17 Bxf7! Bh6 18 Bxg8 Nxg8 19 g4!, or 16 ... Rf8 17 Bf6 Bxf4 18 Rxf4 d6 19 Bg7! Re8 20 Bxf7! leaves White with the advantage.

This position was reached in the correspondence game Lentz-Govarsky (1911-12), which

continued **17 Bxf7** Rf8 18 Ne6+
Bxe6 19 Bxe6 Rxf1+ 20 Kxf1 Ne5
(up to here — all as in Znosko-
Borovsky's analysis) 21 Rf2!, and
White, despite the limited material,
retained for the sacrificed piece an
attack sufficient for a draw.

6.322

14 Nxe7

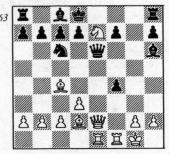

It was in this variation that
Chigorin endeavoured to demon-
strate an advantage for White, but
came to the opposite conclusion.

14 ...   **Qxe7**

14 ... **Qxe2** 15 Nxc6+ bxc6 16 Rxe2
gives White slightly the better
chances, both after **16 ... d5** 17 Bb3
Be6 18 Bxf4 (Chigorin), and after **16
... f3** 17 Rxf3 Bxd2 18 Rxd2 d5 19
Bb3 Be6 20 d4 Kd7 21 Ba4 (Khardin-
Mirotvorsky, corr. 1909).

15 Bc3

Nothing is changed by 15 Qh5 Qg5
16 Bc3! Rg8, which leads merely to
a transposition of moves.

15 ...   **Rg8**

Here too 15 ... Qxe2? 16 Rxe2 Re8
is incorrect, in view of 17 Bf6+ Re7

18 Rfe1 Bf8 19 Bd5 Ke8 20 Bxc6 Re6
21 Bd5, with advantage to White.

16 Qh5!

Other continuations leave White
with inadequate compensation for
the sacrificed piece. For example: **16
Qd2** Qc5+! 17 Kh1 Bg5 18 Bxf7 Rf8
19 Rxf4 d6!, or **16 Qf2** Qg5 17 Bxf7
Rf8 18 Qxf4 Qxf4 19 Rxf4 Ne7, in
both cases with a clear advantage to
Black, while **16 Bd5** Qxe2 17 Rxe2
Ne7 18 Bf6 is met decisively by 18 ...
Bg5!

16 ...   **Qg5**

17 Rf2

This critical position is considered
favourable for Black, but without
sufficient justification.

If, for example, **17 ... Qxh5**, then
by 18 Bf6+ Ne7 19 Bxe7+ Ke8 20
Bd6+ White forces a draw.

Chigorin thought that Black could
gain the advantage by **17 ... Ne7** 18
Qxf7 Rf8 19 Qxh7 d5 20 Rxe7 Bf5,
but instead of 20 Rxe7?, much
stronger is 20 Bb4! Re8 21 Rfe2 Bf8
22 Bxd5, with advantage now to
White.

In the correspondence game Rastochinsky-Mirotvorsky, 1909, **17 ... d5?** 18 Qxf7 Rf8 was played, and now White should have continued 19 Bf6+! Qxf6 20 Re8+ Rxe8 21 Qxf6+ Re7 22 Qxh6, gaining the advantage.

Thus the position in the diagram can be considered equal.

Game No. 4
Chigorin-Davidov
St Petersburg 1874

1 e4 e5 2 f4 exf4 3 Nf3 g5 4 Bc4 g4 5 0-0 gxf3 6 Qxf3 Qf6 7 e5! Qxe5 8 d3

As shown in the theoretical section 6.31, 8 Bxf7+!? deserves serious consideration.

8 ... Bh6 9 Nc3 Ne7 10 Bd2 Nbc6 11 Rae1 Qf5 12 Nd5 Kd8

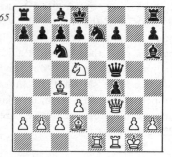

13 Bc3

At that time this move was considered obligatory. Chigorin did not know then of the strongest move 13 Qe2!, to a detailed analysis of which he devoted the last years of his life.

13 ... Re8

13 ... Rf8! is also good (cf. analysis).

14 Bf6 Bg5

On 14 ... Bf8 there could have followed 15 g4 Qg6 16 g5, followed by 17 Nxf4 or 17 Qxf4.

15 g4! Qg6 16 Bxg5 Qxg5 17 h4!

Qxh4

17 ... Qg7 was also possible.

18 Qxf4 d6 19 Nf6 Ne5?

The decisive mistake. Black should have played 19 ... Rf8!, and if 20 Re2, then 20 ... Bf5!, gaining the advantage (pointed out by A. Rabinovich).

Now comes one of Chigorin's wonderful combinations.

20 Rxe5! dxe5 21 Qxe5 Bxg4

21 ... Be6 loses immediately to the obvious 22 Qd4+.

22 Qd4+ Kc8 23 Be6+!!

A study-like interference move — a brilliant concluding stroke! There is no longer any defence.

23 ... Kb8 24 Nd7+ Kc8 25 Nc5+ Kb8 26 Na6+ bxa6 27 Qb4 mate.

7 Greco-Philidor Gambit

1 e4	e5
2 f4	exf4
3 Nf3	g5
4 Bc4	Bg7

This solid continuation is undoubtedly safer than 4 ... g4. Black is prepared now to reinforce his pawn chain by ... h6.

To be considered is Chigorin's idea of **4 ... Nc6**, so as to answer 5 h4 with 5 ... g4 6 Ng5 Ne5 7 Bb3 h6 8 d4 hxg5 9 dxe5 Bg7, with advantage to Black (Mieses-Chigorin, Vienna 1903). In this case White should choose 5 d4 or 5 0-0, which after 5 ... Bg7 leads to the main line.

5 h4

In this way White creates a persistent tension on the K-side, but weakens the position of his own king.

This plan of undermining Black's pawn chain is linked with the name of the legendary chess knight Gioachino El Greco. The given variation was also analysed in the 18th century by André Danican Philidor. For this reason the variation examined below bears the name of the Greco-Philidor Gambit. Many years of tournament practice have shown that, in this branch of the King's Gambit, Black does not experience any great difficulties.

     5 ...   **h6**

5 ... g4? would be completely inconsistent, since by 6 Ng5 Nh6 7 d4 f6 (*7 ... Nc6 8 c3 d6 9 Bxf4* is no better) 8 Bxf4! fxg5 9 Bxg5 Bf6 10 Qd2 White gained a won position in Morphy-Meek (New Orleans, 1855).

     6 d4   **d6**

Here too **6 ... g4?** is unfavourable, in view of 7 Bxf4 gxf3 8 Qxf3, with a very strong attack for White. **6 ... c6** 7 e5 d5 is also inadequate because of 8 exd6 Qxd6 9 hxg5.

7 c3!

It is only after this move, recommended by Philidor, that White gains sufficient compensation for the sacrificed pawn. Other continuations cannot be recommended, for example:

a) 7 hxg5 hxg5 8 Rxh8 Bxh8 9 Qd3 Nh6 (*9 ... Nc6* or *9 ... Kf8* is also good) 10 g3 g4 11 Bxf4 gxf3 12 Bxh6 f2+!, with advantage to Black (Kolisch-Anderssen, 1860).

b) 7 Qd3 Nc6 (*7 ... Kf8 8 hxg5 hxg5 9 Rxh8 Bxh8 10 e5* also led to an advantage for Black after *10 ... dxe5! 11 Qh7 Bg7 12 dxe5 Bg4,* Tartakover-Becker, Vienna 1921) 8 hxg5 hxg5 9 Rxh8 Bxh8 10 e5, and after 10 ... Bg7! 11 Nc3 (White achieves nothing by *11 Qh7 Kf8 12 Qh5 Nh6! 13 Nxg5 Bg4 14 Qh4 Nxd4*) 11 ... Nh6 12 exd6 cxd6 13 Nd5 Kf8 Black gained the advantage (Rosenthal-Neumann, 1869).

c) 7 Nc3 Nc6 8 Ne2 (Schottlander-Muller, London 1891, went *8 Nd5 g4 9 c3 gxf3 10 Qxf3,* when Black should have continued *10 ... Be6!,* consolidating his position and retaining his extra piece) 8 ... Qe7 9 Qd3 Bd7 10 Bd2 0-0-0 11 Bc3 (*11 0-0-0 is well met by 11 ... Nf6! 12 hxg5 Nxe4*) 11 ... Re8 12 d5 Ne5 13 Nxe5 dxe5 14 0-0-0 Nf6, and Black has the advantage (Anderssen-Neumann, 1866).

7 ... **Nc6**

The strongest reply. Other continuations afford White greater possibilities, for example:

a) 7 ... g4 8 Ng1! Qe7 (*8 ... Bf6 9 Bxf4 Bxh4+ 10 g3* favours White) 9 Bxf4! Qxe4+ 10 Qe2 (*10 Ne2 Qxg2 11 Rg1* is also possible) 10 ... Bf5 11 Nd2 Qxe2+ 12 Nxe2, and despite being a pawn down and the queens being exchanged, White retains the advantage.

b) 7 ... c6 8 Qb3 Qe7 9 0-0 Be6 (*9 ... b5 10 Bd3 Nd7* is weaker in view of *11 a4 a6 12 axb5 Rb8 13 Na3,* with advantage to White) 10 Bxe6 fxe6 11 hxg5 hxg5 12 Nxg5 e5 (if *12 ... Qxg5, then 13 Qxb7*). After 13 dxe5 dxe5 Keres considers the position to be roughly equal, but it seems more likely that Bhend, who asserts that 14 Nd2 gives White the better chances, is right.

After the main move 7 ... Nc6 the following position is reached:

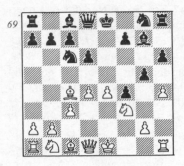

Here two basic continuations deserve consideration: **8 Qb3 (7.1)** and **8 0-0! (7.2)**.

Other moves lead to a clear advantage for Black, for example:
a) 8 hxg5 hxg5 9 Rxh8 Bxh8 10 Qe2 Qe7 11 Na3 Bg4 12 Bd2 0-0-0 13 0-0-0 Nf6, and Black has the advantage (La Bourdonnais — Mac-Donnell, London 1832).

b) 8 Qc2 Qe7 9 hxg5 hxg5 10 Rxh8 Bxh8 11 Na3 g4 12 Ng1 Bf5 13 Bd3 Bxe4!, with advantage to Black (Lukin-Voikovich, Moscow 1965).

c) 8 Na3 g4 9 Ng1 Nf6. This variation, which occurred in Anderssen-Neumann (1866), also leads to the better game for Black.

d) 8 Qd3 Qe7 9 hxg5 hxg5 10 Rxh8 Bxh8 11 e5 f5! 12 Bxg8 dxe5 13 dxe5 g4, and in Marshall-Gunsberg (Vienna 1903) Black obtained an excellent game for the sacrificed piece.

7.1

8 Qb3	Qe7
9 0-0	

9 hxg5 hxg5 10 Rxh8 Bxh8 11 Qb5 g4 12 Ng5 favours Black after the strong reply 12 ... a6!

| 9 ... | Nf6 |

After **9 ... g4** White is not obliged to sacrifice a piece by 10 Bxf4 gxf3 11 Rxf3, which gives him a sufficiently strong attack, but can advantageously continue 10 Nh2! f3 (*10 ... Nxd4? 11 cxd4 Bxd4+ 12 Kh1 Qxh4* is erroneous, in view of *13 Bxf4*) 11 Nxg4! Bxg4 12 Qxb7.

10 hxg5

White achieves nothing by 10 ... e5, when there follows 10 ... dxe5 11 dxe5 Ng4!, with advantage to Black.

| 10 ... | hxg5 |
| 11 Nxg5 | |

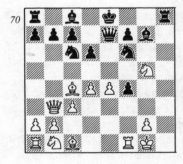

In this critical position of the Greco-Philidor Gambit, which for many decades was considered roughly equal, an important improvement has now been found for Black.

11 ...　　　　　　**Nxd4!**

This is the point. The normal continuation here was **11 ... Nxe4** 12 Nxe4 Qxe4 13 Bxf7+ Kd8 14 Bxf4, which after 14 ... Nxd4 15 Bg5+ Kd7 16 Qd5! Ne2+ 17 Kf2 Qg4 led to a complicated position with chances for both sides. If, for instance, 18 Re1, then 18 ... Be5, while on 18 Nd2 there follows 18 ... c6.

But after the text move Black gains an advantage.

12 Bxf7+

On 12 Qd1 Black replies 12 ... Ne6, retaining the advantage.

12 ...		**Kd8**
13 cxd4		**Nxe4**
14 Bxf4		

14 Nf3 loses to 14 ... Bxd4+! 15 Nxd4 Qh4, when White is defenceless.

14 ...		**Bxd4+**
15 Be3		**Bxe3+**
16 Qxe3		**Nxg5**

After 17 Qc3 Rf8 18 Bc4 Rxf1+ 19 Bxf1 c6! Black retains his extra pawn and winning chances.

7.2

8 0-0!

see diagram 71

This continuation gives White a fully equal game.

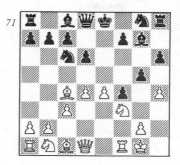

71

8 ...　　　　　　**Qe7**

A complicated game with chances for both sides results after **8 ... Nf6** 9 hxg5 Nxe4 10 Bxf4 d5 (but not *10 ... hxg5? 11 Bxf7+!*) 11 gxh6 Bxh6 12 Bxh6 Rxh6.

8 ... g4 is less promising for Black, in view of 9 Ne1! (*9 Nh2?* is a mistake, on account of *9 ... f3 10 gxf3 g3 11 Ng4 Bxg4! 12 fxg4 Qxh4 13 Kg2 Qh2+ 14 Kf3 h5!*, with a clear advantage to Black) 9 ... f3 10 gxf3 Qxh4 11 f4! g3 12 Nf3, with a promising position for White.

9 a4	**Bd7**
10 a5	**0-0-0**
11 b4	

Anderssen-Riemann (Breslau 1875) continued 11 ... Nb8 12 b5 Nf6 13 e5, with a complicated, double-edged game.

It can be concluded that in the Greco-Philidor Gambit the chances are roughly equal.

8 Hanstein Gambit

1 e4	e5
2 f4	exf4
3 Nf3	g5
4 Bc4	Bg7
5 0-0	

This move leads to the gambit which bears the name of Hanstein, one of the brilliant 'Seven Stars of Berlin' — the first German masters.

White avoids the immediate undermining of his opponent's pawn chain, and in the first instance aims to complete his development, and only then to begin positive action.

Also possible is **5 d4** d6 (but not *5 ... g4? 6 Ng1 Qh4+ 7 Kf1 Nc6 8 c3 Bh6 9 Na3 a6*, in view of *10 g3! fxg3 11 Kg2* with advantage to White, Chigorin-Sellman, London 1883) 6 0-0!, which leads merely to a transposition of moves.

Instead of 6 0-0!, which leads to the main line, 6 Nc3 Nc6 7 Nd5, as occurred in Pillsbury-Schlechter (Vienna 1903), is incorrect. By continuing 7 ... g4! 8 c3 gxf3 9 Qxf3

Be6 10 Bxf4 Qd7 Black retains his extra piece with a solid position.

5 ...	h6
6 d4	

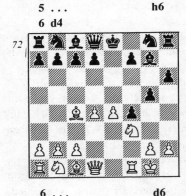
72

6 ...	d6

6 ... Ne7 is also to be considered, so as to answer the undermining 7 g3 with 7 ... d5! 8 exd5 fxg3 9 Ne5 gxh2+ 10 Kh1 0-0, and if 11 d6, then 11 ... Qxd6 or 11 ... Nf5, and Black repels the attack.

But instead of 11 d6 White should play 11 Nxf7! Rxf7 12 Rxf7 Kxf7 13 Bxg5!, with an attack sufficient to equalise, as in Kuindzhi-Men, examined in section 8.2.

In reply to 6 ... Ne7 Keres recommends 7 Nc3, after which Levin-Zamikhovsky (1959) continued **7 ... d6!** 8 g3 Nc6! 9 gxf4 g4! 10 d5, and now, by 10 ... gxf3! 11 dxc6 Bg4 12 Kh1 Nxc6 Black gains the advantage (*E.C.O.*).

Instead of 7 ... d6!, weaker is **7 ... 0-0** 8 g3! fxg3 9 Bxg5! (cf. Game No. 5).

7 c3

7 Nc3 is inadequate, since along with 7 ... Ne7, leading to the variation considered in the previous note, Black has another good alternative: 7 ... Be6 8 Bxe6 fxe6 9 e5 Nc6!, and if 10 Qd3 Nge7 11 exd6 cxd6 12 Re1, then 12 ... e5 13 d5 Qb6+, with advantage to Black.

7 g3? is premature, in view of 7 ... Bh3 8 Rf2 Nc6!, and if 9 Bb5 as in Korchnoi-Malich (Amsterdam 1972), then after 9 ... Nf6 10 d5 a6 or else 9 ... fxg3 Black has a clear advantage. If instead of 9 Bb5 White chooses 9 c3, a variation favourable for Black is reached, considered below in section 8.32.

73

The basic position of the Hanstein Gambit. Here Black has a number of good continuations, the chief of which are: **7 ... Nf6 (8.1)**, **7 ... Ne7 (8.2)** and **7 ... Nc6 (8.3)**.

We will also consider certain other possibilities for Black:

a) 7 ... Be6 8 Bxe6 fxe6 9 Qb3 Nd7! (the old variation *9 ... Qc8 10 h4 g4 11 Nh2 g3 12 Nf3 e5 13 dxe5 dxe5 14 Na3* and *15 Nc4* is clearly in White's favour) 10 Qxe6+ Qe7 11 Qg6+ Qf7 12 Qxf7+ Kxf7 13 g3 g4 14 Nh4 f3, with roughly equal chances (Schiffers-Petrovsky, 1878).

b) 7 ... c6 8 g3 Bh3! (*8 ... g4?* is incorrect in view of *9 Bxf4! gxf3 10 Qxf3*, with a very strong attack for White) 9 Rf2 Nf6!, with a complicated game.

c) 7 ... Qe7 8 Na3 (*8 g3*, as recommended by many opening books, is erroneous in view of *8 ... fxg3* or *8 ... Bh3*, but at this point *8 h4* deserves consideration) 8 ... Nc6 9 b4 **Nf6** 10 b5 Nd8 11 e5! dxe5 12 Nxe5 Be6 13 Bxe6 Nxe6 14 Nac4, with a dangerous initiative for White (Chigorin-Burn, New York 1889).

Instead of 9 ... Nf6, stronger is **9 ... a6!** 10 Qd3 Nf6 11 Bd2 0-0 12 Rae1 Bg4 13 Bb3, with roughly equal chances (Zinkl-Carls, corr. 1899).

8.1

7 ...	Nf6
8 e5	dxe5
9 Nxe5	

9 Qb3 0-0 10 Nxe5 transposes.

9 ...	0-0!

9 ... **Be6** is not good, in view of 10 Bxe6 fxe6 11 Ng6! (but not *11 Qb3 Qd5!*) 11 ... Rg8 12 Bxf4!? gxf4 13 Nxf4 e5 14 Ne6, and in Angelov-Prodanov (match Varna-Odessa, 1974) White gained the advantage.

10 Qb3   Qe8!

This move is the prelude to an exceptionally interesting manoeuvre. Old books also give the variation **10 ... Be6** 11 Bxe6 fxe6 12 Qxe6+ Kh7 13 Qf5+ Kg8 14 Qe6+, with perpetual check, but analysis by Chigorin indicates that by 14 h4! Nd5 15 Qe6+ Kh7 16 hxg5 hxg5 17 Kf2 Rf6 18 Rh1+ Bh6 19 Rxh6+! Rxh6 20 Qxh6+ White can gain a clear advantage.

11 Ng6   b5!

According to Chigorin, 11 ... Nc6

12 Nxf8 Qxf8 is also possible, with sufficient compensation for the sacrificed exchange.

12 Bxb5   Qe4
13 Ne5

It turns out that the black rook is invulnerable, since on **13 Nxf8?** there follows 13 ... Bb7 14 Rf2 Ng4 15 Re2 Bxd4+!, with a decisive attack for Black. For example: 16 cxd4 Qxd4+ 17 Kf1 Nxh2+ 18 Ke1 f3 19 gxf3 Nxf3+ 20 Kf1 Qg1 mate, or 16 Kf1 f3! 17 Rxe4 Nxh2+ 18 Ke1 fxg2 19 Rxd4 g1=Q+ 20 Kd2 Nf3+ 21 Kc2 Ne1+ 22 Kd2 Qf2+, and Black wins.

13 ...   Bb7
14 Nf3

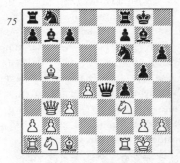

Black has overcome his opening difficulties, and can look to the future with confidence. Blackburne-Mason (London 1892) continued **14 ... Ng4** 15 Re1 Qg6 16 Be2 Qc6 17 Bd3 Nf6 18 Qc2 Nbd7 19 Na3 Rae8 20 Bd2 a6, with roughly equal chances.

8.2

7 ...   Ne7

Many years of tournament practice have shown that this continuation allows White to build up a sufficient initiative.

8 g3

This undermining of Black's pawn phalanx is a standard procedure. **8 h4** is weaker, in view of 8 ... Ng6 9 h5 Ne7 10 g3 (if *10 Qb3 0-0 11 g3*, then *11 ... Bh3!* followed by *12 ... fxg3*, with advantage to Black) 10 ... Bg4 11 gxf4 Bxh5 12 fxg5, as in Morphy-Riviere (Paris 1863), and now, as shown by Maroczy, by 12 ... Qc8! Black could have consolidated his advantage.

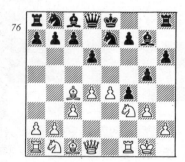

76

8 ...   d5!

Only by this move, suggested by Keres, can Black maintain the balance. Other replies allow White to gain an advantage:

a) 8 ... Qd7 9 gxf4 gxf4 10 Ne1 d5 11 exd5 Nxd5 12 Qf3 c6 13 Bxf4, with good prospects for White.

b) 8 ... fxg3 9 Nxg5! gxh2+ 10 Kh1 hxg5 11 Bxf7+ Kd7 (if *11 ... Kf8*, then *12 Qb3!*) 12 Bxg5, and White has a very strong attack.

c) 3 ... Ng6 9 gxf4 gxf4 10 Kh1! Nc6 11 Ng1 (in Fischer-Smith, Chicago 1964, after *11 Qb3? 0-0 12 Qc2 Nce7 13 Nbd2 Be6* Black gained the advantage) 11 ... Qe7 12 Qf3 Bd7 13 Bxf4 Nxf4 14 Qxf4 0-0-0 15 Nd2 Rdf8. This was the course taken by Dashevsky-Selivanovsky (1961), in which White should have continued 16 Ngf3!, preventing 16 ... f5?, which after 17 Nh4 would have given him a clear advantage.

Instead of 9 gxf4, there is the interesting continuation 9 Ne1!? Qe7 10 Qf3 g4 11 Qd3 f3 12 Nd2, as in Angelov-Kolarov (Sofia 1973). After 12 ... Nc6 13 b4 Nd8 14 b5 h5 15 e5! White built up a strong attack.

d) 8 ... g4. In the past this reply was considered obligatory for Black, but after 9 Nh4 f3 a position is reached, in which White has several highly promising continuations:

77

This is how Chigorin-Schmidt (Berlin 1881) developed: **10 Na3 Nbc6** (*10 ... 0-0* is very strongly met by *11 h3 h5 12 Bg5 Kh8 13 hxg4*, when Black cannot reply *13 ... hxg4*, in view of *14 Ng6+!! fxg6 15 Kf2*, and White wins) 11 Bf4 0-0 12 h3 Na5 13 Qd2 Nxd4 14 Nxc4 h5 15 Bh6 Ng6 16 Nf5, and White gained a clear advantage.

Also after **10 Be3** Nbc6 11 Nd2 0-0 12 h3 h5 13 hxg4 hxg4 14 Ndxf3! gxf3 15 Qxf3 Be6 16 Bxe6 fxe6 17 Qg4! White has a decisive attack (Szekely-Freymann, Abbazia 1912).

Steinitz-Kolisch (Paris 1867) went **10 h3** h5 11 Nxf3 (also good is *11 Qb3 0-0 12 Bg5 Qe8 13 Nd2 Nbc6 14 Bxe7 Nxe7 15 Re1*, with a promising position for White, Weit-Ranken, 1968) 11 ... gxf3 12 Qxf3 Bxh3 13 Qxf7+ Kd7, and now, by continuing 14 Bg5!, White could have gained a very strong attack on the enemy king stuck in the centre.

	9 exd5		fxg3!
	10 Ne5		gxh2+
	11 Kh1		0-0

To maintain his initiative, White must play actively, and not be afraid to sacrifice.

	12 Nxf7!		Rxf7

8.3

	7 ...		Nc6

Theory regards this as the main continuation.

In order to obtain sufficient compensation for the sacrificed pawn, White is obliged to take immediate active measures on the K-side, since otherwise Black gains active counter-play. For example: 8 Na3 (*8 Qb3* is well met by *8 ... Qd7!*) 8 ... Nf6! 9 Qd3 0-0 10 Bd2 d5 11 exd5 Nxd5 12 Bb3 Nde7 13 Rae1 Bf5, with an excellent position for Black (Chigorin-Allies, St Petersburg 1894).

	8 g3		

The strongest continuation here is 8 h4!, which leads to the Greco-Philidor Gambit considered earlier (p.69).

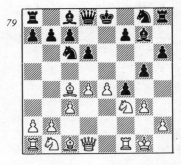

13 Rxf7 Kxf7
14 Bxg5!

This interesting sacrifice of two pieces occurred in Kuindzhi-Men (Batumi 1972). After **14 ... Kg6** (it is dangerous to accept the second sacrifice by *14 ... hxg5*, in view of *15 Qh5+ Kf8 16 Nd2*, or *15 ... Ng6 16 d6+ Kf6 17 Nd2*) 15 Bh4 Bf5 16 Qe2 Bf6 17 Qg2+ Bg5 18 Nd2 Qd6 19 Nf3 Nd7 20 Nxg5 White gained an attack sufficient for a draw.

With the move played White threatens to shatter the opponent's pawn lines on the K-side. Black has two systems of defence: the old **8 ... g4 9 Nh4 f3 (8.31)**, and the modern, counter-attacking **8 ... Bh3! (8.32)**.

We should also touch on one further possibility: **8 ... Nf6 9 gxf4 g4**. *E.C.O.* now recommends that White should continue 10 Nfd2 d5 11 exd5 Nxd5 12 Qe2+ Qe7 13 Ne4, with an unclear position.

However, along with 10 Nfd2 White has the strong manoeuvre 10 Ng5! 0-0 (bad is *10 ... hxg5 11 fxg5 Nxe4 12 Bxf7+*, or *11 ... Bd7 12*

gxf6 Bxf6 13 Bxf7+ !, with advantage to White) 11 e5!, which sets Black difficult problems (Glazkov).

see diagram 80

There can follow:

a) 11 ... dxe5 12 Nxf7! Rxf7 13 Qb3 Qe7 14 fxe5, or

b) 11 ... Ne8 12 e6! hxg5 (if *12 ... fxe6*, then *13 Bxe6+ Kh8 14 Qxg4*) 13 exf7+ Rxf7 14 Qb3, or

c) 11 ... hxg5 12 exf6 Bxf6 13 f5!, with advantage to White in all variations.

d) After 11 ... Nh5 12 Ne4! d5 13 Be2 dxe4 14 Bxg4 Nf6 15 exf6 Qxf6 16 Bxc8 Raxc8 17 f5! White again retains the better chances (analysis by Glazkov).

8.31

8 ...	g4
9 Nh4	f3

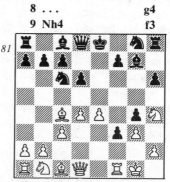

81

The initial position of the variation in question (7 ... Nc6) in its classical treatment. White has two principal ways of developing his initiative: **10 Qb3 (8.311)** and **10 Nd2 (8.312)**.

80

10 Na3 is considered inadequate, on account of 10 ... Bf6 (*10 ... Nf6*, as played in Metger-Englisch, Frankfurt 1887, is weaker in view of *11 Bd3 Qe7 12 Nc2 Bd7 13 Ne3 0-0-0 14 Nef5 Qf8 15 b4 Ne7 16 Nxg7 Qxg7 18 a4*, with the initiative for White) 11 Bf4 Bxh4 12 gxh4 Qxh4 13 e5 dxe5 14 dxe5 a6, and for the two pawns he has given up, White appears to have insufficient compensation.

However, instead of 11 Bf4, stronger is 11 Qb3!, and if 11 ... Qe7, then 12 Bf4, with a good game for White.

8.311
> **10 Qb3   Qe7**

Kaplan-Karpov (Stockholm 1969) is of interest: **10 ... Qd7** 11 Nd2 (*11 Bd3* is better, retaining the important white-squared bishop) 11 ... Na5 12 Qc2 Nxc4 13 Nxc4 Ne7 14 Ne3 Qc6, with a solid position for Black. Instead of 14 Ne3, more promising for White is 14 Bf4!

> **11 Bf4**

The only possibility of fighting for an advantage.

The chances are roughly level after **11 Na3** Nf6 (if *11 ... Bf6*, then *12 Bf4!*) 12 Nf5 Bxf5 13 exf5 0-0-0 (*13 ♟. 0-0 14 Bd3 b6 15 h3 h5* is weaker in view of *16 Bg5 Qd7 17 hxg4 hxg4 18 Nc2* and *19 Ne3*, with advantage to White) 14 Bxf7 Qe2 15 Qc2.

White achieves nothing by **11 Nf5**

Bxf5 12 Qxb7 (if *12 exf5*, then *12 ... 0-0-0*) 12 ... Qxe4 13 Bb5 Kd7! (*13 ... Nge7 14 Qxa8+ Kd7 15 Qxa7! Rb8 16 Qxb8 Bxd4+ 17 cxd4 Qxd4+ 18 Kh1 f2* allowed White in Nosovsky-Astafiev, corr. 1967, to repel the attack by *19 h4!*) 14 Qxa8 Bxd4+ 15 cxd4 Qxd4+ 16 Rf2 Qd1+ 17 Rf1 (*17 Bf1?* loses to *17 ... Qxc1 18 Qb7 Nge7*) 17 ... Qd4+, and Black forces a draw by perpetual check.

Here 18 Kh1? is bad because of 18 ... Nge7 19 Qb7 f2 20 h4 Rb8 21 Qa6 Rxb5 22 Qxb5 Bd3, when Black wins.

Instead of 12 ... Qxe4, the continuation 12 ... Rb8 13 Qxc6+ Bd7 is of interest.   Trofimov-Akimenko (Moscow 1966) continued 14 Qxc7 Rc8 15 Qxa7 Rxc4 16 Bf4 Nf6 17 Nd2 Rc8 18 Qa6 (*18 Qa3* is better) 18 ... Rc6 19 Qa8+, after which Black avoided the repetition of moves by playing 19 ... Qd8 20 Qa3 Bc8, with a complicated and unclear game.

> **11 ...   Nf6**

As Cortlever-Scholten (Leiwarten 1943) showed, **11 ... Bf6** 12 Nf5 Bxf5 13 Qxb7 Rb8 (*13 ... Qxe4*, as in the variation examined above, no longer works, since White's extra tempo *Bf4* enables him to repel the attack) 14 Qxc6+ Qd7 gives White the advantage after 15 Qa6 Bxe4 16 Nd2 Bg6 17 Qxa7 Rxb2 18 Bb3.

12 Nd2　　　　Nh5
13 Be3!

This move, suggested by Euwe, sets Black serious problems. White's pieces are fully mobilized, and he is ready, after sacrificing a knight at f3, to begin a dangerous attack along the f-file.

13 ...　　　　Bf6
14 Ndxf3　　　gxf3
15 Rxf3

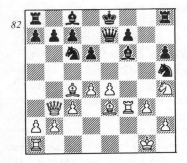

Black's defence is not easy. There can follow:

a) 15 ... Bxh4 16 Rxf7 (*16 Bxf7+* is also good) 16 ... Qxe4 17 Re1 Be7 18 Bd5 Na5 (on *18 ... Qg6* there follows *19 Bf2*) 19 Bxe4 Nxb3 20 Bg6 Kd8 21 Bxh5!, or

b) 15 ... 0-0 16 Bxh6 Bg4 (*16 ... Na5 17 Qb5 Nxc4* is no better, on account of *18 Qxh5*) 17 Bxf8 Rxf8 18 Nf5 Bxf5 (*18 ... Qxe4?* is decisively met by *19 Bd5*) 19 Rxf5 Ng7 20 Rxf6 (*20 Rf2* is also good) 20 ... Qxf6 21 Qxb7 Na5 22 Rxc7, with good winning chances for White in both cases (analysis by Bhend).

8.312

10 Nd2

After this move of Spielmann's, White threatens to begin an immediate attack along the f-file, by sacrificing one of his knights.

10 ...　　　　Bf6

This is the usual continuation, but **10 ... Nf6** also deserves consideration (*10 ... Qe7* is weaker in view of the reply *11 Re1!*), as in Heuer-Villard (Tallinn 1964), which continued 11 Nf5 Bxf5 12 exf5 0-0 13 Bd3 Re8 (*E.C.O.* recommends *13 ... d5 14 h3 h5 15 hxg4 hxg4 16 Nxf3 gxf3 17 Qxf3 Ne4! 18 Bxe4 dxe4 19 Qxe4 Nxd4! 20 f6! Bxf6 21 Qg4+ Bg7 22 Bh6 Ne6 23 Rae1 Qd7 24 Bxg7 f5 25 Qc4*, with a roughly equal game) 14 h3 h5 15 hxg4 hxg4 16 Nxf3 gxf3 17 Qxf3 d5 18 Bg5 Kf8 19 g4 Qd7 20 Bh4, and now, by continuing 20 ... Ne4!, Black would have escaped from his difficulties.

11 Ndxf3

White can also sacrifice his other knight: **11 Nhxf3** gxf3 12 Qxf3, although this does not achieve much. For example: 12 ... Be6 (not *12 ... Bh3? 13 Bxf7+ Kxf7 14 Qh5+*) 13 Bxe6 fxe6 14 e5 dxe5 15 Ne4 exd4! 16 Nxf6+, or 12 ... Qe7 13 e5 Bxe5! 14 Qxf7+ Qxf7 15 Bxf7+ Ke7 16 dxe5 Nxe5, and the chances are roughly equal (Keres).

Instead of the text move, Glazkov's recommendation of avoiding the immediate piece sacrifice by **11 Qb3** deserves consideration, after which the following position arises:

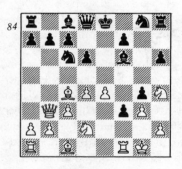

84

These continuations are now possible:

a) **11 ... Bxh4** 12 Bxf7+ Kf8, and now both 13 Nxf3 gxf3 14 Rxf3 Nf6 (on *14 ... Bf6* there follows *15 Bxg8*) 15 gxh4, and 13 Bh5 Qe7 14 Nxf3 gxf3 15 gxh4 Qg7+ 16 Bg5!, give White a decisive attack.

b) **11 ... Qe7** 12 Nf5 Bxf5 13 Qxb7 (*13 exf5 0-0-0 14 Bxf7* is also possible, with a good game for White) 13 ... Rb8 14 Qxc6+ Qd7 15

Qa6 Bg6 16 Qxa7 Rd8 17 a4, with a clear advantage to White.

c) **11 ... Qd7** 12 Nf5 Na5 13 Qc2 Nxc4 14 Nxc4 Qc6 (in the event of *14 ... d5 15 Nce3 dxe4 16 Qxe4+ Ne7* White should play *17 Re1*) 15 Qd3 d5 16 exd5 Qxd5 17 Nce3, with sufficient compensation for the sacrificed pawn.

d) **11 ... Rh7** 12 Nf5 Bxf5 13 exf5 Kf8! 14 Qxb7 Na5 15 Qa6 Nxc4 16 Nxc4, with roughly equal chances.

11 ...	**gxf3**
12 Qxf3	**Bh3**

Grünfeld's recommendation. In Spielmann-Grünfeld (Teplitz-Schonau 1922) Black played the weaker **12 ... Rh7** (Tartakover recommends *12 ... Qe7*), and after 13 Ng6! Rg7 (or *13 ... fxg6 14 Bxg8 Rg7 15 Bb3 Be7 16 Bxh6*, and White wins) 14 Nf4 Bg4 15 Qg2! Bg5 16 h3 Bd7 (*16 ... Bxf4* is no better, in view of *17 Bxf4! Bd7 18 Rae1 Qe7 19 e5 d5 20 Bxd5 0-0-0 21 b4*, with a strong attack for White) 17 Nh5 Rh7 18 e5! dxe5 19 Qe4 f5 20 Rxf5! White won.

13 Rf2	**Qd7**
14 e5	**Bxh4**

According to Keres, 14 ... dxe5 15 dxe5 Bxh4 16 Bxf7+ Ke7 17 Be3! gives White the advantage.

15 Bxf7+	**Kd8**

Bhend recommends 15 ... Ke7, but then there can follow 16 e6! Bxe6 17 Bxe6 Qxe6 18 Re2 Ne5 19 dxe5 Qg6

20 exd6++, with a clear advantage for White.

16	e6		Qe7
17	gxh4		Qxh4
18	Bh5		

In this critical position *E.C.O.* considers that after **18 ... Nf6 19 Qxf6+ Qxf6 20 Rxf6 Rg8+** Black has slightly the better chances.

It is difficult to agree with this evaluation. After **21 Kf2 Rg2+ 22 Kf3 Ke7 23 Rxh6 Rg1 24 Bf4!** the advantage is with White.

This concludes our analysis of the classical continuation 8 ... g4, from which it can be concluded that it affords White good chances of developing his initiative.

8.32

| 8 | ... | | Bh3! |

see diagram 86

The idea of this active continuation, which sets White complicated problems, belongs not to Grünfeld, as all the opening books assert, but to Alapin, who first employed it in a consultation game (St Petersburg 1906). Seeing that the position of

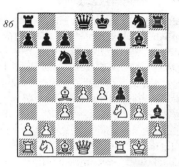

the white king is weakened, Black returns the gambit pawn, aiming to develop an initiative on the K-side.

9 gxf4

To maintain his initiative, White is forced to offer this exchange sacrifice. Moving the rook leads to an advantage for Black, for example:

a) 9 Re1 fxg3 10 hxg3 Qd7 11 Be3 Nf6 12 Qe2 Ng4 13 Nbd2 Nxe3 14 Qxe3 0-0 (Levy-Bisguier, New York 1956), or

b) 9 Rf2 Nf6 10 gxf4 (Tringov-Vukcević, Leningrad 1960, went *10 Qc2 Qd7 11 gxf4 gxf4 12 Kh1 0-0-0 13 Bd3 d5 14 e5 Ne4 15 Bxe4 dxe4 16 Qxe4*, and after *16 ... Bxe5!* Black quickly won) 10 ... Nxe4 11 Re2 (if *11 Qe1*, then *11 ... d5 12 Nbd2 f5!*) 11 ... d5 12 fxg5 Qd7! 13 Nbd2 Qg4+ 14 Kh1 0-0-0 15 Bb5 Nxd2 16 Nxd2 Bg2+! 17 Kg1 Bf3+, and Black won (Sebastian-Szegedy, Budapest 1946).

| 9 | ... | | Qd7! |

In Spielmann-Grünfeld (Karlsbad 1923) Black accepted the exchange sacrifice, **9 ... Bxf1**, and after 10 Qxf1 gxf4 (*10 ... g4 11 Ne1 f5* is weaker, because of *12 Be6!*, with a good game for White, Angelov-Atanasov, Bulgaria 1970) 11 Bxf4 Qf6 12 Bg3 0-0-0 13 Nbd2 Nge7 14 Qh3+ Kb8 15 Rf1 Qg6 16 Nh4 he should have been satisfied with a draw by 16 ... Qg5! 17 Nhf3 Qg6.

10 Rf2

The rook has to move, since 10 f5 Bxf1 11 Qxf1 Nf6 favours Black.

    10 ...   **Nf6**

    11 Qe1

11 Qc2 transposes into Tringov-Vukcević, considered earlier (cf. p.79).

    11 ...   **0-0-0**

    12 Bb5

Relatively best. On 12 f5 there follows 12 ... d5!, while regarding 12 e5, cf. Game No. 6.

    12 ...   **Rhe8!**

    13 Nbd2

Here too 13 e5? is bad because of 13 ... Qg4+ 14 Kh1 dxe5 15 Bxc6 (no better is *15 Nxe5 Nxe5! 16 fxe5 Ne4 17 Re2 Rxe5! 18 dxe5 Rd1!*, or *15 dxe5 Ne4! 16 Qxe4 Rd1+ 17 Ne1 Rxe5!*, with a winning attack for Black) 15 ... bxc6 16 Nxe5 Rxe5! 17 fxe5 Ne4 18 Re2 Qf3+ 19 Kg1 Bxe5!, and White is defenceless, since on 20 dxe5 there follows 20 ... Rd1 21 Qxd1 Qg4+ and mate in three moves, on 20 Be3 Black wins by 20 ... Bf4! 21 Bxf4 gxf4, while on

20 Nd2 Black has 20 ... Nxd2 21 Bxd2 Rxd4! winning decisively (analysis by Estrin).

    13 ...   **gxf4**

    14 Kh1

14 Bf1 is well met by 14 ... Bxf1 15 Rxf1 Nxe4 16 Nxe4 f5, while on **14 e5** there follows 14 ... Ng4 15 Re2 Ne3, with a decisive advantage to Black.

    14 ...   **Nxe4!**

    15 Nxe4   **d5!**

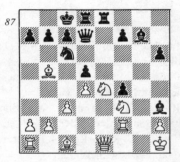

In this critical position Black has an undisputed advantage. For example: **16 Re2** dxe4 17 Rxe4 Qg4, or **16 Bxf4** dxe4 17 Ne5 Bxe5 18 Bxe5 f5!, or **16 Qg1** dxe4 17 Qxg7 e3! 18 Bxe3 fxe3 19 Re2 Bg4! — in all cases with a clear advantage to Black (Glazkov).

Apart from 4 Bc4, White has other possibilities on his fourth move, and these will be examined in the following chapters.

Game No. 5
Glazkov-Smirnov
Kolomna 1973
**1 e4 e5 2 f4 exf4 3 Nf3 g5 4 Bc4 Bg7
5 0-0 h6 6 d4 Ne7 7 Nc3**

This move, recommended by
Keres, is not the strongest. Better is
7 g3, which is examined in the
theoretical section.

7 ... 0-0

Stronger is 7 ... d6! 8 g3 Nc6!, as in
Levin-Zamikhovsky (cf. analysis).

8 g3!

Since Black has delayed playing ...
d7-d6, White can advantageously
undermine his opponent's pawn
chain, thereby opening lines for an
attack.

8 ... fxg3 9 Bxg5!

An unexpected, but perfectly
correct piece sacrifice.

9 ... gxh2+ 10 Kh1

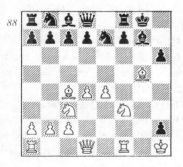

10 ... Qe8

Probably the only move. If Black
accepts the sacrifice by 10 ... hxg5,

he is rapidly crushed after 11 Nxg5
and 12 Qh5.

11 Bxe7 Qxe7 12 Nd5 Qxe4

Black gives up a rook, in the hope
of gaining at least some counter-
play. On 12 ... Qd8 there could have
followed 13 e5 c6 14 Nf6+! Bxf6 15
exf6 d5 (if *15 ... Qxf6, then 16 Ne5*)
16 Bd3 Qxf6 17 Ne5, with a decisive
attack for White.

13 Nxc7

This leads to unnecessary complications, and merely prolongs the
game. White should have continued
his attack by 13 Re1 Qg4 14 Qd3,
with decisive threats.

**13 ... Nc6 14 Nxa8 Nxd4 15 Bd3 Qc6
16 c3 Ne6**

The white knight is doomed, and
so Black, with several pawns for the
lost exchange, can continue to
resist.

17 Qe2 d5?

It was essential to play 17 ... Nf4!
18 Qe4 Nxd3 19 Qxd3 b6, when it
would be Black who had the
winning chances.

18 Nd4 Nxd4 19 cxd4 b6

By blocking the h1-a8 diagonal,
Black has again handed the
initiative to his opponent, who now
gains the opportunity to build up a
winning attack along the open g-
file.

**20 Qxh2 Qxa8 21 Rg1 Qc6 22
Rxg7+! Kxg7 23 Rg1+ Resigns.**

Game No. 6
Issler-Eggman
Correspondence 1966
1 e4 e5 2 f4 exf4 3 Nf3 g5 4 Bc4 Bg7
5 0-0 h6 6 d4 d6 7 c3 Nc6 8 g3

As has already been pointed out in the analysis (p.74), only 8 h4 leads to a double-edged struggle with roughly level chances. After the move played Black gains the opportunity to seize the initiative.

8 ... Bh3! 9 gxf4 Qd7!

An important improvement. In the well-known game Spielmann-Grünfeld (Karlsbad 1923), after 9 ... Bxf1 10 Qxf1 White had perfectly adequate compensation for the sacrificed exchange.

10 Rf2

The murderous 10 ... Qg4+ was threatened.

10 ... Nf6 11 Qe1 0-0-0

Black has a clear lead in development, and his king is safely tucked away on the Q-side. White's position begins to give serious cause for alarm.

12 e5

12 Bb5 would have been answered by 12 ... Rhe8, while if 12 f5, then 12 ... d5! (cf. analysis).

12 ... dxe5 13 Nxe5 Nxe5 14 fxe5 Qg4+

Black turns to positive action.

15 Kh1 Ne4 16 Re2

At first sight White appears to have defended successfully, but now follows a series of surprising and spectacular blows.

16 ... Bxe5!! 17 Nd2

On 17 dxe5 Black has the immediately decisive 17 ... Rd1! 18 Qxd1 Nf2+!

17 ... Rxd4!! 18 cxd4 Bxd4

The tireless rook has nevertheless sacrificed itself, after which Black's threats have become irresistible.

19 Bd5 Re8 20 Bxe4 Rxe4

Black also offers his second rook, the capture of which leads to immediate mate.

21 Qg3 Rxe2 22 Qxg4+ Bxg4

Black has regained with interest his sacrificed material, and remains with a decisive material and positional advantage.

Therefore **White resigned**.

9 Rosentreter Gambit

1 e4	e5
2 f4	exf4
3 Nf3	g5
4 d4	

4 Nc3 can hardly be recommended, in view of 4 ... Bg7! 5 d4 d6 6 g3 (on *6 Bc4* or *6 h4* Black replies *6 ... h6*, transposing into a variation of the Hanstein Gambit unfavourable for White) 6 ... g4 7 Nh4 (*7 Ng1 f3 8 h3 h5* also favours Black) 7 ... f3 8 Bf4 Bf6 9 Nf5 Bxf5 10 exf5 Ne7! 11 Bd3 Nc6, when Black has the advantage.

4 ...	g4

4 ... h6 is considered in chapter 12 (Becker Defence), and **4 ... d6** in chapter 13 (Fischer Defence). If instead Black chooses 4 ... Bg7 then 5 h4 h6! (*5 ... g4 6 Ne5* leads to one of the variations of the Kieseritzky Gambit, chapter 11) 6 hxg5 transposes into the Becker Defence, while 6 Bc4 leads to the Greco-Philidor Gambit, which is acceptable for White.

The text move is of independent significance.

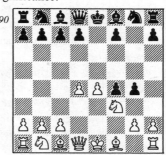

90

Two continuations for White deserve consideration: **5 Ne5 (9.1)** and **5 Bxf4 (9.2)**.

9.1

5 Ne5	Qh4+
6 g3	fxg3
7 Qxg4!	

White offers his opponent a whole rook.

see diagram 91

7 ...	Qxg4

A sound move, which gives Black the better prospects, whereas the

91

tempting continuation **7 ... g2+ 8 Qxh4 gxh1=Q** leads Black into difficulties after Schmidt's strong reply **9 Nc3!**

For example: **9 ... Be7** 10 Qf2 f6 11 Nf3, or **9 ... Qg1** 10 Nd5 Bd6 11 Be3 Qg7 12 Nc4, and Black's defence is extremely difficult.

9 ... Nc6 is also unsatisfactory, in view of 10 Qh5 Nxe5 (*10 ... Nd8 11 Bg5,* or *10 ... Be7 11 Qxf7+ Kd8 12 Bg5* is also clearly to White's advantage) 11 Qxe5+ Ne7 12 Qxh8 Qxh2, and now, according to analysis by Schmidt, by 13 Be3 Qg3+ 14 Kd2 Qg7 15 Qxg7 Bxg7 16 Nb5 Kd8 17 Bc4 a6 18 Nc3 White gains a clear advantage.

Nevertheless, Black has a possibility which promises him equality: **9 ... d6!** 10 Nxf7 Be7! (but not *10 ... Kxf7 11 Qh5+ Kg7 12 Kf2!,* with a decisive advantage for White) 11 Qh5 Nf6 12 Nxd6+ Kd8 (*12 ... Kd7?* loses to *13 Qf5+*) 13 Nf7+, and White is obliged to force perpetual check.

| **8 Nxg4** | **d5** |
| **9 Ne3** | |

Cordel recommended that White should sacrifice a piece by **9 Ne5** f6 10 Bf4 Bg7 11 exd5 fxe5 12 dxe5, but after 12 ... Nd7 13 Bb5 a6 14 Bxd7+ Bxd7 he has insufficient compensation for the piece.

9 ...	**dxe4**
10 hxg3	**Nc6**
11 Bb5	

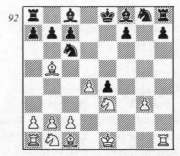

92

Schmidt considers the further continuation **11 ... Bg7** 12 d5 a6 13 Ba4 b5 14 dxc6 bxa4 15 Nd5, in which White gains some compensation for the pawn.

Stronger, however, is **11 ... Bd7!** 12 Bxc6 Bxc6 13 Nc3 0-0-0 14 d5 Bd7. Black returns the pawn, but after 15 Nxe4 Re8 16 Nf2 Bg7 17 Nd3 Nf6 gains the advantage (*Sovremeny Debyut*).

9.2

5 Bxf4

This piece sacrifice gives White more chances than the continuation

5 Ne5 examined above.

According to Schmidt, the similar sacrifice **5 Nc3** gxf3 6 Qxf3 d6 7 Bc4 is insufficient, in view of 7 ... Be6 8 d5 Qh4+! 9 g3 Qg4, when White does not gain sufficient compensation for the piece.

5 ...	gxf3
6 Qxf3	d6

The best defence. 6 ... Nc6 (if *6 ... Bg7*, then *7 Qg3*) 7 Bc4 Bg7 is unsatisfactory after 8 e5! Nxd4 9 Bxf7+! Kxf7 10 Qh5+ Kf8 11 0-0, with a strong attack for White.

7 Bc4	Bg7!

Other replies allow White more attacking possibilities, for example:

a) 7 ... Be6 8 d5 Bc8 9 0-0 (Morphy-Maurian, New Orleans 1869).

b) 7 ... Nf6 8 Bg5 Be7 9 0-0 Nbd7 10 Nc3 c6 11 Rf2 Qa5 12 e5! (Alekhine-Velikanov, Odessa 1916).

c) 7 ... Qh4+ 8 Bg3 Qf6 9 Qb3 Nh6 10 Rf1 Qe7 11 Nc3 (Dahl-Danberg, Sweden 1968) and in all three cases White's attack concluded victoriously.

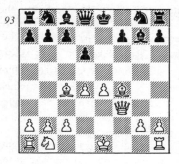

Now White in turn must play accurately, so as to gain sufficient compensation for the sacrificed piece.

8 0-0!

Other moves achieve nothing for White:

a) 8 e5 dxe5 (*8 ... Be6 9 d5 Bf5 10 0-0 dxe5* is less promising for Black after *11 Bxe5 Bxe5 12 Qxf5 Bf6 13 Nc3 Qd6 14 Bb5+ Nd7 15 Rae1+ Kd8 16 Kh1!*, with a dangerous attack for White, Weider-Jansson, France 1977) 9 Bxe5 Nf6 10 0-0 Nbd7 11 Nd2 0-0!, or

b) 8 Bxd6 Be6 9 Bxe6 fxe6 10 Qh5+ Kd7, or

c) 8 Nd2 Be6 9 Rf1 Ne7 10 d5 Bc8 11 Bh6 0-0, and in all cases, according to Bilguer, Black successfully repels the attack.

8 ...	Bxd4+
9 Kh1	Bf6

Now, according to analysis by Nenarokov, **10 e5** dxe5 11 Bxe5 Nd7 12 Bc3 Qe7 13 Re1 Be5 14 Bxe5 Nxe5 15 Qh5 leads to a position with roughly equal chances.

It is difficult to agree with this opinion. After 15 ... Nf6 (or *15 ... Bg4*) 16 Qxe5 Qxe5 17 Rxe5+ Kf8 18 Nc3 White's position is clearly better.

Thus the Rosentreter Gambit affords White no fewer possibilities than the Greco-Philidor Gambit.

10 Allgaier Gambit

1 e4	e5
2 f4	exf4
3 Nf3	g5
4 h4	

This move has the advantage over the continuations considered in the preceding chapters, 4 Bc4 and 4 d4, that Black does not now have time to stabilize the position, but is forced to weaken his pawn phalanx.

4 ...	g4
5 Ng5	

5 Ne5, leading to the Kieseritzky Gambit, is considered in the next chapter.

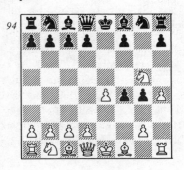

This gambit bears the name of the Viennese player Allgaier. The text move, which leads to a romantic piece sacrifice, was highly popular in the last century, but subsequently practical interest in it fell. The point is that, by initiating such sharp play in the opening, White in a certain sense burns his boats behind him, whereas in the Kieseritzky Gambit he can hope to obtain an attack without any excessive risk.

5 ...	h6

Black has no reason for rejecting the gift offered. By declining the sacrifice, he subjects himself to much greater risk.

For example, after **5 ... d5** White advantageously continues 6 d4! (*6 exd5?* is inconsistent, on which Ponziani recommended *6 ... Nf6*, but *6 ... h6!* is much more convincing, after which both *7 Qe2+ Ne7 8 Ne4 Bg7*, and *7 Ne4 f5! 8 Nec3 Bd6 9 d6 Nf6* lead to an advantage for

Black) 6 ... f6 7 Bxf4 fxg5 8 hxg5 Bg7 9 Nc3 dxe5 (*9 ... c6 10 exd5* transposes into the Alapin Variation in which White also retains the initiative) 10 Bc4 Bf5 11 Nd5 Nc6 12 Nxc7+ Kf8 13 c3, and White's position is clearly better (Chigorin-Fernandez, blindfold game, Havana 1889).

5 ... f6 is of course bad, in view of 6 Qxg4 fxg5 7 Qh5+ Ke7 8 Qxg5+.

The other way of declining the gambit is by **5 ... Nf6**, on which there normally follows 6 e5 Qe7, with two possibilities:

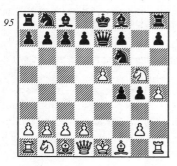

95

a) 7 Be2 Qxe5 8 d4 Qe7 (*8 ... Qd5 9 Bxf4 Qxg2* is weaker, in view of *10 Rf1 d6 11 Nc3 h6 12 Qd3 hxg5 13 Bxg5*, with a very strong attack for White) 9 Bxf4! h6 10 Nc3! d5 11 0-0 c6 (up to here — analysis by Alapin) 12 Qd2! hxg5 13 Bxg5, and after 14 Rae1 White, as Keres shows, has a strong attack.
b) 7 Qe2 Nh5 8 Nc3 Ng3 9 Qc4! Qxe5+ (if *9 ... Nxh1*, then *10 Nd5 Qxe5+ 11 Be2 Bd6 12 d4 Qg7 13*

Ne4, with a strong attack for White) 10 Be2 d5 (*10 ... Nxh1* leads to a clear advantage for White after *11 Qxf7+ Kd8 12 d4 Qg7 13 Bxf4 Qxf7 14 Nxf7+ Ke8 15 Nxh8 c6 16 Bxg4*) 11 Nxd5 Nxe2 12 Qxe2 Qxe2+ 13 Kxe2 Bd6, and now, by continuing 14 Ne4 or 14 b3, White obtains the better chances.

Instead of 8 Nc3, 8 Qxg4 also deserves consideration, so as to answer 8 ... Ng3 with 9 Qxf4 Nxh1 10 Nc3, and 8 ... Qxe5+ with 9 Be2 Ng3 10 d4, in both cases with a dangerous attack for White.

6 Nxf7   Kxf7

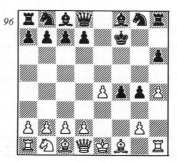

96

The basic position of the Allgaier Gambit.

7 d4

Weak is **7 Qxg4?** Nf6 8 Qxf4 Bd6!, when Black has a clear advantage.

Keres recommends **7 Nc3** f3 (a logical move, breaking up White's K-side; on *7 ... d5* White does best to continue *8 d4!*) 8 gxf3 Be7 9 Bc4+ d5 10 Nxd5 Bxh4+ 11 Kf1 Kg7 12 d3 or 12 f4, with some attacking chances; this has not yet been tested in practice.

7 ... Nc6 (instead of *7 ... f3*) leads to the Hamppe-Allgaier Gambit, which is examined in chapter 4 of the companion volume *King's Gambit Declined*.

The formerly popular continuation **7 Bc4+** d5 8 Bxd5+ appears dubious:

a) 8 ... Ke8 9 d4 Nf6 (less promising for Black is *9 ... f3 10 gxf3 Nf6 11 Nc3 Bb4 12 Bb3! Nc6 13 Be3 gxf3 14 Qd3!*, which according to Keres gives White good chances) 10 Nc3 Nh5! 11 0-0 c6 12 Bb3 Bg7! (Keres considers only *12 ... Qxh4*, which is bad in view of *13 Bxf4*) 13 e5 Rf8 14 Ne4 Qxh4 15 Nd6+ Kd7!, and Black has a winning position (analysis by Shabelsky).

b) 8 ... Kg7 9 d4 f3! 10 gxf3 Nf6 11 Nc3 (after *11 Bb3 Nc6 12 c3, E.C.O.* considers that Black does best to continue *12 ... Qd6! 13 e5 Nxe5! 14 dxe5 Qxe5+*, with the better position) 11 ... Bb4 12 Bc4 gxf3 13 Rg1+ Ng4 14 Qxf3 Qxh4+ 15 Rg3 Rf8 16 Bf4 (Marco-Schlechter, consultation game, Vienna 1903) and now the simple 16 ... Be7! would have led to a clear advantage for Black.

7 ...   d5

On 7 ... d6 there can follow 8 Bc4+ (also possible is *8 Bxf4 Qe8 9 Bd3 Nc6 10 c3 Nf6 11 0-0 Kg7 12 Nd2 Qh5 13 Bg3*, with an active position

for White, Littlewood-Tan, Hastings 1963) 8 ... Kg7 9 Bxf4 Rh7 10 Nc3 Kh8 11 Qd2 c6 12 0-0-0 b5 13 Bd3 Rf7 14 Bg5!, with mounting pressure for White (Anderssen-Amelung, Berlin 1862).

7 ... **f3** is better, and after 8 gxf3 (in the event of *8 Bf4 d5 9 Nc3 c6 10 Qd2 Be6 11 gxf3 Nf6 12 Bd3 gxf3 13 0-0-0 Bb4*, as in a certain correspondence game, Black again has the advantage, but 8 Be3 or 8 Nc3 deserves consideration) 8 ... d5! 9 Bf4 Nf6 10 e5 Nh5 11 fxg4 Nxf4 12 Qf3 Kg7 Black repels the attack, retaining his extra piece (Gunsberg-Bird, London 1889).

8 Bxf4

8 ...   Nf6

8 ... dxe4? is antipositional, in view of 9 Bc4+ Kg6 10 Nc3 Nf6 (in the event of *10 ... Bb4 11 0-0 Bxc3 12 bxc3 Nc6*, as in MacKenzie-N.N., Birmingham 1885, White does best to continue *13 h5+! Kh7 14 Be5!* with a clear advantage) 11 h5+ Kh7 12 Qe2! followed by 13 0-0-0, when

White obtains a very strong attack (Marco-Schlechter, consultation game, Vienna 1903).

8 ... Be6? 9 Bd3 Nc6 is also unsatisfactory, in view of 10 0-0 Ke8 11 Nc3 dxe4 12 Bxe4, when White has numerous threats (Oskam-Maier, Holland 1903).

8 ... Nc6 9 Be2 dxe4 10 d5 Nf6 also seems dubious, in view of the continuation suggested by Keres: 11 0-0 Bc5+ 12 Kh1 Qxd5 13 Qxd5 Nxd5 14 Be5+, with advantage to White.

9 Nc3

Along with this usual move, White can also consider **9 Be2!?** Nc6 (if *9 ... dxe4*, then *10 Nc3*, while on *9 ... Bg7* there follows *10 0-0*) 10 Nc3 Be6 (*10 ... Kg7 11 0-0 dxe4 12 d5!*, or *10 ... dxe4 11 Bc4+* followed by *12 d5* also leaves White with the advantage) 11 0-0 Kg7 12 exd5! Nxd5 13 Nxd5 Qxd5 14 c4!, with a very strong attack (Glazkov).

9 ...   **Bb4**

It is difficult to suggest anything better. For example:

a) 9 ... dxe4 (*9 ... Be6* transposes into a variation considered in the previous note after *10 Be2! Nc6 11 0-0*) 10 Bc4+ Kg7 (or *10 ... Kg6 11 h5+!*) 11 Qd2 Nc6 12 0-0-0 Bd6 13 Rhf1, with a strong attack for White.

b) 9 ... c6 10 Bd3 dxe4 11 Nxe4 Nbd7 (on *11 ... Qxd4* there follows *12 c3 Qb6 13 Nxf6 Kxf6 14 Rf1*) 12

0-0, and in Urusov-Grenishe (corr. 1884-85) White obtained a decisive attack.

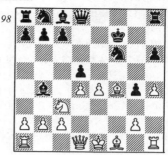

98

10 Be2

In a certain consultation game (London 1904) White tried **10 Be5**, and after 10 ... Nxe4! 11 Bd3! Bxc3+ (if *11 ... Nxc3*, then *12 0-0+*) 12 bxc3 Nc6 (after *12 ... Rf8 13 0-0+ Kg8 14 Bxe4 dxe4 15 Qe2* White again has a very strong attack) 13 0-0+ Ke7 14 Bxh8 Qxh8 15 Bxe4 dxe4 16 Qe2 gained a winning position.

10 Bd3 also deserves consideration, after which Goncharov-Yamont (Moscow 1901) continued 10 ... Bxc3+ 11 bxc3 Re8 (according to Chigorin, *11 ... dxe4 12 Bc4+ Kg7 13 0-0* favours White) 12 e5 Nh5 13 0-0 Nxf4 14 Rxf4+ Ke7 15 Qd2 Be6 16 Rf6 Rf8 17 Raf1 Nd7, and now by 18 Rxe6+! Kxe6 19 Qxh6+ White could have gained a won position.

10 ...   **Bxc3+**

The following continuations have also occurred in practice:

a) 10 ... c6 (if *10 ... dxe4*, then *11 0-0*) 11 0-0 Ke8 (or *11 ... Bxc3 12 Be5*) 12 e5 Bxc3 13 exf6! Bb4 14 Bxg4, and White has numerous threats.

b) 10 ... Be6 11 0-0 Bxc3 (no better is *11 ... Ke7 12 e5 Ne4 13 Nxe4 dxe4 14 c3 Ba5 15 Bxg4 Bc4 16 Qd2*, with excellent attacking chances for White) 12 Be5! Nbd7 13 Bxf6 Nxf6 14 e5 Bb4 15 Rxf6+ Ke7 16 Bxg4, and White won (Gudues-Dimer, corr. 1898).

11 bxc3

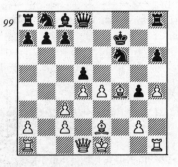

99

In this critical position Black still has his extra piece, but the insecure position of his king gives White good chances for continuing his attack. Here are two examples from practice:

a) 11 ... Kg6 12 e5 Nh5 13 Bc1 Ng3 14 Qd3+ Ne4 15 g3 c5 16 0-0 Nc6 17 Qe3 cxd4 18 cxd4 Ne7 (Gunsberg-Marco, Vienna 1903), and now, according to analysis of Marco, by 19 Rf4! h5 20 Rxe4 dxe4 21 Qg5+ White could have gained the advantage.

b) 11 ... dxe4 12 Qd2 Kg6 13 0-0 Be6 (*13 ... Nc6* is well met by *14 Bg5!*) 14 c4! c6 15 Rab1! b6 16 Rf2 Nbd7 (if *16 ... Ne8 17 Be5 Rh7*, then *18 Qf4*, while on *16 ... Qe7, 17 c5!* is very strong) 17 Bd6! Ne8 18 Qf4! Nef6 19 d5, with a clear advantage to White (Schlechter-Marco, consultation game, Vienna 1903).

With this we conclude our analysis of the Allgaier Gambit. In spite of the extensive practical material available, at present it is difficult to answer the question as to how Black can refute White's bold opening idea.

11 Kieseritzky Gambit

1 e4	e5
2 f4	exf4
3 Nf3	g5
4 h4	g4
5 Ne5	

It should be mentioned that this continuation is the strongest, and that it is of decisive importance for the evaluation of the classical 3 ... g5 defence.

The appropriation of the name Kieseritzky to the entire system is to a considerable degree arbitrary, since the move 5 Ne5 was known at the time of Polerio, and a part in its analysis was played by practically all the leading players of the 19th century.

Four hundred years of practice have revealed for Black five main methods of defence: **5 ... h5 (11.1), 5 ... d5 (11.2), 5 ... d6 (11.3), 5 ... Bg7 (11.4)** and **5 ... Nf6 (11.5)**.

Other continuations are unsatisfactory for Black. For example:

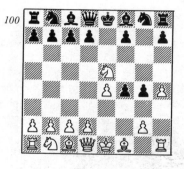

100

a) 5 ... Be7 (this move was known at the time of Polerio) 6 Bc4! Bxh4+ 7 Kf1 d5 (also inadequate is *7 ... Nh6 8 Nxg4*) 8 Bxd5 Nh6 9 d4 Bg5 (*9 ... Qg5* achieves nothing after *10 Nc3*, with the threat of *11 Ne2* or *11 g3*) 10 Nc3! c6 11 Bb3 f6 12 Nd3 Qxd4 13 Bxf4, with a clear advantage to White (Bilguer).

b) 5 ... Qe7 (the Salvio Defence) 6 d4!, and now:

6 ... f5 (*6 ... Bg7 7 Qxg4*, or *6 ... Nc6 7 Nc3* leads to a clear advantage for White) 7 Bc4! Nf6 8 Nc3 d6 9

Bf7+ Kd8 10 Bxf4 Nd7 11 Bb3 Ke8 12 Nf7 Rg8 13 Ng5, and White has a decisive advantage.

6 ... d6 7 Nxg4 f5 (also dubious is *7 ... Qxe4+ 8 Qe2 d5 9 Nf2 Qxe2+ 10 Bxe2 Bd6 11 Nd3 Nc6 12 c3*, with advantage to White, Kieseritzky-Dumonch, Paris 1849) 8 Nf2 Nf6 9 Bxf4 Nxe4 (or *9 ... fxe4 10 d5 Bf5 11 Be2!*) 10 Qh5+ Kd8 11 Be2 Nf6 12 Qf3 Nc6 13 c3, and White has the advantage.

c) **5 ... Nc6** (the Neumann Defence) 6 d4! Nxe5 7 dxe5 d6 8 Bxf4 Bg7 (*8 ... Qe7 is best met by 9 Bb5+! c6 10 exd6 Qxe4+ 11 Qe2*, with advantage to White) 9 Nc3! dxe5 (or *9 ... Bxe5 10 Bxe5 dxe5 11 Qxd8+*) 10 Qxd8+ Kxd8 13 0-0-0+ Bd7 14 Be3, with an excellent position for White (Bilguer).

11.1

5 ...   h5

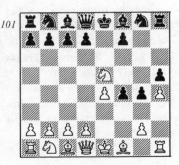

101

It is not known for what reason, but this defence, worked out by Kieseritzky, became known as 'the long whip'. It too is insufficient for equality.

6 Bc4   Rh7

The other way of defending f7 is by the more natural move **6 ... Nh6**, but it too does not give Black equality, for example: 7 d4 d6 8 Nd3 f3 9 gxf3 gxf3 (on *9 ... Be7 either 10 Bf4 Bxh4+ 11 Kd2, or 10 Bg5 Bxg5 11 hxg5 Qxg5 12 f4* can be recommended, with the better prospects for White) 10 Qxf3 Bg4 11 Qf2 Qd7 (no better is *11 ... Qe7 12 0-0 Rh7 13 Nc3 c6 14 e5 d5 15 Bxd5!*, with advantage to White) 12 Nc3 c6 13 Bg5 Na6 14 Kd2 Bg7 15 Raf1 0-0 16 Qe3, and White gained a winning position (Peev-Atanasov, Bulgaria 1954).

7 d4

An essential move. Contrary to the opinion of theory, the immediate capture on f7 does not give White anything: **7 Nxf7** Rxf7 8 Bxf7+ Kxf7 9 d4 f3 10 gxf3 d6 11 Bg5 Be7 12 f4 (*12 Qd2* is possibly better) 12 ... d5 13 e5 Bf5 14 Nc3 Na6 15 a3 c6 16 Ne2 (up to here — a variation by Springfield, 1854, assessed as favourable to White) 16 ... Qd7! 17 Ng3 Kg6, and Black sets up an impregnable position (Glazkov).

see diagram 102

7 ...   f3

Relatively best. The following continuations have also been played:

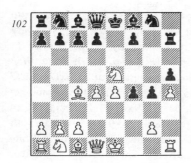

102

a) 7 ... Qf6 8 0-0 Bh6 9 Nc3 d6 (*9 ... c6 10 Nxf7! Rxf7 11 e5! Qxh4 12 Bxf7+ Kxf7 13 Bxf4*, or *9 ... Ne7 10 Bxf4! Bxf4 11 g3 Be3+ 12 Kg2*) 10 Nd5 Qd8 11 Nd3 (*11 Nxf7* is also good) 11 ... f3 12 g3 c6 13 N5f4 Bg7 14 c3, and for the sacrificed pawn White has an excellent attacking position (Duason-Rievs, 1862).
b) 7 ... Bh6 (*7 ... d6* is met by the immediate sacrifice *8 Nxf7!*) 8 Nc3! Nc6 9 Nxf7 Rxf7 10 Bxf7+ Kxf7 11 Bxf4 Bxf4 12 0-0 Kg7 13 Rxf4 Qxh4 14 Qd2 d6 15 Raf1, with a clear advantage to White in Bronstein-Dubinin (Leningrad 1947).

      8 gxf3   **d6**
      9 Nd3

As was shown in note to White's 7th move, with the f-file closed the sacrifice on f7 does not achieve anything for White.

      9 ...   **Be7**
     10 Be3

10 Bf4 also deserves consideration.

     10 ...   **Bxh4+**
     11 Kd2   **Bg5**

After 11 ... gxf3 12 Qxf3 Bg4 13

Qf4, White, despite being a pawn down, has the better prospects.

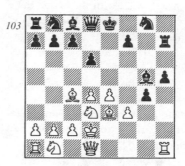

103

The critical position of the 'long whip' system.

At the cost of a pawn White has obtained a highly promising attacking position, as is confirmed by the following examples from practice:
a) 12 Qg1 Nc6 13 Bb5 Bd7 14 Bxc6 bxc6 15 Nc3 Qe7 16 e5 Bxe3+ 17 Qxe3 d5 18 Rag1 (Harrwitz-Anderssen, Paris 1857).
b) 12 f4 Bh6 13 Nc3! Bg7 (*13 ... Nf6* is strongly met by *14 e5*) 14 f5 Nc6 15 Qg1 Bd7 16 Re1 (Kolisch-Anderssen, Paris 1860).
In both games White successfully concluded his attack.

Thus it can be concluded that the 5 ... h5 defence is insufficient for equality.

11.2
      5 ...   **d5**
This, the Brentano Defence, is also not altogether satisfactory.
      6 d4!   **Nf6**

Weak is 6 ... f3 (or *6 ... f6 7 Nxg4 dxe4 8 Bxf4*) 7 gxf3 Be7 8 Be3 Bxh4+ 9 Kd2, with the better game for White (Blackburne-Charlick, Adelaide 1885).

7 Bxf4   Nxe4

7 ... Nh5 8 Qd2 Be7 9 exd5 is also in White's favour.

8 Nd2!

This move, found by Caro, gives White the advantage in all variations.

104

8 ...   Nxd2

The alternatives are:

a) **8 ... Qf6** 9 g3 Bh6 10 Nxe4 dxe4 (Lasker-de Visser, Manhatten 1903) and now, instead of the risky 11 Bc4?! Bxf4 12 Bxf7+ Qxf7!, by 11 Nxg4! Bxg4 12 Qxg4 Bxf4 13 Qxf4 Qxf4 14 gxf4 White could have obtained a position with the better chances.

b) **8 ... f5** 9 Nxe4 fxe4 10 Bb5+ c6 11 0-0! Be6 (if *11 ... cxb5?*, then *12 Nf7!*) 12 Be2, with advantage to White (Bobekov-Pelitov, Sofia 1967).

c) **8 ... Bg7** 9 Nxe4 dxe4 10 Bc4 0-0 11 c3 Nd7 (*11 ... Nc6* is very strongly met by *12 Nxf7! Rxf7 13 Qb3 Qe8 14 0-0*, and if *14 ... Bf5?* Zak's suggestion of *15 Bxf7+ Qxf7 16 Qxb7* gives White the advantage) 12 Nxf7! Rxf7 13 Bxf7+ Kxf7 14 Qb3+ Ke7 15 0-0-0 Nf6 16 d5!, with a decisive attack for White (Lutikov—Shakh-Zade, Tashkent 1950).

9 Qxd2   Bd6

9 ... Be6 10 0-0-0 Nd7 11 Re1 Bd6 leads to the main variation, while after 11 ... Be7? 12 Qe2 Rg8 White wins immediately by 13 Nxf7! Bxf7 14 Bxc7 (Heemskerk-van Rhijn, corr. 1896).

Black's lot is no easier after 11 ... Bg7 12 Nxg4 0-0, in view of 13 Bg5! Nf6 (if *13 ... Qe8*, then *14 Bh6!*) 14 Nxf6+ Bxf6 15 Bd3 Kh8 16 Qf4, with a quick win (Caro-Schiffers, 1897).

Teschner-Dahl (Berlin 1946) went **9 ... Bg7** 10 Bh6 Bxh6 11 Qxh6 Be6 12 Bd3 Nd7, but after 13 Nxf7! Bxf7 14 0-0 Ne5 15 Rae1 Black had to resign.

10 0-0-0   Be6

11 Bd3

see diagram 105

In this critical position White is assured of a persistent initiative. What's more, the presence of Black's extra pawn merely hinders the co-ordination of his pieces.

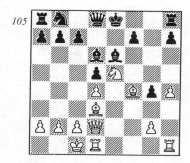

The attempt to win a piece by **11 ... f6** is illusory, in view of 12 Rde1! fxe5 13 Bxe5 Kd7 14 Bxh8 Qxh8 15 Qh6!, while if Black chooses 12 ... Bxe5, then after 13 Bxe5! Kd7 14 Bxf6! Qxf6 15 Rhf1 Qg7 16 Rxe6! White has a decisive attack (Bilguer)

A certain correspondence game went **11 ... Nd7** 12 Rde1 Nxe5 13 Bxe5 Bxe5 14 Rxe5 Qd7, after which Keres' recommendation of 15 Qg5! Qe7 16 Bf5 enables White to regain his pawn while retaining the better chances.

11.3

5 ...   **d6**

While this simple defence does not pretend to be a refutation of the Kieseritzky Gambit, it does give Black good chances of equalizing.

6 Nxg4

Reverting to the Allgaier Gambit by 6 Nxf7 Kxf7 7 Bc4+ Ke8 8 d4 is in the given case too risky, since Black has the strong move 8 ... Bh6.

see diagram 106

6 ...   **Be7!**

After other replies White can expect to obtain the better game. For example:

a) 6 ... h5 (even weaker is *6 ... f5 7 Nf2! Nf6 8 d4 fxe4 9 Bxf4 d5 10 g4*, when White begins a decisive offensive) 7 Nf2 Nf6 8 d4 Bh6 9 Be2 Nc6 10 Nc3 Ng4 11 Nxg4 Bxg4 (on *11 ... hxg4* White continues *12 Nd5 Bg5 13 g3*), and now both 12 Bxg4 hxg4 13 Nd5 f3 14 g3 (Keres), and 12 Qd3 Bxe2 13 Nxe2 Qf6 14 Bd2 followed by 15 0-0-0 give White clearly the better chances.

b) 6 ... Nf6 7 Nf2 (*E.C.O.* recommends *7 Nxf6! Qxf6 8 Nc3 c6 9 Be2! Rg8 10 Bf3 Bh6 11 d4 Na6 12 e5! dxe5 13 Ne4 Qe7 14 0-0*, with a strong attack for the sacrificed material) 7 ... Rg8 8 d4 Bh6 9 Nc3 Nc6! (the best move), when there can follow:

10 Nd3 Bg4 11 Be2 Bxe2 12 Nxe2! Qe7 13 Bxf4 Bxf4 14 Ndxf4 Qxe4 15 Qd2 0-0-0 16 0-0-0 Nd5, with a roughly equal game, or

10 Nd5 Nxd5 11 exd5 Qe7+ 12

Be2 Nb4 13 c4 Rxg2! 14 Kf1 Rg3 15 Qa4+ Bd7 16 Qxb4 0-0-0, with an unclear position, in which Black has a dangerous attack for the piece. These variations suggested by Korchnoi deserve practical testing.

Instead of 9 ... Nc6, Planinc-Korchnoi (Moscow 1975) went **9 ... Qe7 10 Nd3!** Bg4 11 Be2 Bxe2 12 Qxe2 Nc6, and now, by continuing 13 Nxf4! Nxd4 14 Qd3 Bxf4 15 Bxf4 White would have gained the better chances.

7	d4	Bxh4+
8	Nf2	Qg5

8 ... Bg3 9 Qf3! Qf6 is weaker, in view of 10 Nc3 Qxd4 11 Bxf4 Qxf2+ 12 Qxf2 Bxf2+ 13 Kxf2 Be6 (if *13 ... Nc6*, then *14 Nb5*) 14 e5!, when White's initiative compensates for the pawn (A.Rabinovich).

9 Qf3

The alternative is **9 Nc3** Nf6 10 Qf3 Ng4! 11 Nd1 Nxf2 12 Nxf2 Nc6 13 c3 Bg3 14 Kd1 (in Mortimer-Rosenthal, Paris 1878, *14 Be2 Bd7 15 Bd2 0-0-0* lead to a slight advantage for Black) 14 ... Be6 15 Nh3 Qg7, which Bilguer assesses as favourable for Black, but in fact after 16 Be2! White maintains the balance.

see diagram 107

9	...	Nc6!

Black's entire defence is based on this move of Rosenthal, since the old continuation 9 ... Bg3 is not altogether satisfactory, on account

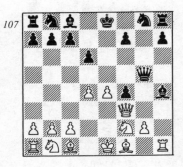

107

of 10 Nc3, and now:

a) 10 ... Nc6 11 Bb5 Bd7 12 Bxc6 bxc6 13 Ne2 Bg4 14 Qxg3 fxg3 15 Bxg5 gxf2+ 16 Kxf2, with the better prospects for White (variation by Kieseritzky).

b) 10 ... Nf6 11 Bd2! Nc6 (*11 ... Rg8 12 0-0-0, and 11 ... Bd7 12 Bd3 Nc6 13 Ne2 Nxd4 14 Nxd4 Qe5 15 Kf1* are also favourable for White) 12 Bb5! Bd7 13 Bxc6 bxc6 14 0-0-0 0-0-0 15 Nh3, with the better chances for White (Steinitz-Green, London 1864).

10	Qxf4!	Bxf2+
11	Kxf2	Qxf4+
12	Bxf4	Nxd4
13	Nc3!	

The position has simplified; Black has an extra pawn, but White's pieces are more actively placed.

13	...	Be6

13 ... Nxc2? is unsatisfactory, in view of 14 Nd5! Kd8 (or *14 ... Nxa1 15 Nxc7+ Kd8 16 Nxa8 Nc2 17 Bxd6*) 15 Rc1, with advantage to White.

14 Nb5	Nxb5
15 Bxb5+	Bd7

Weaker is 15 ... c6 16 Bd3.

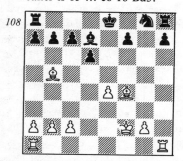

In this critical position White's positional advantage compensates for the pawn.

A correspondence game Ressegnier-Lentz (1912) continued **16 Be2** Nf6 17 e5 Ne4+ 18 Ke3 d5 19 c4 c6 20 Rad1 Be6 21 Bf3 f5! 22 exf6 Nxf6 23 Be5!, and soon ended in a draw.

11.4

5 ...	Bg7

This defence of Paulsen's used to be considered one of the best, but recent research has somewhat undermined its reputation.

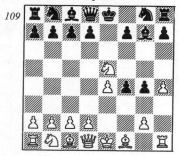

6 d4

Schlechter considered **6 Nxg4** to be the simplest reply to Black's system of defence, but after 6 ... d5 White cannot, in our opinion, achieve full equality. For example:

a) 7 Nf2 (*7 exd5?* loses to *7 ... Qe7+*) 7 ... dxe4 8 Nxe4 Qe7 9 Qe2 Nc6 10 c3 Nh6, or

b) 7 Qf3 Nc6 8 Bb5 Ne7 9 Qxf4 Bxg4 10 Qxg4 0-0, and in each case Black's position is better.

c) 7 d4 dxe4 8 Bxf4 Qxd4 9 Qxd4 Bxd4 10 c3, and now, according to analysis by Panov, 10 ... Bg7! 11 Nf2 f5 12 Bxc7 Nc6 gives Black the better chances.

d) Gheorghiu-Kavalek (Bucharest 1966) went **7 Qe2** dxe4 8 Qxe4+ Qe7 9 Nf2 Bf5 10 Qxe7+ Nxe7 11 c3 Nd7 12 d4 c5, which also proved to be to Black's advantage.

6 ...	Nf6

Here **6 ... d6** deserves consideration, with the following alternatives:

a) 7 Nxf7 Kxf7 8 Bc4+ Ke8 (less good is *8 ... d5 9 Bxd5+ Ke8 10 Bxf4 Ne7 11 Nc3 c6 12 Bb3 Qxd4 13 Qe2*, with an attacking position for White, Pillsbury-Gunsberg, Vienna 1903) 9 Bxf4 Qf6! 10 Be3 (Pillsbury-Marco, Vienna 1903), and now *E.C.O.* considers that Black could have replied 10 ... Be6!, after which White appears to have no satisfactory continuation of the attack. Therefore, instead of 9 Bxf4, it would be interesting to try 9 Nc3!, which rules out this defence for Black.

b) 7 Nxg4 Bxg4 8 Qxg4 Bxd4 9 c3 Be5 10 Bxf4 Nf6 11 Qf3 Bxf4! (stronger than the continuation given in *E.C.O., 11 ... Nbd7 12 g3 Qe7 13 Nd2 0-0-0*, with an equal game) 12 Qxf4 Qe7!, and Black's position is to be preferred (Glazkov).

However, in this case too, by following Euwe's recommendation of 9 Nc3! (instead on 9 c3), White attains a promising position.

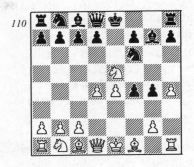

110

Here White has a choice between two main continuations: **7 Bc4 (11.41)** and **7 Nc3! (11.42)**

Also to be considered is **7 Bxf4** d6 8 Nxf7 (*8 Nd3 Nxe4* leads to a variation considered in section 11.52) 8 ... Kxf7 9 e5! dxe5 (if *9 ... Nh5*, then *10 Bg5*) 10 Bc4+ Be6 11 Bxe6+ Kxe6 12 Bxe5 Nc6 13 Qe2, when, according to Leonhardt, White has sufficient compensation for the sacrificed piece.

7 Nxg4, which was at one time popular, allows Black good counter-play after 7 ... Nxe4, and if 8 Nc3, then Black should reply 8 ... d5! (but not *8 ... Ng3? 9 Bxf4! Nxh1 10 Bg5 f6 11 Nxf6+! Bxf6 12 Qh5+*, and White wins) 9 Bxf4 0-0!, and if 10 Ne3, then 10 ... Nc6 11 Ncxd5 Bxd4 12 Nxc7 Bxe3, with the advantage.

Instead of 8 Nc3, **8 Bxf4** looks rather better, with the following possibilities:

a) 8 ... Qe7 9 Qe2 (*9 Be2* is best met by *9 ... Nc6! 10 c3 d5 11 0-0 Qxh4 12 Bxc7 Rg8*, which, according to analysis by Zukertort and Chigorin, gives Black the advantage after *13 Rf4 Qe7* or *13 Ne3 Bh6*, while after *9 Ne3 Qb4! 10 Nd2 Qxd4 11 Ndc4! Qxd1+ 12 Rxd1*, White, as shown by *E.C.O.*, has sufficient compensation for the pawn) 9 ... d6! 10 Ne3 Be6 11 c3 0-0 12 Qf3 d5 13 Bd3 (Walbrodt-Burn, Berlin 1897), and after 13 ... f5! 14 Nd2 Nd7 15 0-0-0 c5! a double-edged position is reached (Glazkov).

b) 8 ... 0-0! (this forgotten move of Paulsen's gives Black the better chances) 9 Nc3 (on *9 Be2* there can follow *9 ... Re8 10 g3 d5 11 0-0 c5*, with the initiative for Black) 9 ... Re8 10 Ne3 d5 (*10 ... Ng3!* is even more convincing), and after 11 Ncxd5? Ng3 12 Nxc7 Rxe3+ 13 Kf2 Nxh1+ 14 Kxe3 Nc6! Black gained a won position (Malkov-Aleksandrov corres. 1902-3).

11.41

7 Bc4

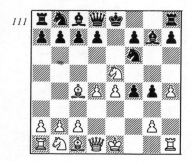

111

7 ...   **d5**

The natural move, but for the system of defence chosen by Black the following variation is also important: 7 ... 0-0 8 Nc3 (*8 Nxf7 Rxf7 9 Bxf7+ Kxf7 10 e5 Nd5* gives Black the better game) 8 ... d6 9 Nxf7 Rxf7 10 Bxf7+ Kxf7 11 Bxf4 Qe8:

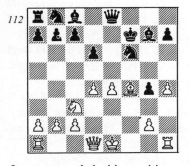

112

Lange regarded this position as favourable for White. A consultation game Cordel-Mikhaelson (Memel 1879) continued 12 0-0 Kg8 13 Qd3 Nc6, and now, by continu-

ing 14 Rae1 Qg6 (if *14 ... Bd7*, then *15 Nd5 Rc8 16 Bh6!*) 15 Nb5 Nh5 16 c3, White would have gained the better chances.

12 Qd3 is also possible, which after 12 ... Kg8 13 0-0 Nc6 leads to a transposition of moves. The *E.C.O.* recommendation of 12 ... Bf5? 13 0-0 Bxe4 is incorrect, in view of 14 Nxe4 Qxe4 15 Qc4+! Kg6 (if *15 ... d5*, then *16 Qb4!*) 16 Rae1 Qc6 17 Qd3+, with a clear advantage to White (Estrin).

8 exd5

Now two moves deserve consideration: **8 ... 0-0 (11.411)** and **8 ... Nh5 (11.412)**.

8 ... Nxd5? is bad because of 9 Nc3!

11.411

       8 ...   **0-0**

       9 0-0

The natural 9 Bxf4 leads to a roughly equal game after 9 ... Nh5 10 Qd2 c5! 11 Nc3 cxd4 12 Ne2.

       9 ...   **Nxd5**

Black achieves nothing by **9 ... c5**, in view of 10 dxc5 Nh5 11 Nxg4 Qxh4 12 Be2!, with advantage to White, while on **9 ... Nh5?** there can follow 10 Nxg4! Qxh4 11 Nh2 Qf6 12 Qxh5 Qxd4+ 13 Kh1 Qxc4 14 Bxf4 Bxb2 15 Bh6, with a clear advantage to White.

       10 Bxd5   **Qxd5**

       11 Bxf4   **c5**

On 11 ... Nc6 Lange recommended 12 Nxc6 Bxc6 13 Be3, followed by 14 Nc3 and 15 Qd2.

113

The game Steinitz-Zukertort (London 1872) continued **12 c3 cxd4 13 Nxg4 Qe6** (if *13 ... Nc6 14 Bh6!*) **14 Nf2 Qb6 15 c4 Be6 16 Nd2 Nd7 17 Nd3 Nc5**, with roughly equal chances.

Four years later, in a game against Blackburne (London 1876), Steinitz preferred a different continuation: **12 Nc3 Qxd4+ 13 Qxd4 cxd4 14 Nd5 Nc6** (*14 ... Na6 is weaker in view of 15 Ne7+ Kh8 16 Rad1*, with the initiative for White) **15 Nxc6 bxc6 16 Ne7+ Kh8 17 Nxc6 Bb7 18 Ne5 Rac8**, and now Cordel recommends that White should have continued **19 c3! dxc3 20 bxc3 Rxc3 21 Nxg4 Rc2 22 Ne3 Bd4 23 Be5+!**, which would have led to simplification and equality.

11.412

    8 ...   Nh5

114

    9 0-0!

Other continuations fail to give White a satisfactory game. For example:

a) 9 Nxg4? Qe7+!,

b) 9 Nxf7 Kxf7 10 d6+ Kg6,

c) 9 Bxf4 Nxf4 10 0-0 Ng6! 11 Nxf7 Qxh4 12 Qe2+ Qe7, in all cases with advantage to Black.

d) 9 Nc3 0-0 10 Ne2 (if *10 Nxg4, then 10 ... Ng3*, while on *10 Ne4 Nd7 11 Nxf7* Black advantageously replies *11 ... Qe8!*) 10 ... c5!, and now:

11 dxc6 Nxc6 12 Nxc6 bxc6 13 Bxf4 Nxf4 14 Nxf4 Re8+ 15 Ne2 Qf6, with advantage to Black.

11 c3 cxd4 12 cxd4 Nd7 13 Nxd7 Bxd7, and Black gained a clear advantage (Steinitz-Zukertort, Vienna 1882).

11 Bxf4? b5!, and White loses a piece.

11 Nxf4 Ng3 12 Ne6 fxe6 13 dxe6 Bxe6! 14 Bxe6+ Kh8 15 Qxg4 Qxd4! (stronger than *15 ... Nxh1 16 Be3*

gaining a very strong attack for the exchange) 17 ... g3 18 Qd2! White has the advantage, since on 18 ... Qf2+ 19 Kd1 g2 there follows 20 Qg5+, while 18 ... Bg4+ 19 Ke1 g2 20 Qxg2 Nc6 is unsatisfactory in view of 21 Be2 Re8 22 Rf1!, when White wins.

Thus the variation considered casts doubts on the 5 ... Bg7 system of defence.

11.5

    5 ...   Nf6

The so-called Berlin Defence. Theory regards this continuation as one of the strongest replies to the Kieseritzky Gambit.

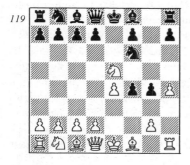

White now has two possibilities for developing his initiative: **6 Bc4** (11.51) and **6 d4** (11.52).

6 Nxg4 has also been played, but Black replies 6 ... Nxe4!, with the following possibilities:

a) 7 Nc3 (bad is *7 d4 Be7!*) 7 ... Ng3 8 Nd5 (Khardin) is refuted by 8 ... Bg7!

b) 7 Qe2 Qe7 8 Nc3 Ng3, and Black has the advantage after both 9 Nd5 Nxe2 10 Nxe7 Ng3 11 Nd5 Nxh1, and 9 Qxe7+ Bxe7 10 Rh2 d5 11 Ne5 c6 12 d4 Nf5!

c) 7 d3 Ng3 8 Bxf4 Nxh1 9 Qe2+ Qe7 10 Nf6+ Kd8 11 Bxc7+ Kxc7 12 Nd5+ Kd8 13 Nxe7 Bxe7, and Black, with three pieces for the queen, has clearly the better chances.

11.51

    6 Bc4

In former times this continuation was the most popular, but subsequent tournament practice has shown that Black has sufficient possibilities for obtaining equality.

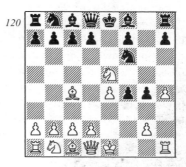

    6 ...   d5

After this counter-sacrifice Black can hope for full equality.

Philidor's recommendation of **6 ... Qe7** 7 d4 d6 has not justified itself, as White has two ways of attaining an excellent position:

a) 8 Nxf7 Qxe4+ 9 Kf1 (on *9 Kf2*

there follows *9 ... d5! 10 Re1 Kxf7)*
9 ... f3 (*9 ... Nh5 10 Kf2*) 10 g3 f2 11
Kxf2 Qf5+ 12 Bf4 Ne4+ 13 Kg2 d5
14 Nxh8, with a clear advantage to
White (Girshbakh, 1864).

b) 8 Bxf7+ Kd8 9 Bxf4 dxe5 10
dxe5+ Bd7 11 Bb3 (*11 0-0 is also
good*) 11 ... Qb4+ 12 Nd2 Nxe4 13
c3 Nxc3 14 Bg5+, and White has a
clear advantage (*E.C.O.*).

7 exd5   Bd6

After 7 ... Bg7 8 d4 (*8 Bb5+ is bad
because of 8 ... c6 9 dxc6 0-0!*) 8 ...
Nh5 positions from section 11.412
are reached.

8 d4

8 0-0 Bxe5 9 Re1 leads to the
so-called Rice Gambit, which after
detailed analysis was pronounced
not altogether correct.

This gambit owes its existence to
the American chess patron,
professor Isaac Rice, at the expense
of whom tournaments were held,
where all the games were played
with his gambit, analyses were
published, and brochures and books
produced.

In his notes to his game against
Zhukovsky, played by correspondence in 1908-9, Alekhine suggested
that this gambit was essentially of
no theoretical importance, although
(like Chigorin) he remarked that the
Rice Gambit "is nevertheless of
some interest, since it leads to
exceptionally complex positions,
and thus gives cause for instructive

analytical searchings".

After 9 ... Qe7 10 c3 the following
position is reached:

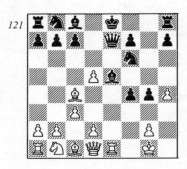

It should be mentioned that all the
games from a thematic tournament
in St Petersburg, 1905, began from
this position.

Here Black has various possibilities:

a) 10 ... f3 11 d4 Ne4 12 Rxe4 Bh2+
13 Kxh2 Qxe4 14 g3 0-0 (all the
games of an analytical match
Lasker-Chigorin, played in
Brighton in 1903, began from this
position) 15 Bf4 Qg6 16 Nd2 c6 17
dxc6 Nxc6 18 Nf1 Ne7 19 Ne3 Nf5,
and Black's material advantage
gradually became decisive (Gelbak-
Chigorin, St Petersburg 1905).

b) 10 ... g3 11 d4 Ng4 12 Bxf4! (on
12 Nd2 Black replies *12 ... Ne3*) 12
... Bxf4 13 Rxe7+ Kxe7 14 Qf3
Be3+ 15 Kh1 Nf2+, with a draw by
perpetual check.

c) 10 ... Nh5 11 d4 Nd7, and now:
12 Qxg4 Ndf6 13 Qe2 (*13 Qxc8+
Rxc8 14 Rxe5 Rd8 also favours

Black, while on *13 Qg5*, in the game Koyalovich-Chigorin, St Petersburg 1905, there followed *13 ... Bxd4+! 14 Kf1 Qxe1+! 15 Kxe1 h6 16 Qxh5 Nxh5 17 cxd4 Bg4*, and Black won) 13 ... Ng4 14 Qxe5 Nxe5 15 Rxe5, and now both 15 ... Be6 16 dxe6 f5!, and 15 ... Rg8 (consultation game Capablanca-Gajet, 1913) give Black the advantage.

12 Bb5 Kd8 13 Bxd7 Bxd7 14 Rxe5 Qxh4 15 Rxh5 Qxh5 16 Bxf4 Re8!, and the advantage is again with Black (Matulin-Chigorin, St Petersburg 1905, and Marshall-Napier, London 1905).

12 dxe5 Nxe5 13 b3 0-0 14 Ba3 Nf3+! 15 gxf3 Qxh4 16 Re5! Bf5! 17 Nd2 Qg3+ 18 Kf1 Qh2, and according to analysis by Bird, Capablanca and Ed. Lasker, Black has a dangerous attack which assures him of at least a draw. Keres points out that in the event of 19 Bxf8 g3 20 Bc5 g2+ 21 Ke1 Qh4+ 22 Ke2 Ng3+ 23 Kf2 Ne4++ 24 Kxg2 (on *24 Ke2?* there follows an elegant mate by *24 ... Nxc3*) Black has to be content with perpetual check.

8 d4 leads to the following position:

see diagram 122

8 ...   Nh5

8 ... 0-0 has also been played (weaker is *8 ... Qe7 9 Bxf4 Nh5 10 g3!*, and if *10 ... f6*, then *11 0-0*, with a strong attack for White), and now:

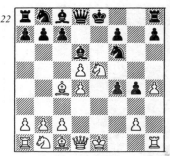

122

a) 9 0-0! Nh5 10 Nxg4 Qxh4 11 Nh2 Ng3 (after *11 ... Re8* White is not bound to go in for Bilguer's variation, *12 Nf3 Qf6 13 Nc3 Bg4*, with an equal game, but can follow Alapin's more interesting recommendation of *12 Nc3! a6 13 Qf3 Ng3 14 Bxf4 Nxf1 15 Rxf1*, with sufficient initiative for the sacrificed exchange) 12 Re1 Nd7 13 Nd2 Nf6 14 Ndf3 Qh5 15 Re5! Bxe5 16 dxe5, with a dangerous initiative for White (Neustadtl-Pierce, corr. 1903).

b) 9 Bxf4 (this is less good) 9 ... Nh5 10 g3 f6 11 Nd3 Nxg3 12 Bxg3 Bxg3+ 13 Kf1 Qe8, with advantage to Black (Pillsbury-Chigorin, Vienna 1903).

see diagram 123

9 0-0!

The strongest move, assuring White of the initiative. Other continuations are unpromising for White, for example:

a) 9 Bb5+ c6! 10 dxc6 bxc6! 11 Nxc6 Nxc6 12 Bxc6+ Kf8 13 Bxa8 Ng3 14 Rh2, and now:

123

14 ... Qe7+ 15 Kf2 Ne4+!, and Black has a very strong attack.

14 ... Bf5 15 Bd5 Kg7, when Rosanes-Anderssen (Breslau 1863) continued 16 Nc3 Re8+ 17 Kf2 Qb6 18 Na4 Qa6 19 Nc3 Be5! 20 a4 Qf1+! 21 Qxf1 Bxd4+ 22 Be3 Rxe3, with inevitable mate.

b) 9 Bxf4 Nxf4 10 0-0. This piece sacrifice is refuted by 10 ... Ng6! 11 Nxf7 Qxh4.

c) 9 Nc3 Qe7!, with the alternatives: **10 Bb5+** c6! 11 dxc6 bxc6 12 Nd5 Qe6 13 Nc7+ Bxc7 14 Bc4 Qe7 15 Bxf7+, and Black gains the advantage by 15 ... Qxf7! 16 Nxf7 Kxf7.

10 0-0 Bxe5 11 Bb5+ (*11 Nb5* fails to the reply suggested by Keres: *11 ... 0-0 12 dxe5 a6*) 11 ... c6 12 dxc6 bxc6 13 Nd5 Qxh4 14 dxe5 0-0!, and Black has the advantage.

9 ...   **Qxh4**

After 9 ... 0-0 10 Nxg4 we reach a position examined in the notes to Black's 8th move.

9 ... Bxe5 is antipositional: 10 dxe5

(*10 Qe1 0-0 11 Qxe5* is also good) 10 ... Qxh4 11 Qd4 g3 12 Rxf4, and, despite the loss of the exchange, White has a clear advantage (Bilguer).

10 Qe1   **Qxe1**

On 10 ... Qe7, according to Keres, White continues 11 Qf2, with a good game.

11 Rxe1   **0-0**

12 Nc3

The alternative is **12 Bd3**, with the threat of 13 c4 or 13 Nc4, but after 12 ... Re8 13 Bd2 (if *13 c4*, then *13 ... f6 14 Nf3 Rxe1+ 15 Nxe1*, and now Keres' move *15 ... c5!* gives Black the advantage) 13 ... f6 14 Nc4 Rxe1+ 15 Bxe1 Bf8 16 Nc3 c6 Black has sufficient counter-play (Pitschel-Anderssen, Vienna 1873).

12 ...   **Bf5**

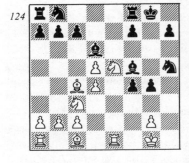

124

The critical position. White is better developed, and has strong points in the centre, which compensate for the pawn. Cordel here recommends **13 Ne4** Bxe4 (if *13 ... Re8*, then *14 Bd3*) 14 Rxe4 f6 15

Nxg4 f5 16 Nh6+ Kg7 17 Re6 Rf6 18 Rxf6 Kxf6 19 Bd3, with a roughly equal game.

In a correspondence game Robinow-Neustadtl (1903) White preferred **13 Bd3**, and after 13 ... Bxd3? 14 Nxd3 Nd7 15 Nb5 Rfe8 16 Bd2 Nb6 17 b3! Nxd5 18 c4 Ne3 19 c5 a6 20 cxd6 he gained the advantage. According to analysis by Alapin, Black should have continued 13 ... Bxe5! 14 dxe5 Bxd3 15 cxd3 Na6 16 Rf1 Nb4 17 d4 c5 18 dxc6 Nxc6, with equal chances.

11.52

6 d4

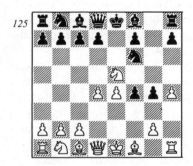

The idea of this variation is that, after the exchange of the e4 and f4 pawns, despite the further simplification and possible exchange of queens, White retains a persistent initiative, and Black's defence is by no means as easy as it appears at first sight.

6 ...   **d6**

7 Nd3

Here, as in the majority of the variations of the Kieseritzky Gambit, the sacrifice 7 Nxf7 is incorrect. After 7 ... Kxf7 8 Bxf4 (or *8 Bc4+ d5 9 exd5 Bd6 10 0-0 Nh5*) 8 ... Bg7 9 Bc4+ d5 10 exd5 Re8+ Black has a clear advantage.

7 ...   **Nxe4**

7 ... f3 8 gxf3 g3 is weak, in view of 9 Nc3 Nc6 10 Be3 d5 11 e5 Nh5 12 f4 Ng7 13 Qf3, with advantage to White (Shefc-Louma, Bratislava 1948).

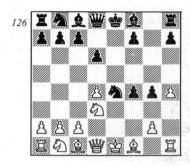

8 Qe2

The simplest. **8 Bxf4** Bg7 **9 c3!** Qe7! (but not *9 ... 0-0 10 Nd2 Re8 11 Nxe4 Rxe4+ 12 Kf2 Qf6 13 g3 Bh6 14 Qd2!* followed by *15 Bg2*, with advantage to White) 10 Qe2 leads to the main variation, although 10 Be2 is also possible.

In Spassky-Fischer (Mar del Plata 1960), instead of 9 c3! White played the weaker **9 Nc3** Nxc3 10 bxc3, and after 10 ... c5 11 Be2 (according to analysis by Aronin, Black has the advantage after *11 Qe2+ Be6! 12 d5*

Bxc3+ 13 Bd2 Bxa1 14 c3 Qf6) 11 ...
cxd4 12 0-0 Nc6 13 Bxg4 0-0 14 Bxc8
Rxc8 15 Qg4 f5 (Fischer considers
15 ... Kh8! to be stronger) 16 Qg3
dxc3 17 Rae1 (*17 Bxd6* is bad in view
of *17 ... Rf6 18 Bf4 Rg6)* Black, as
shown by Kmoch, could have
gained the advantage by 17 ... Qd7!
18 Bxd6 Rfe8 19 Nc5 Qf7.

    8 . . .   **Qe7**

After 8 ... d5 9 Bxf4, or 8 ... f5 9
Nc3, White's position is no worse,
in Keres' opinion, than in the main
variation.

    9 Bxf4   **Bg7**

Regarding 9 ... Nc6, cf. Game No.
7 (p.109).

    10 c3   **h5**

Other replies achieve nothing for
Black. For example:
a) 10 ... **Bf5** 11 Nd2 Nc6 (or *11 ...
Nxd2 12 Qxe7+! Kxe7 13 Kxd2 Nc6
14 g3*, with a good position for
White) 12 0-0-0 0-0-0 13 Nc4!, with
an excellent game for the sacrificed
pawn (Keres).
b) 10 ... **Nc6** 11 Nd2 Nxd2 12 Kxd2
Qxe2+ 13 Bxe2, and now 13 ... h5
leads to the main variation.

    11 Nd2

On 11 g3 Philidor recommended 11
... d5 (*11 ... Bh6* is better) 12 Bg2 f5
13 Nd2 Be6, but Rubinstein's move
14 Nc5! gives White sufficient
compensation for the pawn.

    11 . . .   **Nxd2**

After **11 ... d5** White advantageously continues 12 Nxe4 dxe4 13

Ne5, while on **11 ... f5** there follows
12 Bg5 Nxg5 13 Qxe7+ Kxe7 14
hxg5 and 15 Nf4, with an excellent
game for the pawn.

    12 Kxd2   **Qxe2+**
    13 Bxe2

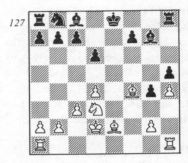

127

For all its apparent harmlessness,
the resulting critical position can
cause Black considerable dis-
comfort.

An example is provided by Stoltz-
Sämisch (Swinemünde 1932) which
continued **13 ... Bf5** 14 Rhf1 Nd7 15
Nb4 Nf6 16 Bb5+ Bd7 17 Rae1+
Kd8 18 Bg5! Bxb5 19 Rxf6, and
Black resigned.

Black has better chances of
equalizing after **13 ... Nc6** 14 Rae1
Be6, as in Schmidt-Batshinsky
(Prague 1943).

It can be concluded that after 6 d4
White attains a promising position,
which fully compensates for the
sacrificed pawn.

With this we conclude our examin-
ation of the Classical Defence 3 ...
g5. From the analysis given it

is apparent that this defence is perfectly playable, but requires of Black considerable theoretical knowledge.

Game No. 7
Hajek-Bures
Correspondence 1962
1 e4 e5 2 f4 exf4 3 Nf3 g5 4 h4 g4 5 Ne5 Nf6 6 d4 d6 7 Nd3 Nxe4 8 Bxf4 Qe7 9 Qe2 Nc6

Black decides not to waste time on the unnecessary move 9 ... Bg7, preferring to develop his Q-side pieces as quickly as possible, and to castle long.

10 c3 Bf5 11 Nd2 0-0-0 12 0-0-0 Re8

12 ... Bg7 would have led after 13 Nc4 to familiar positions, which are considered in the theoretical section. The move played conceals a masked threat, which White overlooks.

13 g3?

A routine move. White should have replied 13 Re1, with sufficient compensation for the sacrificed pawn.

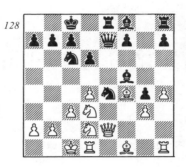

13 ... Nxc3!

This unexpected blow leads to a decisive advantage for Black.

14 Qxe7 Nxa2+ 15 Kb1 Rxe7 16 Kxa2 Bxd3 17 Bxd3 Nb4+ 18 Kb3 Nxd3

Black has regained his piece, and remains with three extra pawns.

Therefore **White resigned**.

12 Becker Defence

1 e4	e5
2 f4	exf4
3 Nf3	h6

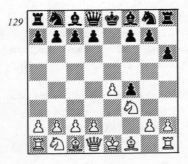

129

Black attempts to transpose into the Classical Defence, while avoiding the dangerous Allgaier and Kieseritzky Gambits, but White can exploit the fact that the move is rather slow to give the play a different trend.

4 d4	g5

Here two main continuations deserve consideration: **5 h4 (12.1)** and **5 Nc3 (12.2)**.

If White plays **5 Bc4**, then after 5 … Bg7 play transposes into the Hanstein or Greco-Philidor Gambits.

The immediate **5 g3** allows the strong counter-blow 5 … d5!, which after 6 gxf4 g4 7 Ne5 Qh4+ 8 Ke2 Nf6, or 6 exd5 Qxd5 7 Nc3 (*7 Bg2 g4*) 7 … Bb4 is favourable for Black.

12.1

5 h4	Bg7

130

6 g3	

The other way to develop the initiative is by **6 hxg5** hxg5 7 Rxh8 Bxh8 8 g3!, and now:

a) 8 ... g4 9 Nh2 fxg3 10 Qxg4, and White's attack is very dangerous.

b) 8 ... d5! 9 gxf4! g4 10 Ng5 f6 11 f5 (*11 Nh3 dxe4*) 11 ... fxg5 12 Qxg4 Bxd4 (Rellstab-Pfeiffer, Hamburg 1954, went *12 ... Nf6 13 Qh3 Bg7*, when White should have replied *14 Bxg5! dxe4 15 Nc3*, with dangerous threats) 13 Nc3 Bxc3+ 14 bxc3 Qe7, with advantage to Black, according to *E.C.O.*

It is difficult to agree with this last assessment. By continuing 15 Bxg5! Qxe4+ 16 Qxe4 dxe4 17 Bc4 White forces his opponent to return the piece by 17 ... Bxf5!, which leads to a roughly equal game. 17 ... Kf8 is extremely risky, in view of 18 f6 Nd7 19 f7 Ngf6 20 0-0-0, while on 17 ... Ne7 there follows 18 f6 Ng6 19 f7+ Kf8 20 0-0-0! Nc6 21 Rh1, in both cases with a decisive advantage for White (Glazkov).

6 ...   **g4**

Apart from this natural reply, the counter-blow **6 ... d5!?** 7 exd5 Qxd5 also deserves consideration.

E.C.O. continues **8 hxg5** hxg5 9 Rxh8 Bxh8 10 gxf4 g4 11 Ne5, and judges the position to be in White's favour. But Black can play more strongly: 8 ... Bg4! (instead of *8 ... hxg5*), when there can follow 9 Bg2 Nc6 10 Nc3 (or *10 Qe2+ Kf8*) 10 ... Qe6+ 11 Qe2 Bxf3 12 Bxf3 Nxd4 13 Qxe6+ fxe6 14 Bxb7 Rd8 15 Be4 fxg3, and Black retains his extra pawn (Glazkov).

After **8 Nc3** Qe6+ 9 Qe2 g4 10 Qxe6+ Bxe6 11 Ne5 fxg3 Black's chances are again better.

7 Nh2

The piece sacrifice **7 Ne5** d6 8 Nxf7 Kxf7 9 Bc4+ is incorrect. The game Cheremisin-Volovich (Moscow 1964) continued 9 ... d5 10 Bxd5+ Ke8 11 Bxf4 Ne7 12 Nc3, and now, according to analysis by Keres, Black beats off the attack by 12 ... c6! 13 Bb3 Qxd4 14 Qe2 Ng6.

Padevsky against Planinc (Cacak 1969) chose a different way: 9 ... Ke8 10 Bxf4 Nc6 11 c3 (*11 Be3 Nf6 12 Nc3* is no better, in view of *12 ... Qe7*) 11 ... Qe7 12 0-0 Nf6 13 Nd2 Rf8, and also gained a clear advantage, having retained his extra piece.

7 ...   **fxg3**
8 Nxg4   **d6**

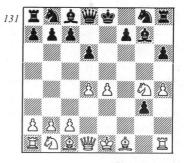

131

Denk-Sämisch (Prague 1943) continued: **9 c3** (the immediate *9 Be3* followed by *10 Nc3* should be considered) 9 ... Nf6 10 Nxf6+ Qxf6, and now White should have played 11 Be3!, with roughly equal chances.

12.2

5 Nc3!

This move, which prevents ... d7-d5, sets Black the most difficult problems.

5 ...   d6

5 ... Bg7 6 g3 fxg3 (if *6 ... d6*, then *7 gxf4*) 7 h4! transposes.

6 g3

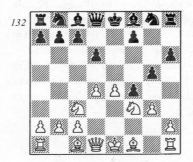

132

6 ...   fxg3

6 ... g4 is inconsistent, in view of 7 Bxf4!? (*7 Ng1 f3 8 h3* should also be considered) 7 ... gxf3 8 Qxf3 Nc6 (Eppinger-Engert, 1969), and now by 9 0-0-0! White gains a strong attack for the sacrificed piece.

A position which is important for the assessment of the variation arises after **6 ... Bg7** 7 gxf4 g4 8 Ng1 Qh4+ 9 Ke2 g3 (*9 ... Nf6 10 Be3 Nh5 11 Kd2 Ng3* is refuted by *12 Bb5+ c6 13 Bf2*) 10 Nf3 Bg4, when Black, by returning the extra pawn, attempts to seize the initiative.

White does best to continue 11 Be3, when after 11 ... gxh2 12 Kd2 Qg3 13 Be2 Nc6 14 Nxh2, or 11 ... Nc6 12 Kd2! Qh5 (if *12 ... Bxf3 13 Qxf3 Nxd4*, then *14 Qxg3*) 13 Be2 g2 14 Rg1 Qh3 15 d5 Ne7 16 Nd4 he retains the advantage (Bhend).

7 h4!

Only by this energetic advance can White succeed in breaking up his opponent's defences.

7 ...   g4

Black achieves nothing by 7 ... Bg4 8 hxg5 Nc6, with the aim of gaining time for the development of his pieces. By continuing 9 Nd5! Bxf3 10 Qxf3 Nxd4 11 Qc3 Bg7 12 Nxc7+ Kf8 13 Nxa8 Qxa8 14 gxh6 White gains a clear advantage.

Instead of 8 ... Nc6, no better is 8 ... Bg7 9 gxh6 Bxh6, in view of 10 Bg2!, and if 10 ... Nc6, then 11 Bg5.

8 Ng1   g2

A curious position arises after 8 ... Be7 (in the event of *8 ... Qf6 9 Be3 Be7, 10 h5!* is very strong) 9 Bg2 Bxh4 10 Bf4 Qf6 11 Qd2, when, in spite of the opponent's three extra pawns, White's position is to be preferred.

9 Bxg2   Be7

10 h5

see diagram 133

In this critical position White undoubtedly has sufficient compensation for the sacrificed pawn. There can follow **10 ... Bh4+** 11 Ke2 Bg5 12 Bxg5 Qxg5 13 Qd2, when if

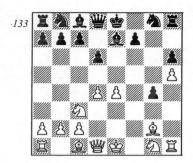

133

Black attempts to win a further pawn by **13 ... Nf6 14 Rf1 Nxh5**, White sacrifices the exchange by **15 Rxh5! Qxh5 16 Nd5**, with the better chances. For example: 16 ... Qh2 17 Kd1 Na6 18 Qf2 Be6 19 Nf6+ Kd8 20 Ne2, threatening to win the queen.

Therefore Black is forced by **13 ... Qxd2+ 14 Kxd2 Ne7 15 Nge2** to go into an ending, in which, despite his extra pawn, he has a difficult task to draw (Zak).

Thus White's pawn attack with 6 g3 and 7 h4 (after *5 Nc3!*) can prove a highly effective weapon against the Becker Defence.

Game No. 8
Cheremisin-Volovich
Moscow 1964
1 e4 e5 2 f4 exf4 3 Nf3 h6 4 d4 g5 5 h4 Bg7 6 g3

Regarding 6 hxg5, cf. the theoretical section.
6 ... g4 7 Ne5

A risky move. The usual continuation 7 Nh2 leads to a roughly equal game.
7 ... d6 8 Nxf7!?

This sacrifice is practically forced, since after 8 Nxg4 or 8 Nd3 White would lose his central d4 pawn.
8 ... Kxf7 9 Bc4+ d5

The immediate 9 ... Ke8 is safer, retaining the pawn, as in Planinc-Padevsky (Cacak 1969) — cf. analysis.
10 Bxd5+ Ke8 11 Bxf4 Ne7 12 Nc3 Rf8

This move allows White to gain the initiative. Keres recommended the immediate 12 ... c6! 13 Bb3 Qxd4 14 Qe2 Ng6, when Black repels the attack.
13 0-0 c6 14 Be5!

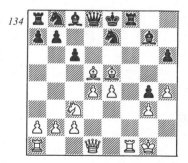

134

This is the point! As a result of Black's delay the picture has changed sharply. By this unexpected intermediate move White obtains a very strong attack.
14 ... Bxe5
Black has nothing better.

15 Rxf8+ Kxf8 16 Qf1+ Nf5 17 dxe5

White's attack develops un-impeded.

17 ... Qb6+ 18 Kh2 cxd5 19 exf5

Black is still a piece up, but the open position of his king and his lack of development give White a decisive advantage.

19 ... Qxb2 20 Qf4!

An elegant move, after which there is no longer any defence. White's pieces penetrate into the enemy rear.

20 ... Qxc2+ 21 Kg1 Qxf5 22 Qxh6+ Ke8 23 Rf1 Qxe5 24 Qf8+ Resigns.

13 Fischer Defence

1	e4	e5
2	f4	exf4
3	Nf3	d6

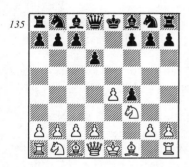

135

This defence pursues the same aims as the Becker Defence, but the resulting modification to the 'Classical Defence' is in this case more favourable to Black.

Fischer considers this to be the best defence to the Knight's Gambit, but it is difficult to agree with him.

Two basic continuations should now be considered: **4 Bc4 (13.1)** and **4 d4 (13.2)**.

4 b3 is not in the spirit of the position, in view of 4 ... Be7 5 Bb2 Bh4+ 6 Ke2 Bf6, with advantage to Black (Basman-Kolarov, Varna 1971).

Bhend's suggestion of **4 d3** g5 5 h4 is rather passive, and leads to a roughly equal game after 5 ... g4 6 Nd4 Bg7.

Of interest is the variation **4 Nc3** g5 5 h4 g4 6 Ng5 f6! 7 Nh3 gxh3 8 Qh5+ Kd7 9 Qf5+, when the strongest is 9 ... Ke8! 10 Qh5+ Kd7, with a draw by repetition, whereas after 9 ... Ke7? (but not *9 ... Kc6?? 10 Qb5 mate*) 10 Nd5+ Kf7 11 Qh5+ Kg7 (if *11 ... Ke6, then 12 Bc4!*) 12 gxh3 Ne7 13 Rg1+ Ng6 14 Nxf4 Qe8 15 Qd5 White gains a won position (analysis by Bhend).

13.1

	4 Bc4	h6

But not **4 ... g5?** 5 h4 g4 6 Ng5 Nh6 7 d4 f6 8 Bxf4 fxg5 9 Bxg5, with a decisive attack for White (Morphy-Tilghman, Philidelphia 1859).

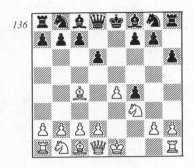

136

5 d3

Along with this move, suggested by Bhend, other continuations have occurred in tournament practice:

a) 5 h4 (preventing ... *g7-g5*) 5 ... Nf6 6 Nc3, and now:

6 ... Be7 7 d3 Nh5 8 Ne5!? (on *8 Ne2* Black should reply *8 ... Bg4 9 Nxf4 Bxh4+ !*) 8 ... dxe5 9 Qxh5 0-0 10 Qxe5 Bd6 11 Qd4, with a roughly equal game (Suls-Grseskovjak, corr. 1966).

6 ... Bg4 7 d4 Nh5 8 Ne5 dxe5 9 Qxg4 Nf6 10 Qf5, when White has a dangerous attack (Levy-Hess, Sparks 1972).

b) 5 b4 Nf6 6 e5 dxe5 7 Nxe5 Nd5 8 0-0 Be6 9 Qe2 Nc6 10 Bb2 Nxe5 11 Bxe5 c6 12 Nc3, with a complicated game, in which the chances are roughly equal (Planinc-Tukmakov, Vrnjacka Banja 1965).

c) 5 b3 Nc6 6 Bb2 Nf6 7 Nc3 Be7 8 Qe2, and White has adequate compensation for the pawn (Bhend-Gostely, corr. 1969).

d) 5 d4 g5 6 g3!? (after *6 c3 Bg7 7*

0-0 the Hanstein Gambit is reached, while on the immediate *6 0-0* there can follow *6 ... Bg4!? 7 c3 c6! 8 Qb3 Qd7*, with equal chances, Glazkov-Sherman, Moscow 1976) 6 ... Nc6 7 gxf4 g4 8 Ng1 Qh4+ 9 Kf1 Nf6 10 Nc3 g3 11 Kg2 gxh2 12 Rxh2 Rg8+ 13 Kh1.

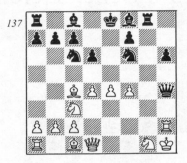

137

Spassky-Portisch (Budapest 1967) continued 13 ... Qxh2+ 14 Kxh2 Ng4+, and after 15 Qxg4 Bxg4 16 Nd5 0-0-0 17 c3 Be7 18 Ne3 White gained the better chances.

Many commentators consider that 13 ... Qg3 14 Be2 Ng4 (*14 ... Bg4* is weaker, in view of *15 e5* and *16 Ne4*) 15 Bxg4 Bxg4 gives Black the advantage, but White's reply 16 Qd3! gives him counter-play. For example: 16 ... Qxg1+ 17 Kxg1 Be2+ 18 Kf2 Bxd3 19 cxd3 Nxd4 20 Nd5 0-0-0 21 Be3, or 16 ... Qxd3 17 cxd3 Nxd4 18 Nd5 0-0-0 19 Be3 Nf3 20 Rc2, and in both cases White has sufficient compensation for the pawn (analysis by Thimann).

5 ... **g5**

6 g3   Nc6

The opening of lines by **6 ... fxg3** 7 hxg3 favours White, for example:

a) 7 ... **Bg7** 8 Nxg5! hxg5 9 Rxh8 Bxh8 10 Qh5 Qf6 11 Nc3 c6 12 Bxg5 Qg7 13 0-0-0, or

b) 7 ... **Bg4** 8 Bxg5! hxg5 9 Rxh8 Nh6 10 Nc3 Qf6 11 Rxf8+ Kxf8 12 Nd5! (Bhend-Issler, corr. 1970), in each case with advantage to White.

According to Bhend, **6 ... g4** 7 Nd4 f3! 8 c3 Nc6 9 Qb3 Ne5 10 Bf4 Nxc4 11 dxc4 Bg7 12 Nd2 leads to a roughly equal game.

7 gxf4

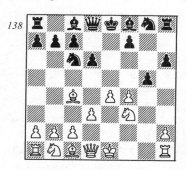

138

If now Black continues 7 ... **g4** 8 Ng1 Qh4+ 9 Kf1 Nf6, then by 10 Kg2 Nh5 (*10 ... Rg8 11 Nc3 g3* is no better, because of *12 h3 h5 13 Nce2*) 11 Nc3 g3 12 Qe1! Rg8 13 h3 White gains the advantage.

According to analysis by Bhend, best is 7 ... **Bg4** 8 0-0 Nd4 9 Nbd2 gxf4 10 c3 Ne6!, with a roughly equal game.

13.2

4 d4

The most natural continuation.

4 ...   g5

4 ... Nf6 is inconsistent, and leads after 5 Nc3 Nh5 6 Be2 Bg4 7 0-0 g6 8 Nd5! to the better game for White.

5 h4   g4

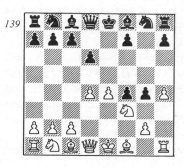

139

6 Ng1

An important moment. Formerly only **6 Ng5** was played, which after 6 ... h6 7 Nxf7 led to a form of the Allgaier Gambit favourable to White.

Doubts were cast on the bold knight move by the game Heuer-Randviir (Tallinn 1949), in which Black played 6 ... f6! 7 Nh3 gxh3 8 Qh5+ Kd7! 9 Qf3 Qe8, and gradually beat off the opponent's attack.

The other form of the sacrifice is also insufficient: 7 Bxf4 fxg5 8 Bxg5 (or *8 hxg5 Bg7 9 Bc4 Nc6 10 c3 Nge7*) 8 ... Be7 9 Qd2 Be6! 10 Nc3 Nd7, with a solid position for Black (*E.C.O.*).

6 ...   Bh6

After **6 ... f3** 7 gxf3 Be7 White gains clearly the better chances by 8 Be3 Bxh4+ 9 Kd2 Nc6 10 Nc3 Bf6

11 Kc1.

On **6 ... Nf6** White has the strong reply 7 Qd3!, preventing 7 ... Nh5, in view of 8 Qb5+.

6 ... Qf6 is also insufficient after 7 Nc3, and now:

a) 7 ... c6 8 e5! dxe5 9 Ne4 Qe7 10 dxe5 Qxe5 11 Qe2, with dangerous threats (Nei).

b) 7 ... Ne7 8 Nge2 Bh6 9 Qd2 Bd7 10 g3 Nbc6 11 gxf4 0-0-0 12 Bg2 Qg7 13 d5 Ne5 14 Qe3 Kb8 15 Qf2, and White gained a clear advantage (Planinc-Portisch, Ljubljana 1973).

7 Nc3   c6

Regarding 7 ... Nc6, cf. Game No. 9.

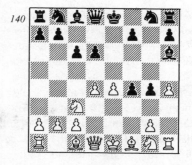

140

White has several ways to develop his initiative:

a) 8 Bd3 Qf6 9 Bd2 (the *E.C.O.* recommendation of *9 e5?! dxe5 10 Ne4 Qe7 11 dxe5 Qxe5 12 Qe2* fails to *12 ... Be6 13 Bd2 f3!*, with advantage to Black) 9 ... Qxd4 10 Nce2 Qb6 11 Bc3 f6 12 Rb1, and the chances are roughly equal (Bhend-Issler, corr. 1969).

b) 8 Nge2 Qf6 9 g3 f3 10 Nf4 Nd7 11 Bc4 Nb6 12 Bb3 Qe7 13 Kf2, with a complicated game.

c) 8 Be2 Nf6 9 h5 Qe7 10 Qd3 b6! (*10 ... 0-0* followed by *11 ... Re8* is also good) 11 b4 Ba6 12 b5 cxb5 13 Nxb5 (Glazkov-Vaganov, Moscow 1980), and now by 13 ... 0-0! Black could have gained the advantage.

d) 8 Qd3 Qf6 9 Bd2, and now Black should not play 9 ... Na6, as recommended by Bhend, because of 10 0-0-0!, with the threat of 11 e5!, opening the central files, but 9 ... b6! followed by 10 ... Ba6, which parries the opponent's immediate threats.

Game No. 9
Planinc-Gligorić
Ljubljana 1977
1 e4 e5 2 f4 exf4 3 Nf3 d6 4 d4 g5 5 h4 g4 6 Ng1

As shown in the theoretical section, after 6 Ng5 f6! White does not obtain sufficient compensation for the sacrificed piece.

6 ... Bh6 7 Nc3 Nc6

A new continuation, which was first employed in the present game. The usual move 7 ... c6 is considered in the analysis.

see diagram 141

8 Nge2

As often happens, at the board a player fails to find the correct reply

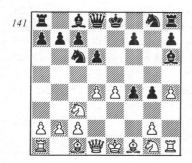

141

to an innovation by the opponent. White should have played 8 Qd3!, and after 8 ... Nf6 9 Nge2 d5 (not *9 ... Nh5? 10 Qb5*) 10 exd5 Nxd5 11 Nxd5 Qxd5 12 Bxf4 Bxf4 13 Nxf4 Qxd4 14 Qxd4 Nxd4 15 0-0-0 Ne6 16 Nd5 h5 17 Bc4 he gains sufficient compensation for the sacrificed pawn.

Less promising for White, instead of 10 exd5, is 10 e5 Nh5 11 g3, in view of 11 ... Ne7!, while after 11 Qb5 Black advantageously returns the pawn by 11 ... 0-0 12 Qxd5 Be6! The immediate 10 g3 deserves consideration.

8 ... f3 9 Nf4 f2+ 10 Kxf2 g3+!

By returning his extra pawn and sacrificing another one, Gligorić opens important lines for his pieces, and creates dangerous threats against the enemy king.

11 Kxg3 Nf6 12 Be2 Rg8+ 13 Kf2 Ng4+ 14 Bxg4 Bxg4 15 Qd3 Bg7 16 Be3 Qd7 17 Nce2

Since all the same White is unable to prevent the undermining ... f7-f5,

he should have played 17 g3.

17 ... 0-0-0 18 Ng3 f5!

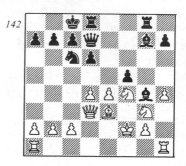

142

By the sacrifice of a further pawn, Black opens the f-file, on which White's king is subjected to a very strong attack.

19 Nxf5 Rdf8 20 Nxg7 Qxg7

It is well known that opposite-coloured bishops merely help the stronger side to mount an attack.

21 Ke1

White tries to evacuate his king from the danger zone. On 21 g3 there could have followed 21 ... Bh5! 22 Rhg1 Qg4, with a very strong attack.

21 ... Nb4! 22 Qc3 Qe7 23 Qxb4 Rxf4!

This way, since on 23 ... Qxe4 White could have replied 24 Qb3, indirectly attacking the rook at g8.

24 Kd2

24 Bxf4 loses immediately to 24 ... Qxe4+.

24 ... Qxe4 25 Rag1?

The decisive mistake. 25 Rhg1 was better, so as to use the other rook for the defence of the e-file.

25 ... Bf5 26 Qb3 Rg3!

The most elegant solution. Clearly, 26 ... Rxg2+ would also have won.

27 Rh2 Rf2+ and **White resigned.**

He is mated after 28 Bxf2 Rxb3 29 axb3 Qxc2+ 30 Ke3 (or *30 Ke1 Bg4*) 30 ... Qd3+ 31 Kf4 Qe4+ 32 Kg5 Qg4+ 33 Kf6 Qg6+ 34 Ke7 Qg7+ 35 Ke8 Bd7 mate.

14 Euwe Defence

1 e4	e5
2 f4	exf4
3 Nf3	Be7

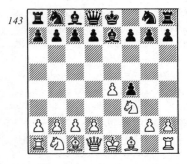

143

This move has been known since the time of Greco, but it was not especially popular until the 1940s, when Max Euwe associated it with a new and interesting idea.

Two main continuations should now be considered: **4 Bc4 (14.1)** and **4 Nc3 (14.2)**.

The following continuations have also occurred:

a) **4 d4** d5! (*4 ... Bh4+ gives White an excellent game after 5 Ke2 d5 6 e5*

Be7 7 Bxf4 c5 8 Kf2!, Pachman-Petrik, Zlin 1943) 5 e5 g5 6 Be2 c5 7 0-0 Nc6 8 c3 Be6, with advantage to Black (Martin-Euwe, corr. 1962).

b) **4 Be2** Nf6 (*4 ... d5 5 exd5* leads to the Petroff Gambit), and now:
5 e5 Ng5 6 d4 (Kenink-Erlandson, 1962), and Black could have equalized by 6 ... Ne3! 7 Bxe3 fxe3 8 Qd3 d5.
5 d3 d5 6 e5 Ng4 7 Bxf4 f6 8 d4 0-0 9 0-0 fxe5 10 Nxe5 Nxe5 11 Bxe5, with roughly equal chances (Bronstein-Ivkov, Baden 1957).

14.1

4 Bc4

For a long time this move was considered obligatory, and normally used to have favourable consequences for White.

see diagram 144

4 ...   **Nf6!**

The point of Euwe's plan. In former times **4 ... Bh4+** was played here, but on the basis of modern

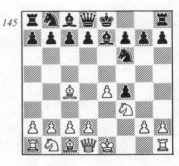

analysis this gives White the advantage.

After **5 Kf1** d5 (*5 ... Bf6, 5 ... Nh6 and 5 ... d6* also leave White with the advantage after *6 d4*) 6 Bxd5 Nf6 7 Bb3! White has an excellent game. On 7 ... Nxe4 there follows 8 Qe2!, with a clear advantage for White.

Less promising for White is the tempting **5 g3**. This move is associated with the name of Cunningham, although it was known back at the start of the 17th century. There can follow 5 ... fxg3 6 0-0, and now:

a) 6 ... gxh2+ 7 Kh1 d5 8 Bxd5! Nf6 9 Bxf7+ Kxf7 10 Nxh4 Rf8! 11 Qf3 Kg8 12 d3, with a roughly equal position.

b) 6 ... d5! 7 Bxd5 (if *7 exd5*, then *7 ... Bh3*) 7 ... Nf6 8 Bxf7+ (*8 Nxh4 Nxd5 9 exd5 Qxh4 10 Qe2+ Kd8* also favours Black) 8 ... Kxf7 9 e5 (or *9 Nxh4 Qd4+*) 9 ... Bh3 10 exf6 Bxf1 11 Qxf1 gxh2+ 12 Kh1 Bxf6, with a clear advantage to Black (Krejcik-Schlechter, Vienna 1918).

5 e5

In the event of **5 d3** d5 6 exd5 Nxd5 7 Bxd5 Qxd5 8 Bxf4 0-0 Black equalises without difficulty.

5 Nc3 is also inadequate, in view of the standard reply 5 ... Nxe4!, when after 6 Ne5 (*6 Bxf7+ Kxf7 7 Ne5+ Kg8! 8 Nxe4 Bh4+ 9 g3 Qe7*, or *6 0-0 Nf6! 7 d4 d5 8 Bd3 0-0 9 Bxf4 Nc6* also favours Black) 6 ... Ng5! 7 d4 d6 8 Nd3 f3! 9 gxf3 Black has two ways of gaining an advantage:

a) 9 ... Nh3 10 Be3 0-0 11 Kd2 (*11 Qe2* is well met by *11 ... Bh4+ 12 Nf2 Re8*) 11 ... Nc6 12 Qf1 Bf6 (Nei-Chukayev, 1956).

b) 9 ... 0-0 10 Be3 Re8 11 Kd2 Bf6 12 Qf1 Nc6 13 d5 Rxe3! 14 Kxe3 Bh3 (Zweigberk-Oechslein, corr. 1962).

To be considered is **5 Qe2** 0-0 (to *5 ... d5* the correct reply is *6 Bxd5!*) 6 0-0 d5 7 Bxd5! (but not *7 exd5 c6!* with good prospects for Black) 7 ... Nxd5 8 exd5, when the chances are roughly equal.

5 ...   Ng4

5 ... Nh5 is less convincing, in view

of 6 Nc3 (*6 0-0* is also possible) 6 ... d6 7 exd6 (*7 d4 Bg4 8 Nd5* is dubious in view of *8 . .. dxe5! 9 dxe5 Nc6*, with a good game for Black) 7 ... Qxd6 8 d4 Nc6 9 0-0 0-0 10 Be2 Bg4 11 Ne4 followed by 12 Nf2, which gives White good chances.

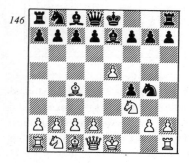

146

Here two systems of development should be considered: **6 0-0 (14.11)** and **6 Nc3 (14.12)**.

Other continuations fail to give White an advantage, for example: **a) 6 d4** d5, and now both **7 Bb3** Bh4+ 8 Kf1 b6 followed by 9 ... Ba6 (Kramer-Euwe, Liwarden 1941), and **7 Bd3** Bh4+ 8 Ke2 Nf2 9 Qe1 Nxd3 10 Qxh4 Nxc1+ 11 Rxc1 Qxh4 12 Nxh4 Nc6 13 c3 0-0 14 Kf2 f6 (Lutikov-Estrin, Leningrad 1951) lead to an advantage for Black.

In the event of **7 Be2** Ne3 8 Bxe3 fxe3 9 Qd3, or **7 exd6** Bxd6 (after *7 ... Qxd6 8 Nc3 Be6 9 Bd3 Ne3 10 Qe2* White gains slightly the better chances) 8 Qe2+ Qe7 9 Qxe7+ Kxe7 10 0-0 White, in Euwe's opinion, has chances of equalizing.

b) 6 Qe2 0-0! 7 Nc3 d6 8 d4 dxe5 9 dxe5 Nc6 10 Bxf4 Nd4 11 Nxd4 Qxd4 12 Nd5 Bh4+! 13 g3 Qxb2 14 Rd1 (if *14 0-0*, then *14 ... Bd8 15 h3 c6*, with advantage to Black), as in Pietzsch-Fuchs (Halle 1961), and now by 14 ... Bd8! (*E.C.O.*) Black could have gained the better chances.

14.11

6 0-0

147

6 ...   Nc6

Here the **6 ... d5** counter-blow is not so convincing as after 7 exd6!:
a) 7 ... Bxd6 8 Re1+ Kf8 9 d4 g5, Hindre-Rozenfeld, Tallinn 1949, when Keres considers that after 10 h3! White has sufficient compensation for the pawn.
b) 7 ... Qxd6 8 d4 0-0 9 Nc3 Ne3 (*9 ... c6* is well met by *10 Qd3! g6 11 Ne4*) 10 Bxe3 fxe3 (Bronstein-Koblents, Moscow 1945), and now, as pointed out by Boleslavsky, White should continue 11 Nb5! Qd8 (after *11 ... Qb6* White gains the

advantage by *12 Ne5 Be6 13 Bxe6 fxe6 14 Rxf8+ Bxf8 15 Qf3*) 12 Ne5 Bf6 (no better is *12 ... Be6 13 Bxe6 fxe6 14 Rxf8+* and *15 Qg4*, with advantage to White) 13 Nxf7 Rxf7 14 Qh5, with a won position for White.

7 d4

Romanovsky's recommendation of 7 Re1 is refuted by 7 ... Bc5+ 8 d4 (or *8 Kf1 Nd4*) 8 ... Nxd4! 9 Nxd4 Qh4, when Black wins.

7 ...   d5

8 exd6

Here too bishop moves are less promising for White:

8 Be2 Ne3 9 Bxe3 fxe3 10 Qd3 Nb4!

8 Bb5 g5 9 c4 a6 10 Ba4 dxc4 11 Bxc6+ bxc6 12 h3 Nh6, with a slight advantage for Black (Kolobov-Zhuravlev, 1965).

After **8 Bb3** Black should continue 8 ... g5!, and now:

a) 9 h3 h5! 10 hxg4 (no better is *10 Na3 Ne3 11 Bxe3 fxe3 12 c4 g4*, with advantage to Black) 10 ... hxg4 11 Nh2 g3 12 Ng4 Rh4 13 Nf6+ Bxf6 14 exf6 Qxf6 15 Re1+ Kf8, and White resigned (Kutyonok-Akimov, Kiev 1954).

b) 9 c4, and after either **9 ... dxc4** 10 Bxc4 Nxd4 11 Qxd4 Qxd4 12 Nxd4 Bc5 13 Rd1 Nxe5 (Romanovsky), or **9 ... Be6** 10 cxd5 Bxd5 11 Bxd5 Qxd5 12 Nc3 Qd7 13 h3 h5! 14 hxg4 hxg4 15 Nh2 g3!, Black has a clear advantage.

8 ...   Bxd6

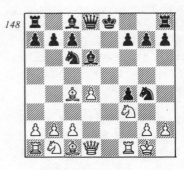

148

9 Qe1+!

This move has been deeply studied by Bhend, who has employed it in a number of correspondence games. Other moves are less promising, for example:

a) 9 Re1+ Ne7 10 h3 (Rozenfeld's recommendation of *10 Nc3 0-0 11 h3 Nf6 12 Ne5* should be met by *12 ... Ng6!*, when *13 Qf3 Bxe5 14 dxe5 Qd4+ 15 Qf2 Qxc4 16 exf6 Bf5* gives Black the advantage) 10 ... Nh6! 11 Ne5 (Thomas-Euwe, Plymouth 1948), and now Euwe considers that, by continuing 11 ... Bxe5! 12 Rxe5 Nhf5 13 c3 0-0 Black could have gained the advantage.

b) 9 Nc3 0-0 10 Ne2 (*10 Nd5* is well met by *10 ... Be6! 11 Bb3 g5*) 10 ... Ne3 11 Bxe3 fxe3 12 Qd3! (in Keres-Alatortsev, Moscow 1950, Black gained the advantage after *12 a3? Qf6 13 Qd3 Qh6*), and now:

12 ... Na5 13 Bb3 Nxb3 14 axb3 Qe7, with the better chances for Black (Bhend).

12 ... **Qe7** 13 Rae1 Bg4, which is less promising, in view of 14 Ng3 Rae8 15 Nf5, with approximate equality.
12 ... **Nb4** 13 Qb3 Bf5 14 a3, and Black has to waste time on the retreat of his knight.

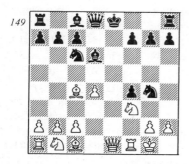

149

For the sacrificed pawn White has sufficient compensation.

The following examples from practice are of interest:

a) 9 ... Kf8 10 Nc3 g5 (*10 ... Nxd4 11 Nxd4 Bc5 12 Rxf4 Bxd4+ 13 Kh1* led to a clear advantage for White in Bhend-Muller, Basel 1963) 11 h3 Nh6 12 Ne4 Be7 13 d5, with good attacking chances for White (Bhend-Schmidt, corr. 1964).

b) 9 ... Ne7 10 h3 Nh6 (weaker is *10 ... Nf6 11 Ne5 Bxe5 12 Qxe5 0-0 13 Qxf4 Ng6 14 Qf2*, with advantage to White) 11 Ne5 g5 12 h4 f6 (Bhend-Fischli, corr. 1970), with a roughly equal game, according to Bhend. In our opinion, by continuing 13 hxg5 fxg5 14 Nf3 White gains the better chances.

c) 9 ... Qe7 10 Nc3 0-0 11 Qxe7

Nxe7 12 Bb3, with a roughly equal game (Bhend).

14.12

6 Nc3

In this way White prevents the freeing advance ... d7-d5.

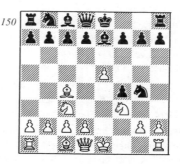

150

6 ...   **d6**

Other possibilities for Black should also be considered:

a) 6 ... d5?! 7 Bxd5! Bh4+ 8 Kf1 Nc6 9 Bxc6+ bxc6 10 d3 0-0 11 Bxf4 f6 12 e6 f5 13 Nxh4 Qxh4 14 Qe1, and, according to Keres, White's position is preferable.

b) 6 ... Bh4+? 7 Kf1!, when 7 ... Nf2? is bad in view of 8 Qe1, while after 7 ... 0-0 8 d4 Ne3+ 9 Bxe3 fxe3 10 Qd3 Bf2 11 h4!, or 7 ... d6 8 exd6 cxd6 9 Qe2+ Be7 10 d4 (*E.C.O.*), or 7 ... c6 8 Qe2 0-0 9 d4 b5 10 Bd3 Nf2 11 Bxh7+! (Glazkov-Efimov, Moscow 1963), White has clearly the better chances.

After 7 Kf1! 0-0 8 d4 the Bulgarian master Tsvetkov has suggested 8 ... Kh8? (the question mark is attached by the authors of this book), on which White should continue 9 g3!, forcing the retreat of the enemy bishop, since after 9 ... fxg3 10 hxg3 Bxg3, 11 Ng5! is decisive, while after 10 ... Be7 White again achieves a won position by 11 Qd3 h6 12 Qe4 d6 13 Bxh6!

Instead of 7 Kf1!, less promising for White is the sharp continuation 7 g3?! fxg3 8 0-0 Nf2 9 Qe2 Nh3+ 10 Kh1 Nf4 11 Bxf7+ Kf8 12 Bb3!?, as occurred in Pypel-Ivanov, 1959. Black should have accepted the queen sacrifice, since after 12 ... Nxe2! White has no more than perpetual check (cf. Game No.9).

c) 6 ... Nc6 7 d4, and now:

7 ... d6 8 Bxf4 dxe5 9 dxe5 0-0 10 h3 Nh6 11 Qxd8 Bxd8 12 0-0-0, with a clear advantage for White, Glazkov-Vorkin, Moscow 1971.

7 ... d5!? 8 Bxd5! (*8 Nxd5 Bh4+ 9 Kf1 Na5 10 b3 c6* leads to a complicated game with chances for both sides, Wade-Bouwmeester, Vevey 1955), when Keres recommends 8 ... Bh4+ 9 Kf1 Bf2 10 Bxf4 Be3. However, after 11 Bg3 Ne7 12 Be4! White has an obvious advantage.

7 d4

The following continuation also appears highly attractive: **7 exd6!?** Bxd6 (*7 ... Qxd6 can be met by 8 Qe2 0-0 9 d4 Nc6 10 Nd5*, with a promising position for White, Cheremesin-Shishov, 1958, al-

though the immediate *8 d4* is also good) 8 Qe2+, and now:

a) 8 ... Qe7 9 Qxe7+ Kxe7 (*9 ... Bxe7? 10 d4 Bd6* is clearly unsatisfactory, in view of *11 Ne4 Nd7 12 Nxd6+ cxd6 13 Bxf4*, with a clear advantage for White, Bronstein-Lemoine, Munich 1958) 10 0-0! f6 11 Nd5+ Kd8 12 d4 Ne3 13 Nxe3 fxe3 14 Bxe3, with a slight advantage for White (Genike-Konke, Hamburg 1975).

b) 8 ... Kf8 9 0-0 Nc6, and now by 10 d4! White again attains an advantage. For example: 10 ... Nxd4 11 Nxd4 Bc5 12 Bxf4 Qxd4+ 13 Kh1 Nf2+ 14 Rxf2 Qxf2 15 Qxf2 Bxf2 16 Rf1, or 10 ... Bf5 11 Nd5 Qd7 12 Nxf4 Bxf4 13 Bxf4 Nxd4 14 Qd1, and if 14 ... Nxc2, then 15 Qxd7 Bxd7 16 Rad1, and White has a dangerous initiative (Euwe).

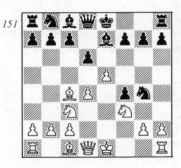

151

7 ...   dxe5

Instead of this exchange, Euwe has recommended 7 ... Bh4+ 8 Kf1 Ne3+ 9 Bxe3 fxe3 10 Qd3 Bg5 (after *10 ... dxe5 11 Qxe3 0-0 12 dxe5 Be7*

13 Rd1 White has excellent chances) but after 11 exd6! c6 (*11 ... cxd6 12 Qe4+ Be7 13 Ng5*, with a won position, Leuta-Bulgakov, corr. 1971) 12 Qe4+ Kf8 13 Re1 g6 14 Nxg5 Qxg5 15 Rxe3 White has clearly the better chances (Schevchik-Hanneman, corr. 1975).

After **7 ... Ne3** 8 Bxe3 fxe3 a position is reached from Spassky-Kholmov (Leningrad 1964), which continued 9 0-0 (*9 Qd3* and *10 0-0-0* also deserves consideration) 9 ... 0-0 10 Qd3 Nc6 11 exd6 cxd6 (*11 ... Bxd6* can be met by *12 Ne4 Be7 13 Qxe3*) 12 Rae1 Bg4 13 Rxe3 Kh8 14 Nd5, and White gained the advantage.

7 ... 0-0 8 Bxf4 c5 9 h3 Nh6 10 Bxh6 gxh6 11 0-0 Nc6 12 d5! also gives White the advantage.

    8 dxe5   **Qxd1+**

In Glazkov-Matveev (Tambov 1954), 8 ... 0-0 9 Bxf4 Be6 10 Qe2! gave White a slight but definite advantage.

    9 Nxd1

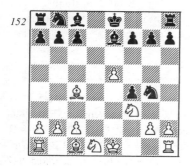

In spite of the simplification that has occurred, it is not easy for Black to solve his development problems.

Bronstein-Kholmov (Moscow 1961) continued 9 ... Be6 (after *9 '.. Bf5 10 Bxf4 Bxc2 11 e6!* White again has good prospects) 10 Bxe6 fxe6 11 h3 Nh6 12 Bxf4, when White had a slight but persistent advantage.

14.2

    4 Nc3

This unusual continuation, which resembles the Mason Gambit, also gives White good chances of gaining an opening advantage.

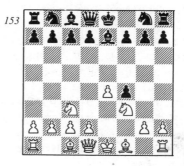

    4 ...   **Bh4+**

Another continuation to occur in tournament practice is **4 ... Nf6**, and now:

5 e5!? Ng4 6 d4, when 6 ... Bh4+ 7 Ke2 d6 (or *7 ... Nf2 8 Qe1*) 8 Bxf4 Nf2 9 Qe1 Bg4 10 exd6! favours White (Thimann), while 6 ... Ne3 7 Bxe3 fxe3 8 Bc4 d6 9 0-0 leads to a position from Spassky-Kholmov, mentioned in the note to Black's 7th move (cf. section 14.12).

5 d4 d5 6 Bd3, with the possibilities:

a) 6 ... Bb4 7 e5 Ne4 8 0-0 Nxc3 (Filtser-Vasilchuk, Moscow 1961), and now by 9 bxc3! Bxc3 10 Rb1 Nc6 11 Bxf4 Nxd4 12 Ng5 Nf5 13 Nxf7 Kxf7 14 g4 White gains the advantage.

b) 6 ... dxe4 7 Nxe4 Nxe4 (Lukin-Faibisovich, Leningrad 1965, continued *7 ... Nc6 8 Bxf4 0-0 9 c3 Nxe4 10 Bxe4 Bh4+ 11 Kf1 Bg4 12 Qd3*, with advantage to White) 8 Bxe4 Bd6 9 0-0, with two alternatives:

9 ... 0-0 10 Ne5! Bxe5 11 dxe5 Qxd1 12 Rxd1 Nc6 (*12 ... g5 is bad, in view of 13 h4 h6 14 hxg5 hxg5 15 g3!*) 13 Bxf4, with a minimal advantage for White (Euwe).

9 ... Nd7 10 Qd3 h6 11 c4 c5 12 b4! cxd4 13 c5 Be7 14 Bxf4 0-0 15 Nxd4 Nf6 (Spassky-Najdorf, Varna 1962) and now by 16 Rad1! White could have gained a definite advantage.

5 Ke2   d5

Black also has the following possibilities:

a) 5 ... f5 6 d3! fxe4 7 dxe4 d6 8 Bxf4 Bg4 9 Qd3 Nc6 10 Kd2, with a good game for White.

b) 5 ... Be7 6 d4 g5 7 Kf2 d6 8 Bc4 Nf6 (after *8 ... Nh6 9 h4 g4 10 Ng5 Bxg5 11 hxg5 Qxg5 12 Nd5* White has a splendid position) 9 h4 Nxe4+ 10 Nxe4 d5 11 hxg5 dxc4 12 Bxf4, with a clear advantage for White

(analysis by Cheremisin).

c) 5 ... Bg5 6 d4 Bh6, and now:

7 g3 fxg3 8 hxg3 d6 9 Bf4 Nc6, Heuer-Uusi, Tallinn 1963, and now White should have continued 10 Kf2! Nce7 11 Bc4 Bxf4 12 gxf4, with a promising position.

7 Kf2 Nf6 (on *7 ... g5* there follows *8 Bc4 d6 9 h4!*) 8 Bc4 Ng4+ 9 Kg1 0-0 10 h3 Ne3 11 Bxe3 fxe3 12 Kh2 d6 13 Rf1, with a clear advantage for White (analysis by Euwe).

d) 5 ... d6, with two alternatives:

6 d4 Bg4 7 Bxf4 Nc6 8 Qd3 Nge7 (or *8 ... Bg5 9 Bxg5 Qxg5*, Popovich-Kaufman, 1972, and now White could have gained the better chances by *10 Qe3!*, according to Keres) 9 Kd2 Bxf3 10 gxf3 Qd7 11 Rd1 0-0-0 12 Kc1 Kb8 13 Qe3, and White's chances are preferable (Planinc-Ivkov, Yugoslav Championship 1978).

6 d3 Bg4 7 Bxf4 Ne7 8 h3 Bxf3+ 9 gxf3 Nbc6 10 Kd2 0-0 (Bhend-Unzicker, Vienna 1972), and now, as indicated by Unzicker, after 11 Kc1! Ng6 12 Be3 a double-edged position is reached, with roughly equal chances.

6 Nxd5   Nf6
7 Nxf6+   Qxf6
8 d4

On 8 e5 Euwe recommends 8 ... Qa6+! 9 d3 Bg4 10 Bxf4 Nc6 11 c3 0-0-0, with an active position for Black.

8 ...   Bg4

Hartston-J.Littlewood (England 1965) went 8 ... 0-0 9 Qd3! Bg4 10 e5 Qb6?, and now by 11 g3! White could have gained a clear advantage.

9 c3   Nc6

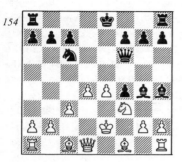

154

This critical position was reached in Kavalek-Gerink (Prague 1959), in which Black gained a dangerous attack after **10 Kd3?** 0-0-0 11 Kc2 Rhe8 12 Bd3 Bf2 13 Qf1 Bxf3 14 gxf3 Bxd4! 15 cxd4 Nb4+ 16 Kb1 Rxd4.

White should have continued **10 Qd2!**, after which both 10 ... 0-0 11 Kd1 Rfe8 12 Bd3 Rad8 13 Kc2, and 10 ... g5 11 Kd1 0-0-0 12 Kc2 Qh6 13 Nxh4 Qxh4 14 g3! fxg3 15 Qg2! give him a clear advantage.

It can be concluded that the Euwe Defence affords White good chances of developing the initiative.

Game No. 10
Pypel-Ivanov
Riga 1959
1 e4 e5 2 f4 exf4 3 Nf3 Be7 4 Bc4

Nf6 5 e5 Ng4 6 Nc3 Bh4+?

A move in the style of players from the last century. Stronger, as shown in the analysis, is 6 ... d6.
7 g3?!
This leads to double-edged play, whereas the quiet 7 Kf1 assures White of an advantage.
7 ... fxg3 8 0-0 Nf2
On 8 ... gxh2+ White can advantageously play either 9 Kh1, or 9 Nxh2.
9 Qe2 Nh3+ 10 Kh1 Nf4
Now White gains the opportunity to carry out an interesting and unexpected combination.
11 Bxf7+! Kf8
Not, of course, 11 ... Kxf7 12 Qc4+.
12 Bb3!

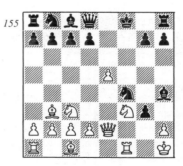

155

A beautiful queen sacrifice, the acceptance of which, however, leads only to a draw.
12 ... Bf6
On 12 ... Nxe2 there could have followed 13 Nxh4+ Ke8! (*13 ... Ke7? loses to 14 Nf5+ Kf8 15*

Nd6+ !) 14 Bf7+ Kf8!, and White is obliged to force the draw.

13 exf6 Nxe2

The result is that Black has captured the queen in a much less favourable situation, since now all the opposing pieces fall upon his unprotected king.

14 Nxe2 g2+ 15 Kxg2 d5 16 d4

White has only two minor pieces for the sacrificed queen. But Black is completely undeveloped, and is in no position to oppose his opponent's superior forces on the K-side.

16 ... Bf5 17 Ng3 Bg6 18 Ng5 Qd7 19 Bd2

White's last minor piece comes into play with decisive effect.

19 ... Nc6 20 Rae1 h6

20 ... Re8 looks sounder, but after 21 Rxe8+ Kxe8 (or *21 ... Bxe8 22 f7*) 22 f7+ Kf8 23 Ba4!, threatening 24 Bb4+, Black loses quickly.

21 Ne6+ Kg8 22 fxg7 Kh7 23 gxh8=Q+ Kxh8

White now has a decisive material advantage. The rest is clear.

24 Rf8+ Rxf8 25 Nxf8 Qf7 26 Nxg6+ Qxg6 27 Bxd5 Qxc2 28 Re8+ Resigns.

Game No. 11
Lutikov-Estrin
Leningrad 1951
1 e4 e5 2 f4 exf4 3 Nf3 Be7 4 Bc4

Nf6 5 e5 Ng4 6 d4

This move does not give White any advantage. 6 0-0 or 6 Nc3 is more promising.

6 ... d5 7 Bd3

7 Bb3 would be met by the same reply. As shown in the theoretical section, 7 Be2 gives White an equal game.

7 ... Bh4+ 8 Ke2 Nf2 9 Qe1 Nxd3 10 Qxh4 Nxc1+ 11 Rxc1 Qxh4 12 Nxh4 Nc6 13 c3 0-0 14 Kf2

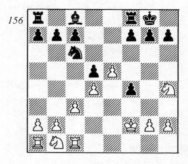

156

It is readily apparent that Black, with his lead in development and extra pawn, has a clear advantage, and with his next move he consolidates it.

14 ... f6! 15 Re1

White loses his head. He should have continued 15 exf6 Rxf6 16 Nf3 Bg4 17 Re1, making it difficult for Black to realize his extra pawn. But now Black succeeds in strengthening his position.

15 ... g5 16 Nf3 g4 17 Ng1

17 Nh4 would have been met by 17

... fxe5 18 dxe5 Re8, when White has to part with another pawn.

17 ... fxe5 18 dxe5 Bf5

Now 18 ... Re8 19 Ne2 leads to unnecessary complications.

19 h3 g3+ 20 Kf3 Rae8

On 20 ... Be4+ there would have followed 21 Rxe4 dxe4+ 22 Kxe4 Rae8 23 Nf3. Black aims to win the exchange in a more favourable situation.

21 Nd2 Be4+

The simplest. Now 22 Nxe4 fails to 22 ... Nxe5+ 23 Ke2 dxe4, when White is defenceless.

22 Rxe4 dxe4+ 23 Kxe4 Rxe5+ 24 Kd3 Re3+ 25 Kc2 b5

Black now has a decisive material and positional advantage. There followed:

26 Rf1 Ne5 27 Ra1 Nd3 28 Ngf3 Rd8 29 Rf1 c5 30 a4 Re2 31 axb5 Ne5 32 Kc1 Nxf3 33 Nxf3 Rxg2 White resigns.

15 Schallopp Defence

1 e4	**e5**
2 f4	**exf4**
3 Nf3	**Nf6**

This defence was especially popular at the start of the present century, when it appeared to have claims to being a refutation of the Knight's Gambit. But with the passage of time, sound ways have been found for White to develop an initiative.

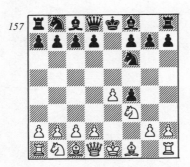

157

4 e5

A popular alternative to this natural move is **4 Nc3** d5 5 e5 (*5 exd5 or 5 Nxd5* leads to the Modern Defence, Chapter 16), and now:

a) **5 ... Nh5!** This is Black's best reply, leading to a favourable line of the main variation.

b) **5 ... Ne4.** This is recommended by all the opening guides, but it gives Black nothing after 6 d3! (*6 Ne2 is well met by 6 ... Bg4! 7 Nxf4 Bc5*, while after *6 Be2 g5! 7 0-0 Nc6 8 Bb5 a6 9 Bxc6+ bxc6 10 d3 Bc5* the advantage is again with Black, Spielmann-Bogoljubov, Berlin 1919) 6 ... Nxc3 7 bxc3 g5 8 h4! (after *8 d4 g4 9 Ng1 Qh4+ 10 Ke2,* Gunsberg-Mieses, 1903, Black could have gained a clear advantage by *10 ... Bh6!*) 8 ... g4, and now 9 Nd4 Bh6 10 Ba3 or 10 g3 gives White a good game.

4 ...	**Nh5**

4 ... Nd5 is inadequate, in view of 5 c4 Nb6 6 d4 d6 7 exd6!, while on **4 ... Ne4** there can follow 5 d3 (Keres recommended here *5 d4 d5 6 Bxf4 c5 7 Nbd2 Nc6 8 Bd3!*) 5 ... Ng5 6 Bxf4 Ne6 (*6 ... Nxf3+ 7 Qxf3 d6 8 Qg3!*

also favours White) 7 Bg3 d5 8 Nc3 d4 9 Ne4 Nc6 10 Be2 Be7 11 0-0 0-0 12 Qd2, with a good game for White (Tolush-Averbakh, Kislovodsk 1960).

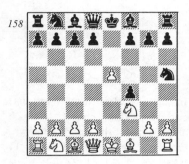

158

The basic position of the Schallopp Defence, in which four main continuations should be considered for White: **5 Nc3 (15.1), 5 d4 (15.2), 5 Be2 (15.3)** and **5 Qe2 (15.4)**.

White achieves nothing by **5 g4** (the Tashkent Variation) 5 ... fxg3 6 d4, in view of 6 ... d5! (*6 ... h6!? is also possible*) 7 Ng5 g6 8 Qf3 (*on 8 hxg3 Nxg3 9 Qf3 Nf5 10 Nxh7 there follows 10 ... Be7!*) 8 ... f6! 9 hxg3 (*9 e6 Qe7 10 hxg3 fxg5 11 Rxh5 Qxe6+, or 9 exf6 Qxf6 10 Qe3+ Be7 11 hxg3 Nc6 also favours Black*) 9 ... fxg5 10 Rxh5 g4! 11 Qh1 gxh5 12 Qxh5+ Kd7, and Black beats off the attack, remaining with a material advantage (Cheremisin).

15.1
5 Nc3

After this move Black has to play

very exactly, so as to avoid ending up in an inferior position.

Here two replies for Black have been played: **5 ... d6 (15.11)** and **5 ... d5 (15.12)**.

15.11
    5 ...   d6
    6 Bc4

6 Qe2 led to a double-edged position after 6 ... d5 7 d4 Nc6 8 Bd2 Be6 9 0-0-0 Be7 10 Qf2 0-0 11 Be2 g6 12 g3 in Bhend-Wirtenson, corr. 1970.

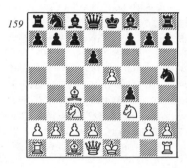

159

    6 ...   Nc6
The most accurate reply.

6 ... Bg4 7 0-0 Nc6 was played in Hay-Wiener (Sydney 1963), and gave White the advantage after 8 h3! Bxf3 9 Qxf3 dxe5 10 Bb5 Nf6 11 Bxc6+ bxc6 12 Qxc6+ Nd7 13 d4!

6 ... Be6 7 Bxe6 fxe6 8 Qe2 leads after 8 ... Nc6! to the main variation, whereas 8 ... d5 9 d4 Nc6, as occurred in Pillsbury-Mieses (Vienna 1903), is clearly bad in view of 10 g4! fxg3 11 Ng5 g6 12 hxg3

Qe7 13 Qg4!, with a won position for White.

7 Qe2

7 d4 dxe5!, examined in section 15.22, is favourable for Black. The text move is suggested by Glazkov.

Euwe's recommendation of **7 exd6** Bxd6 8 d4 0-0 9 0-0 Bg4 10 Ne4 also deserves consideration, when White has certain compensation for the sacrificed pawn.

7 ...   Be6

In the event of **7 ... Be7** White gains the advantage by 8 exd6 cxd6 9 Ng5 Ne5 10 Nxf7 Nxf7 11 Qxh5 0-0 12 0-0.

Stronger is **7 ... dxe5!**, which after 8 Nxe5 Nxe5 9 Qxe5+ Qe7 10 Qxe7+ (after *10 d4 Qxe5+ 11 dxe5*, *11 ... Bf5!* is good) 10 ... Bxe7 11 Be2 Nf6 12 d3! Bd6 13 Nb5 Nd5 14 Nxd6+ cxd6 15 Bf3 Nb4 16 Kd1 g5 17 Bd2! leads to an equal game.

8 Bxe6   fxe6
9 d4!

A strong move, suggested by Bhend. After 9 exd6 Bxd6 10 Qxe6+ the chances are equal, while in the event of 9 ... Qxd6 10 Ng5 Qe5 11 Qxe5 Nxe5 12 d4 Nf7 13 Nxe6 Bd6 14 Nb5 Kd7 15 Nxd6 Nxd6! (*E.C.O.*) White again cannot hope for more than equality.

9 ...   dxe5

But not 9 ... d5? 10 g4! (cf. the note to Black's sixth move).

10 dxe5

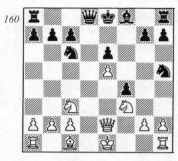

In this critical position White has good attacking chances, which compensate for the sacrificed pawn.

On **10 ... Be7** there can follow 11 Bd2 Bh4+ 12 g3 fxg3 13 0-0-0, while after **10 ... Bc5** 11 Bd2 Qe7 12 Ne4 White, who is threatening to open lines by g2-g4, again has the better chances.

15.12

5 ...   d5

This move, blocking the centre, would appear to be the strongest, although of interest is Moiseev's idea, 5 ... Be7, so as to prevent White from castling after ... Bh4+. In this case White should play 6 Qe2.

6 d4

see diagram 161

6 ...   g5

Here the relatively new move **6 ... c6!** deserves serious consideration. After 7 Be2 (*7 g3* is well met by *7 ... g5!*) 7 ... Rg8! (if *7 ... g5*, then *8*

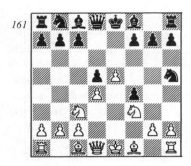

161

Nxg5!) 8 0-0 g5 9 Qd3 Rh8! 10 g3 Black returns the gambit pawn by 10 ... Ng7! 11 gxf4 Bf5 12 Qd1 g4 13 Ne1 Qh4!, obtaining the better game.

Another alternative is **6 ... Nc6** 7 Be2 g5 8 0-0 (in the given situation *8 Nxg5 Qxg5 9 Bxh5* favours Black, in view of *9 ... Qh4+! 10 Kf1 b6!*), and now:

a) 8 ... g4 9 Bb5 (much weaker is *9 Ne1? Nxe5! 10 dxe5 Bc5+ 11 Kh1 Ng3+! 12 hxg3 Qg5*, when Black won, MacEwan-Kitts, corr. 1964) transposing into Chigorin-Mieses (Vienna 1903), which continued 9 ... gxf3 10 Qxf3 Qh4 11 Nxd5 Kd8 12 Qc3 Bd7 13 Bxf4 Rg8 14 g3 Bh6 15 e6! Nxf4 (*15 ... fxe6* is bad because of *16 Bxh6!*, with the threat of *17 Rf8+*) 16 Rxf4 Qg5 (after *16 ... Bxf4 17 exf7!* Black loses his rook) 17 exf7 Rf8 18 Bc4, with an excellent position for White.

b) 8 ... Rg8, Aurbach-Freymann (Abbazia 1912), when White should have continued 9 Qd3! Rg6 10 Qb5

g4 11 Ne1 a6 12 Qxd5 Nxd4 13 Bd3, gaining an advantage.

c) 8 ... Ng7 9 Nxg5 Qxg5 10 Nxd5 Kd8 11 Bxf4 Qg6 12 Nf6 followed by 13 d5, and again White stands better.

7 g4!?

Dudarukov's interesting idea.

Formerly **7 Be2** Rg8 8 0-0 was considered obligatory, which after 8 ... c6! favours Black. But **7 Bd3** Nc6 8 0-0 is perfectly possible, leading after 8 ... g4 9 Bb5! to the Chigorin-Mieses game considered in the previous note.

7 ...   Ng7

In Dudarukov-Tretyakov (Krasnodar 1952) 7 ... Bxg4 8 Rg1 f5 9 h3 Bxf3 10 Qxf3 g4 led to a won position for White after 11 hxg4 Nc6 12 Qh3!

8 h4   Bxg4

After 8 ... Be7 White gains a clear advantage by 9 hxg5 Bxg5 10 Nxg5 Qxg5 11 Nxd5!

9 hxg5   Ne6

10 Bh3

162

Dudarukov-Filipenko (corr. 1947) now continued **10 ... Bxf3** 11 Qxf3 Nxd4 12 Qh5!, and White won quickly.

Sokolsky's recommendation of **10 ... Bxh3** 11 Rxh3 Nc6 looks stronger, but even here Keres considers that after 12 Ne2 White gains sufficient compensation for the sacrificed pawn.

15.2

5 d4

The evaluation of this move depends upon whether or not White can maintain his position in the centre.

163

Two main replies should be considered for Black: **5 ... d5** (15.21) and **5 ... d6** (15.22).

5 ... g5 is risky, in view of 6 Nfd2! Ng7 7 Ne4 Be7 8 h4!, when White gains the advantage (Pachman-Lakes, Prague 1943).

15.21

5 ...   d5

6 c4

In this way White undermines his opponent's central pawn, but also to be considered is **6 Be2**, which after 6 ... g5 7 0-0 (*7 Nxg5 Qxg5 8 Bxh5 Qh4+! 9 Kf1 b6!* gives Black dangerous counter-play) 7 ... Rg8 leads to a variation considered below, in section 15.3.

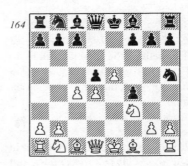

164

6 ...   Nc6

The most popular, but not the only reply. Other possibilities:

a) 6 ... Bb4+ 7 Nc3 Nc6 8 Be2 0-0 9 0-0 Bxc3 (*9 ... dxc4 10 d5 Bc5+* leads to an advantage for White after *11 Kh1 Ne7 12 Ng5 Nf5 13 Nce4*) 10 bxc3 Bg4 11 Ne1 (or *11 cxd5 Qxd5 12 h3!*) 11 ... Bxe2 12 Qxe2 g6 13 Bxf4, with advantage to White (Muchnik-Dzhalalov, Moscow 1952).

b) 6 ... Bg4 7 cxd5 Be7 8 Be2 Bh4+ 9 Kf1 0-0 10 Nc3 Nd7 11 Bd2 Re8 12 Rc1 Nb6 13 a4 Be7 14 Qb3, with a good game for White (Freeman-Haygarth, corr. 1960).

c) 6 ... Be7 7 Be2 Bh4+ 8 Kf1 Be7 9

cxd5 Qxd5 10 Nc3 Qd8 11 d5, with a sharp game (Bronstein-Hukl, Bratislava 1946).

d) 6 … g5 7 Be2 g4 8 0-0 gxf3 9 Bxf3, and White has a strong attack for the sacrificed piece.

e) 6 … c6 7 Nc3, and the threat of 8 Qb3 gives White a good game.

      7 cxd5   Qxd5
      8 Nc3   Bb4

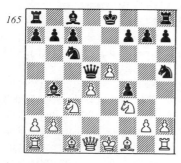

165

For a long time this position was considered roughly equal, but it has recently been re-evaluated. White has two good continuations:

a) 9 Kf2 Bxc3 10 bxc3 Bg4 11 Be2 0-0 (after *11 … 0-0-0 12 c4! Qd7 13 d5 Nb8 14 Qd4* White gained a clear advantage in Malyuzhinets-Glazkov, Moscow 1950), and now, instead of 12 Ng5 Bxe2 13 Qxe2 f6!, which in Reti-Nyholm (Abbazia 1912) led to a roughly equal game, Keres considers that White gains the advantage by 12 h3! Bc8 13 Re1!

b) 9 Be2 Qa5 (on *9 … Bg4 10 0-0 Bxc3 11 bxc3 0-0* White has the good continuation *12 h3!*, which is considered above in the note to Black's 6th move, variation 'a') 10 Bd2 Bg4 11 a3 Bxc3 12 bxc3 0-0, and now in Glazkov-Malyuzhinets (Moscow 1950) there followed 13 Ng5 Bxe2 14 Qxe2 g6 15 g4! fxg3 16 hxg3 Nxg3 17 Nxh7!, with a quick win.

15.22

      5 …   d6
This move, undermining White's centre, has also been re-evaluated. The latest researches show that White has good prospects.

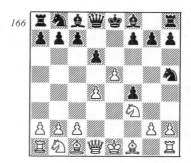

166

The following three continuations will be considered: **6 Bc4 (15.221)**, **6 g3 (15.222)** and **6 Qe2! (15.223)**.

Reti-Szekely (Abbazia 1912) went instead **6 Nc3** dxe5 7 Qe2 Bg4 8 Qxe5+, and after 8 … Qe7? 9 Nd5 Nc6 10 Nxe7 Nxe5 11 Nxe5 Be6 12 d5 White gained the advantage.

However, instead of 8 … Qe7? Black should play 8 … Be7!, and now:

a) 9 Nd5 Nc6 10 Bb5 0-0! 11 Nxe7+

Nxe7 12 0-0, Vukcevic-Karaklajic (Belgrade 1958), and now by 12 ... Ng6! Black could have consolidated his advantage.

b) 9 Bxf4 (or *9 h3 Nd7 10 Qe4 Ndf6*) 9 ... 0-0 10 Qxc7 Bxf3 11 gxf3 Qxd4, and again Black has an excellent game.

15.221

6 Bc4

In this way White provokes his opponent into playing 6 ... d5, so as after 7 Be2 to transpose into a variation considered below in section 15.3.

6 ...   Nc6

On **6 ... Be6** White advantageously continues 7 Bxe6 fxe6 8 g4! fxg3 9 Ng5! g6 10 Qf3, while after **6 ... Bg4** there follows 7 0-0, threatening the extremely unpleasant 8 h3, when 7 ... dxe5? is strongly met by 8 Bxf7+!

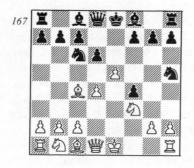

167

7 0-0

7 Nc3 used to be played here, but is unsatisfactory in view of 7 ... dxe5 8

Qe2 (if *8 0-0 Bg4*, while *8 d5* is strongly met by *8 ... Na5* or *8 ... Nd4!*) 8 ... Bg4!, and now:

a) 9 d5 Bxf3 10 Qxf3 Qh4+ 11 g3 Nd4 12 Qe4 Nxg3 13 hxg3 Qxg3+ 14 Kd1 0-0-0, and for the sacrificed piece Black has more than adequate compensation.

b) 9 Bb5 Bd6 10 dxe5 0-0 11 Bxc6 bxc6 12 0-0 Bc5+, with an excellent game for Black (Bhend).

7 ...   dxe5
8 Re1

8 d5 loses to 8 ... Bc5+ 9 Kh1 Nd4 10 Nxd4 Qh4!

In Marshall-Schlechter (Vienna 1903) White continued **8 Qe2** (if *8 Nc3*, then *8 ... Bg4*) 8 ... Bg4 9 Nc3, when Black should have chosen 9 ... Bxf3! 10 Rxf3 Qxd4+ 11 Be3 and now 11 ... Qd7! (Glazkov), with good chances of a successful defence.

8 Nxe5 Nxe5 9 Re1 leads to the main variation.

8 ...   Be7
9 Nxe5   Nxe5
10 Rxe5

see diagram 168

In this critical position there can follow **10 ... Bg4** 11 Be2 (*11 Qxg4? is bad because of 11 ... Qxd4+ 12 Re3 Nf6! 13 Qxg7 0-0-0*) 11 ... Bxe2 12 Qxe2 Nf6 (but not *12 ... Qxd4+? 13 Kf1!*) 13 c3 Nd7 14 Re4 Nf6, or **10 ... Nf6** 11 Bxf4 0-0, in both cases with a roughly equal game.

In Bhend-Wirtenson (corr. 1970)

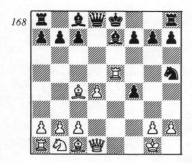

10 ... g6!? 11 Nc3 0-0 led to a somewhat more comfortable game for Black.

15.222

6 g3

A little-studied continuation, suggested by Bhend.

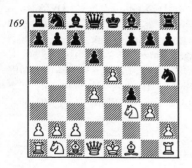

6 ...   Be7

To equalize it is sufficient for Black to play **6 ... dxe5** 7 Nxe5 Nf6. **6 ... fxg3** is risky, since 7 Ng5 g6 transposes into an unfavourable version for Black of the Tashkent Variation examined earlier. Airapetov-Ginger (Tashkent 1952)

continued 8 Qf3 f6 (after *8 ... Bf5* both *9 hxg3* and *9 Bc4* are good) 9 Bc4 Qe7 10 hxg3 fxg5 11 Rxh5 gxh5 12 Qxh5+ Kd7 13 Bxg5 Qg7 14 e6+, and White gained a decisive attack.

7 Nc3   fxg3

Also good here is **7 ... Bg4** 8 exd6 Bxd6 9 Qe2+ Qe7 10 Qxe7+ Kxe7. Bhend indicates that after 11 Nd5+ Ke8 (weaker is *11 ... Kd7 12 Be2*, with the threat of *13 Ne5+*) 12 Ne5 Bxe5 13 dxe5 Bf3 a position is reached with roughly equal chances. However, in reply to 11 Nd5+ Black should play 11 ... Kd8!, retaining his extra pawn.

8 Be3   Bg4

Also possible is the preliminary **8 ... gxh2** 9 Rxh2, and only now 9 ... Bg4, which after 10 Bc4 Nc6 11 Rg2 leads to a double-edged position.

Less promising for Black is **8 ... Bh4** 9 Kd2 g2 (if *9 ... dxe5 10 Nxh4 Qxh4*, then *11 hxg3!*, and Black cannot play *11 ... Qxh1?* because of *12 Bb5+*) 10 Bxg2 dxe5 11 Nxe5 Bg5 12 Re1, when White has the advantage (Bhend-Wirtenson, corr. 1970).

9 h3   Bf5

9 ... Be6 10 d5 Bc8 11 Bb5+ c6 12 Bc4 also leads to a complex and unclear position.

10 Bc4	**g2**
11 Rg1	**Bh4+**
12 Kd2	**Bxh3**

see diagram 170

Bhend considers that **13 Nxh4**

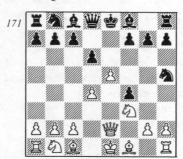

170

Qxh4 14 Qf3 0-0 15 Nd5 leads to a sharp game with chances for both sides. However, it is difficult to agree with this, since by 15 ... dxe5! 16 Nxc7 exd4 Black gains a decisive advantage, while after **13 exd6** cxd6 14 Nxh4 Qxh4 15 Qf3 0-0 16 Nd5 Nc6 the advantage is again with Black (Estrin).

For a definitive assessment, all these variations require testing in practice.

15.223

6 Qe2!

171

6 ...   d5
White also has the better prospects after 6 ... dxe5 7 Qxe5+ Qe7 8 Be2 Bg4 9 Bxf4.

7 c4
A very logical continuation, but 7 Nc3 is also possible, transposing into a position from section 15.11.

7 ...   Be6
8 cxd5
Keres recommends the immediate 8 Nc3.

8 ...   Bxd5
9 Nc3   Nc6
10 Bd2!
10 Nxd5 Qxd5 11 Qc4 is bad in view of 11 ... Bb4+ 12 Kf2 Qxc4 13 Bxc4 Nxd4!, when Black retains his extra pawn.

10 ...   Bb4
11 Nxd5   Qxd5
12 0-0-0!   Qxa2
12 ... 0-0-0 is weaker in view of 13 Qc4 Bxd2+ 14 Rxd2 Qxc4 15 Bxc4, and if 15 ... f6, then 16 Be6+ Kb8 17 Bg4 g6 18 Bxh5 gxh5 19 e6!, with advantage to White.

13 d5!

see diagram 172

E.C.O. rightly considers this critical position to favour White, and gives the following two variations:

a) **13 ... Qa1+** 14 Kc2 Qa4+ 15 Kb1 Ne7 (*15 ... Bxd2* is weaker because of *16 dxc6*) 16 Qb5+ Qxb5 17 Bxb5+ c6 18 Bxb4, with an overwhelming position for White.

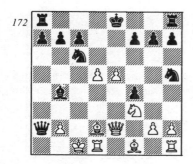

172

b) 13 ... Bxd2+ 14 Nxd2! Qxd5 15 Qxh5 Qxe5 16 Qxe5 Nxe5 17 Re1 f6 18 Nc4 0-0-0 19 Nxe5 fxe5 20 Rxe5, with slightly the better chances for White.

15.3
5 Be2

White directly attacks the knight at h5. Up till 1965 this variation was considered favourable for Black, but then it was established that White has sufficient counter-chances.

173

5 ... g5

This is considered best. In the last game of the Chigorin-Steinitz match

(Havana 1892) Black tried **5 ... g6**, on which there followed 6 d4 Bg7 7 0-0 d6 8 Nc3 0-0, and now, according to analysis by Chigorin, by 9 ... exd6! cxd6 (or *9 ... Qxd6 10 Ne5!*) 10 Ne1! White could have forced 10 ... Nf6, winning back the gambit pawn with the better prospects.

The alternative is **5 ... d6** (if *5 ... d5*, then *6 0-0!*, when on *6 ... g5?*, *7 Nxg5* is good) 6 0-0 dxe5 7 Nxe5 Bc5+ (on *7 ... Qd4+ 8 Kh1 Nf6* White does best to continue *9 Nd3 Bd6 10 c3!*) 8 Kh1 Nf6, and now:

a) 9 c3 Nbd7 (Prins-Jackson, Hastings 1935), when, according to *E.C.O.*, White should continue 10 Nxd7! Bxd7 11 d4 Bd6 12 Bxf4 Bxf4 13 Rxf4 0-0 14 Bd3, with a considerably superior position.

b) 9 Nd3 (*9 Rxf4* is unsatisfactory, in view of *9 ... Bd6 10 d4 Nbd7!*) 9 ... Bb6 10 Nxf4 0-0 (Chigorin-Marco, Vienna 1903), and now Marco considers that White should have played 11 d3, with a roughly equal game.

6 0-0

The usual move.

In the past **6 Nxg5** was often played, with these possibilities:

a) 6 ... Qxg5 7 Bxh5 Qg2 (*7 ... Qh4+ 8 Kf1 b6!* should also be considered) 8 Qf3 (no better is *8 Bf3 Qg5 9 d4 d6*, with advantage to Black), but Nenarokov's continuation 8 ... Qxf3! 9 Bxf3 Nc6 10 Bxc6

dxc6 11 d4 Bh6 12 Rf1 Bf5 13 c3
Rg8 gives Black the better chances.
b) 6 ... Ng3 7 hxg3 Qxg5, and now
White is recommended to play 8 g4,
which received a practical testing in
Malyuzhinets-Glazkov (Moscow
1959). After 8 ... h5 9 d4? d6 10 0-0
dxe5 11 gxh5 Nc6 12 Nc3 Nxd4 13
Bxf4 Bc5! 14 Bxg5 Nf3++ Black
announced mate in three. White
should have continued 9 Nc3!, when
Black has no useful moves.

6 d4!? is interesting, and now:
a) 6 ... d5, when 7 Nxg5 Qxg5 8
Bxh5 is inadequate, in view of 8 ...
Qh4+! 9 Kf1 b6, but 7 g4!? Bxg4 8
Rg1 Bxf3 9 Bxf3 Ng7 10 c4! deserves
consideration, with good attacking
chances for White.
b) 6 ... g4 7 0-0 gxf3 (Black is forced
to accept the piece sacrifice, since *7
... Rg8 8 Ne1! d5 9 Nd3* is clearly to
White's advantage) 8 Bxf3 Ng7 9
Nc3 Be7 10 Bxf4 0-0 11 Bh6 d6 (*11
... Bg5 is bad because of 12 Nd5!
Bxh6 13 Nf6+ Kh8 14 Qd3*), and in
Glazkov-Rogachenko (Engels 1954)
a draw was agreed after 12 Bxb7
Bxb7 13 Qg4 Bg5 14 Bxg5 Qd7! 15
Qg3 Nf5 16 Qg4 Ng7 17 Qg3.

see diagram 174

6 ...   Rg8

In the middle of the last century it
was thought that, after this move,
Black, with an extra pawn, gained a
strong attack on the enemy king
position (cf. the diagram after
Black's 9th move).

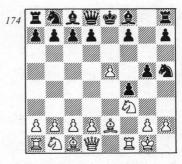

174

Other moves have also been
played, for example:
a) 6 ... Nc6 7 d4! (*7 Nxg5? is refuted
by 7 ... Bc5+ 8 Kh1 Ng3+! 9 hxg3
Qxg5*) 7 ... Rg8, and now, according
to analysis by Lasker, very strong is
8 Nfd2! Ng7 (or *8 ... g4 9 Bxg4 Qg5
10 Bf3 Nxd4 11 Ne4 Nxf3+ 12 Qxf3
Qxe5 13 Nbc3*, with the threat of
Qxh5) 9 Ne4 Be7 10 Nbc3 d5 11
exd6 cxd6 12 Nd5, when White has
an excellent attacking position.
b) 6 ... Ng7 7 d4 d5 8 c4 c6 9 Nc3
Be6, and after 10 cxd5 cxd5 11 Qb3
Nd7 12 Nxd5 Be7 13 Qxb7 0-0 14
Nc7 White gained a clear advantage
in Lutikov-Kuzmin (Sochi 1970).
c) 6 ... d6, when Keres recommends
7 Nxg5! Qxg5 8 Bxh5 dxe5 9 d4!
with advantage to White.

7 d4

After this move Black blocks the
centre. Of interest is the attempt by
White to prevent this by **7 c4!?**,
after which Lacis-Mickevic (corr.
1971) continued 7 ... g4 8 d4! d6 9
Nc3 gxf3 10 Bxf3 Qg5 11 exd6! Kd8

(the threat was *12 Qe2+* and *13 Bxh5*) 12 dxc7+ Kxc7 13 Nd5+ Kd8 14 Qe2, and for the sacrificed piece White gained a very strong attack. After 14 ... Bg4 15 Re1 Bd6 16 c5 Nc6 17 cxd6 Kd7 18 Bxf4 White won easily.

7 ...   **d5**

The most logical move. The attempt to seize the initiative by 7 ... g4 appears rather naîve; White has:

a) 8 Ne1 (the simplest; *8 c4!?* is another possibility) 8 ... d5 9 Nd3! (*9 Bxf4 Nxf4 10 Rxf4* is weaker, after which *10 ... Bh6* gives Black a strong counter-attack), and if now 9 ... f3, then simply 10 Bxf3! gxf3 11 Qxf3, with a clear advantage to White.

b) 8 Nc3 (this is also strong) 8 ... d5 (after *8 ... gxf3 9 Bxf3* White gains an overwhelming position for the piece) 9 Ne1 Bh6, and now 10 Nd3! Qh4 11 Nxf4 g3 12 Bb5+ c6 13 Qxh5 gives White a clear advantage.

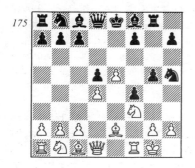

175

8 Qd3

Along with this move, White has

other, no less effective, ways of developing his initiative:

a) 8 Ne1 Ng7 9 c4 (Winawer-Pitschel, Berlin 1881, went *9 Qd3 Ne6 10 c3 Bg7 11 Qxh7 Rh8 12 Qd3 Nd7*, with a complicated game) 9 ... Nc6 10 Nc3 Be6 11 Bf3 Ne7 12 Nd3 c6 13 Nc5 Qc7 14 Qa4 Kd8 15 Bd2, and White has a clear advantage (Listengarten-Ovanesov, Baku 1973).

b) 8 c4 c6 9 Nc3 Be6 (*9 ... g4* is inconsistent, in view of *10 cxd5 gxf3 11 Bxf3 Qg5 12 Ne4 Qg6 13 Qe2*, with a strong attack for White) 10 cxd5 cxd5 11 Qd3 (*11 Qb3 Qd7 12 g4!?* deserves consideration, whereas *12 Ne1 Ng7 13 Bf3 Nc6! 14 Nxd5! Bxd5 15 Bxd5 Nxd4 16 Qxb7* leads to a roughly equal ending) 11 ... Rg6 12 Nh4 Rh6 13 Nf5 Bxf5 14 Qxf5 Ng7 15 Qd3 Nc6.

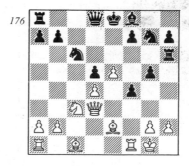

176

An important position for the assessment of the variation. On **16 Qb5** Black has the good reply 16 ... Nf5, while on **16 Bg4** there follows 16 ... Ne6.

Euwe considers that by continuing **16 Bf3** White gains slightly the better chances, in view of the weakness of the opponent's d5 square. But by 16 ... Ne6! 17 Nxd5 Bg7! Black gains sufficient counter-play.

In our opinion, White should continue **16 g3!** fxg3 17 hxg3, with the better chances.

        8 ...   **Rg6**

        9 Nh4

The new possibility **9 e6!?** fxe6 10 Ne5 Rh6 is of interest, when White can either force a draw after **11 Ng4** Rg6 12 Ne5, or else attempt to continue the attack by **11 g3**, when 11 ... fxg3? is bad in view of 12 Bxh5+ Rxh5 13 Qf3, and White wins.

        9 ...   Rh6

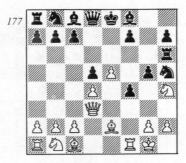

177

For a long time this position was thought by theory to favour Black, since after **10 Nf5** Bxf5 11 Qxf5 Ng7 he retains his extra pawn, with good chances.

White, however, can play more strongly: **10 Bxh5!** Rxh5 11 Nf5 Bxf5 (if *11 ... Qd7*, then *12 g4 fxg3 13 Nxg3*, and White gains strong pressure on the f-file, which gives him the better chances) 12 Qxf5 Rh6 (*12 ... Qd7? is bad because of 13 Rxf4!*), and after 13 g3 Qd7! 14 Qxd7+ Nxd7 15 gxf4 gxf4 16 Bxf4 Re6! 17 Nc3 c6 followed by 18 ... f6 the chances are equal.

Also of interest is a new possibility: **10 g4!?** Ng7 (*10 ... fxg3?* loses to *11 Bxh5 Rxh5 12 Qf3*) 11 Ng2 Rg6 12 h4, leading to a complex and unclear game.

15.4

        5 Qe2

This move, which contains an unusual idea, was first employed in Keres-Alekhine (Salzburg 1942). After reinforcing his centre, White threatens to break open the position by g2-g4.

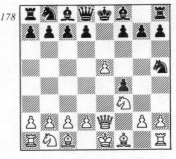

178

        5 ...   **Be7**

Black has a very limited choice of good replies. Apart from the text

move, only **5 ... g6** 6 d4 deserves
consideration, and now:

a) 6 ... Bg7? 7 g4!, and Black loses
a piece (Koblents-Zagoryansky,
Vilnius 1946), since 7 ... fxg3? loses
immediately to 8 Bg5!

b) 6 ... Be7! 7 Nc3 (*7 g4 fxg3 8 Nc3!
d5 9 exd6 Qxd6 10 Bg5 f6 11 Ne4*
leads to a double-edged game) 7 ...
d5 (*7... 0-0 8 g4! fxg3 9 Bh6 Re8 10
Nd5 c6 11 Nxe7+ Qxe7 12 0-0-0,*
with a dangerous attack for White)
8 exd6 (on *8 Bd2* Black should reply
8... 0-0! 9 0-0-0 c6) 8 ... Qxd6 9 Nb5
Qd8 10 Qe5 0-0 11 Qxc7 Bh4+ 12
Kd1 Bg4, and Black has a good
game (Bhend).

On **5 ... g5** White again continues
advantageously 6 g4!, and if 6 ...
Ng7, then 7 h4, while on 6 ... fxg3
there follows 7 Qg2!

6 d4

This move is considered obligatory, although 6 Nc3 also deserves
consideration.

6 ...	**0-0**

6 ... Bh4+ 7 Kd1 0-0 is weak in
view of 8 g4! fxg3 9 Qg2 Be7 10
hxg3, and White gained a strong
attack in Randviir-Tepaks (Tallinn
1946).

7 g4

Basman-Griffiths (Bognor Regis
1968) went **7 Nc3** d6 8 Bd2 (cf.
Game No.12), and now Keres
considers that Black could have
gained the better chances by 8 ...
Nc6! 9 0-0-0 Bg4.

7 ...	**fxg3**

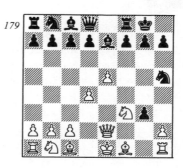

179

Three continuations for White
deserve consideration: **8 hxg3**
(15.41), 8 Nc3 (15.42) and **8 Qg2**
(15.43).

15.41

8 hxg3	

White sacrifices the exchange,
which is a risky way of conducting
the attack. Practice has shown that
in this case Black has a reliable
method of defence.

8 ...	**Nxg3**
9 Qh2	**Nxh1**
10 Bd3	**f5!**

The only move, but good enough.
10 ... h6? loses to 11 Bxh6!, while
on 10 ... g6 White advantageously
continues 11 Qh6 or 11 Bh6.

11 Bc4+

On **11 exf6** g6! 12 Bxg6 (after the
immediate *12 Ng5 h5 13 Bxg6
Bxf6!*, Black, according to
Alekhine, has a decisive advantage)
12 ... hxg6 13 Ng5 Black replies 13
... Bb4+ 14 c3 Re8+ 15 Kd1 Qxf6,

obtaining a clear advantage.

Bronstein recommends **11 Nc3!?**

11 ...	**Kh8**
12 Nc3	**b5!**

This move is significantly stronger than Bhend's recommendation of 12 ... d6 13 Bf4 Nc6, since after 14 Ke2 White retains certain threats.

13 Nxb5	**d5**

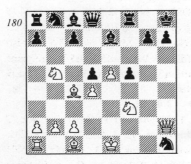

E.C.O. correctly points out that after 14 exd6 cxd6 15 Bd5 Bd7! Black has a clear advantage.

15.42

8 Nc3

This move leads to double-edged

play.

8 ...	**d5**

On **8 ... Bh4** White advantageously continues 9 hxg3!, and after 9 ... Bxg3+ (or *9 ... Nxg3 10 Qh2 Nxh1 11 Nxh4*) 10 Kd1 Nf4 11 Qe4 Ng6 12 Qg4 Bf2 13 Qh5 gains a very strong attack.

9 Qg2

Also to be considered is **9 Bg2** Nc6 10 Be3 Bg4 11 0-0-0, with a very sharp game.

9 Be3 is weaker, in view of 9 ... f5! 10 0-0-0 f4, with a solid position for Black, while Keres-Alekhine (Salzburg 1942) went **9 Bd2** Nc6 10 0-0-0 Bg4 11 Be3 f6!, again with the better chances for Black.

9 ...	**Bg4**
10 hxg3	**Nc6**
11 Bd3	

White achieves nothing by the tempting 11 Nh2, in view of 11 ... Qd7! 12 Be3 Rad8.

11 ...	**g6**
12 Bh6	

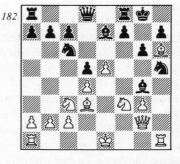

For the sacrificed pawn White has

sufficient compensation.

15.43

8	Qg2	d6
9	hxg3	Bg4

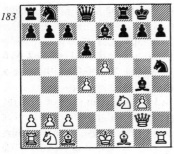
183

10 Nh2

Spielmann's move, which is considered strongest.

Randviir-Tolush (Tallinn 1945) went **10 Be3**, but after 10 ... Nc6 11 Nc3 dxe5 12 d5 Nb4 13 Nxe5 Qc8 14 Kd2 Qf5! (this move would also have followed on *14 a3*) this led to a won position for Black.

10 Bd3 deserves consideration, and now:

a) 10 ... Nc6 11 Nh2 Bd7 12 Nf3 Bg4, Emami-Birman—Ratjen (Hamburg 1975), and White could have forced a draw by repetition of moves.

b) 10 ... dxe5 11 Nxe5 Qxd4 12 Qe4 Qxe4 13 Bxe4 Nxg3! (*13 ... f5?* is not so good, since after *14 Bxb7 Nxg3 15 Bxa8* White has the advantage) is considered by Bhend to give Black the advantage. How-

ever, after 14 Bxh7+ Kh8 15 Rh2 Nh5 (but not *15 ... Bh5 16 Bg6!*, with advantage to White) 16 Bd3! Bd6 17 Nxg4 Bxh2 18 Nxh2 a position is reached with chances for both sides.

10 ... **Nxg3!**

The only way. After 10 ... Qc8 11 Nxg4 Qxg4 12 Be2 Qxg3+ 13 Qf2! Qxf2+ 14 Kxf2 Nc6 (*14 ... g6 15 Bxh5 gxh5 16 Bh6*, or *14 ... dxe5 15 dxe5 Bc5+ 16 Kg2 Nc6 17 Rxh5* also favours White) 15 Rxh5 White gains the advantage (Nei-Bannik, Rostov 1952).

11 Rg1

11 Nxg4 Nxh1 12 Qxh1 dxe5 (or *12 ... Bh4+ 13 Kd1 Nc6*) 13 Bd3 is weak in view of 13 ... Bh4+ 14 Kd1 Nc6 15 Be3 e4! 16 Qxe4 f5, when Black wins (Gusev-Sherbakov, Rostov 1949).

11 ... **Bf5**

According to analysis by Rozenfeld, **11 ... Bh5** 12 Bf4 Nf5 13 Bd3, **11 ... Bc8** 12 Bf4 Nf5 13 Bd3 g6 14 Ng4, and **11 ... h5** 12 Nxg4 hxg4 13 Bf4 followed by 14 Qxg4 all allow White a strong attack.

12 Nf3

In Wade-Alexander (London 1951) after 12 Bf4 Be4! 13 Nf3 Nh5 Black beat off the opponent's attack.

12 ... **Nh5**
13 Rh1 **Bg6**

Diagram 184

In this critical position White has active play for the two sacrificed

184

pawns. Keres recommends 14 Be2 or 14 Be3, while Bhend advises 14 Nc3.

These continuations require practical testing.

It can be concluded that the Schallopp Defence leads to a complicated, double-edged game.

Game No. 12
Spielmann-Reti
Abbazia 1912
1 e4 e5 2 f4 exf4 3 Nf3 Nf6 4 Nc3

At that time it was difficult to know whether to give preference to this move or to 4 e5. From the viewpoint of modern theory, the move chosen by White allows the counterblow 4 ... d5, after which Black can successfully battle for equality. Regarding 4 e5, see the following game.

4 ... d5 5 e5

5 exd5 Nxd5 6 Nxd5 Qxd5 7 d4 Be7 leads to a position considered in section 16.121.

5 ... Ne4

As is shown in the analysis, 5 ...

Nh5 is sounder.

6 Be2

In 1912 Spielmann could not yet have known that only 6 d3 gives White a good game.

6 ... Nc6

Black should definitely have continued 6 ... g5!, threatening 7 ... g4, and only after 7 0-0 have played 7 ... Nc6, as in Spielmann-Bogoljubov (Berlin 1919). Now White gains the opportunity to drive off the centralized enemy knight.

7 d3 Nxc3 8 bxc3 g5

As will subsequently become apparent, ... g7-g5 does not now have the same force.

9 0-0 Rg8

A hasty move. Black prematurely aims for a counter-attack, instead of thinking about the development of his forces and the consolidation of his position.

10 d4 g4 11 Ne1 f3 12 Bd3 Qh4 13 Bf4!

Black's premature attack has reached an impasse. All White's pieces are excellently developed.

13 ... fxg2 14 Nxg2 Qh5 15 Rb1 Nd8

see diagram 185

All Black's pieces, with the exception of his queen, are on the back rank, which allows Spielmann to seize the initiative.

16 c4 Be6 17 Ne3 dxc4 18 Be4 c6 19 d5!

19 Rxb7 would have been answered

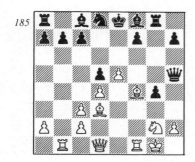

185

not by 19 ... Nxb7, but by 19 ... Bh6!, with counter-play for Black.

19 ... Bc5

After 19 ... cxd5 20 Nxd5 Bxd5 21 Qxd5 Black would have been in a critical position. With the move played he sacrifices a piece, aiming to seize the initiative, but this is clearly insufficient.

20 Kh1!

The simplest. White is not tempted into accepting the sacrifice, but prepares to be the first to land a decisive blow against the opposing king, which is caught in the centre.

20 ... Bxe3 21 dxe6!

This is the point! Now Black is helpless.

21 ... Nxe6 22 Bxe3

As a result White has won a piece, while retaining numerous threats. The remainder is simple.

22 ... Qxe5 23 Bxh7 Rh8 24 Rxf7!

A spectacular concluding stroke.

24 ... Rd8

Obviously, 24 ... Kxf7 is decisively met by 25 Qd7+ and 26 Rf1+.

25 Qxg4 Qxe3

If 25 ... Kxf7, then 26 Rxb7+.

26 Bg6! Resigns.

Game No.13
Basman-Griffiths

Bognor Regis 1968

1 e4 e5 2 f4 exf4 3 Nf3 Nf6 4 e5 Nh5 5 Qe2

This relatively new continuation of Keres prevents Black's freeing advance ... d7-d5.

5 ... Be7 6 d4 0-0 7 Nc3

This move was first played in the present game. White aims to castle Q-side as quickly as possible.

7 ... d6

7 ... d5 8 g3 fxg3 leads to a position from Keres-Alekhine (Salzburg 1942), examined on p. 146.

8 Bd2 dxe5

As is shown in the analysis, the strongest continuation is 8 ... Nc6! 9 0-0-0 Bg4, with the better chances for Black.

9 dxe5 Bh4+?

A fundamental error. 9 ... Be6 would have given Black a roughly equal game.

10 g3 fxg3 11 0-0-0 Bd7 12 hxg3 Nxg3 13 Qh2!

see diagram 186

White has sacrificed two pawns, one after the other, and now offers also the exchange, obtaining in return a very strong attack.

13 ... Nxh1 14 Nxh4 Bg4 15 Bd3!

186

By sacrificing a second exchange, White creates decisive threats against the hostile king.

15 ... Bxd1 16 Nf5!

White is a rook and the exchange down, but his last, 'quiet' move, although obvious, demonstrates that it is time for Black to resign.

16 ... Qxd3

Black has no defence. On 16 ... g6 there would have followed 17 Qh6 gxf5 18 Bxf5, with mate in a few moves.

17 cxd3 Bg4 18 Nh6+ gxh6 19 Qxh6 Nd7 20 Nd5 Rae8 21 Nf6+ Resigns.

16 Modern Defence

1 e4	e5
2 f4	exf4
3 Nf3	d5

Almost all the defences examined earlier have the common idea of retaining the gambit pawn. The aim of the present system is radically different: to return the pawn, hinder the creation of White's centre, and aim for rapid development.

4 exd5

This move is necessary, since after 4 e5? g5 5 h3 Nh6 6 d4 Nf5 Black retains his extra pawn with the better position (Gunsberg-Pillsbury, Vienna 1903).

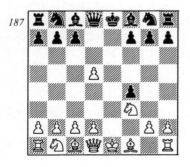

Here Black has various replies. In the main we will examine the most popular move **4 ... Nf6 (16.1)**, and also **4 ... Bd6 (16.2)**.

Other continuations are also played:

a) 4 ... Qxd5. After this White's initiative develops without any hindrance. There can follow 5 Nc3 Qe6+ 6 Be2 (also good is the old move *6 Kf2*, with the threat of *7 Bb5+* and *8 Re1*) 6 ... Bd6 7 0-0 Ne7 8 d4 0-0 9 Ng5, with an excellent game for White (Solntsev-Kamishov, Moscow 1946).

b) 4 ... Be7 (on *4 ... g5?* there follows *5 Qe2+ !*) 5 Bb5+ c6 6 dxc6 bxc6 7 Bc4 Bh4+ 8 Kf1! (in the well known game Morphy-Lichtenhein, New York 1857, White played the risky *8 g3?! fxg3 9 0-0*, after which Black had the strong reply *9 ... Bh3!*) 8 ... Bf6 9 d4, with advantage to White.

c) 4 ... c6 5 d4 Bd6 (after *5 ... cxd5* White gains slightly the better position by *6 Bxf4 Nf6 7 Bd3 Bd6 8*

Qe2+ Be6 9 Bxd6 Qxd6 10 0-0 0-0 11 Nbd2 Nbd7 12 c3) 6 dxc6 Nxc6 7 Bd3 Nf6 (Muchnik-Bakulin, Moscow 1967), and now by 8 Qe2+! White could have gained some advantage.

16.1

4 ...   Nf6

White now has various possible replies: **5 c4 (16.11)**, **5 Nc3 (16.12)**, **5 Bc4 (16.13)** and **5 Bb5+ (16.14)**.

After **5 Be2** a position is reached from the Petroff Gambit (p. 27).

16.11

5 c4

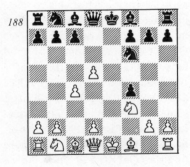

5 ...   c6

The most popular reply.

5 ... b5 is best met by 6 Nc3! (*6 d4 Bb4+! 7 Nc3 0-0 8 Bxf4 Re8+ 9 Be2 bxc4 10 0-0 Bxc3 11 bxc3 Nxd5*, Kramer-Euwe, Leeuwarden 1940, leads to a position which is more comfortable for Black) 6 ... bxc4 7 Bxc4 Bd6 8 d4 Nbd7 (Sämisch-Thelen, Prague 1943), and after 9

0-0! 0-0 10 Ne5 White's position is preferable.

6 d4

6 dxc6 Nxc6 7 d4 is not good, since by 7 ... Bg4 8 d5 Bxf3 9 Qxf3 Nd4 10 Qd3 Bc5 and 11 ... 0-0 Black gains a very strong attack.

6 Nc3! is stronger, and now:

a) 6 ... Be7 7 dxc6! Nxc6 8 d4 0-0 9 Be2 Bg4 10 d5 Bxf3 11 gxf3 Ne5 12 Bxf4, with the better game for White, Basman-Balchan, Dresden 1969.

b) 6 ... cxd5 (this looks sounder) 7 cxd5 Bd6 (on *7 ... Nxd5* White advantageously continues *8 Qb3* or *8 Qe2+*, when Black cannot reply *8 ... Be7?* because of *9 Qb5+*) 8 Bb5+ Nbd7 9 Qe2+ Qe7 10 Qxe7+ Kxe7 11 0-0 Rd8 12 Bc4! Nb6 13 b3 a6 (if *13 ... Bc5+ 14 d4 Bb4, then 15 d6+!*) 14 Bb2 Kf8, with roughly equal chances (Lacis-Makarov, corr. 1971).

6 ...   Bb4+

Weaker is **6 ... cxd5** 7 c5!, and now:

a) The plan of undermining White's pawns by **7 ... b6** 8 b4 a5 leads after 9 Ne5 Bd7 10 Nxd7 Qxd7 11 Nc3 axb4 12 Bb5 Nc6 13 Na4 bxc5 14 Qe2+ Ne4 15 Nb6 to an advantage for White (Litvin-Bruch, corr. 1966).

b) **7 ... Be7** 8 Bxf4 0-0 9 Nc3 Nc6 (as shown by Keres-Schmidt, Salzburg 1942, the undermining plan *9 ... b6* does not work at the present moment, in view of *10 b4 a5 11 Na4 Nfd7 12 Bb5*, with advantage to White) 10 Bb5 Ne4! (better than *10 ... Nh5 11 Be3*, when White has a good game, Johanessen-Jimenez, Leipzig 1960) 11 0-0 Bg4.

Tolush-Averbakh (Leningrad 1959) now continued 12 Qa4?, and after 12 ... Bxf3 13 gxf3 Ng5 14 Bg3 Ne6 Black firmly seized the initiative. White should have played 12 Bxc6! bxc6 13 Qa4, maintaining the balance.

7 Nc3   cxd5
8 Bxf4

After 8 Bd3 Black gains the better chances by 8 ... dxc4 9 Bxc4 Nd5 (Lujk-Pruun, Tallinn 1949).

8 ...   0-0
9 Bd3

If White avoids the main line by 9 Be2 dxc4 10 0-0, Black gains the advantage by 10 ... Bxc3 11 bxc3 Be6.

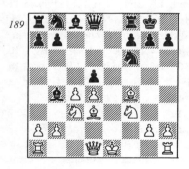

189

9 ...   dxc4

On 9 ... Nc6 10 0-0 Bg4 White has the strong rejoinder 11 a3! dxc4 12

Bxc4 Ba5 13 d5!, and if 13 ... Bb6+ 14 Kh1 Nd4, then 15 Na4! Bxf3 16 gxf3 Rc8 17 Nxb6 Qxb6 18 Rc1, when White's position is preferable (Chepukaitis-Zhukovitsky, Baku 1956).

In the event of **9 ... Re8+** White has a choice of two continuations:
a) 10 Ne5 Be6! (Sämisch-Schmidt, Prague 1943, went *10 ... dxc4 11 Bxc4 Be6 12 Bxe6! Rxe6 13 0-0 Bxc3 14 bxc3 Nc6 15 Qb3 b6*, and now by *16 Nxc6! Rxc6 17 Bg5* White could have gained some initiative) 11 0-0 dxc4 12 Bxc4 Bxc4 13 Nxc4 Nc6 14 a3 Bxc3 15 bxc3.

This variation was successfully employed for a number of years by Heuer, but in 1966 A.Zaitsev in a game against him played 15 ... Qd5!, and after 16 Ne3 Qe4 17 Qf3 Rac8 Black had the better prospects.
b) 10 Be5! Nc6! 11 0-0 Nxe5 12 Nxe5 (on *12 dxe5* Black should reply *12 ... dxc4!*) 12 ... dxc4 13 Bxc4 Be6, and theory considers the chances to be equal.

On 14 Qd3 Black should play 14 ... Bxc4, but not 14 ... Qb6?, in view of 15 Bxe6 Rxe6 16 Rxf6!, with advantage to White (Kirinnis-Yumetal, corr. 1966).

10 Bxc4   Nd5
see diagram 190

In this critical position Black's chances are to be preferred. **11 Bg5?**, for example, loses to 11 ... Nxc3! 12 bxc3 Bxc3+ and 13 ...

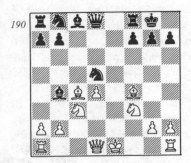

190

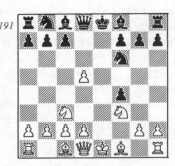

191

Qc7.

Obukhovsky-Manovsky (Moscow 1960) went **11 Bd2** Bxc3 (Zak considers that *11 ... Nb6 12 Be2 Nc6* or *12 Bb3 Re8+ 13 Ne5 Be6* also favours Black) 12 bxc3 Re8+ 13 Ne5, and now by 13 ... Rxe5+! 14 dxe5 Qh4+ Black could have won immediately.

White should continue **11 Bxd5** Qxd5 12 0-0 Bxc3 13 bxc3, although even in this case Black retains the better prospects by 13 ... Nc6 or 13 ... Be6!

16.12

    5 Nc3

Now Black has several sound systems of defence, which assure him of a good game.

It should be mentioned that this same position can also arise in the Schallopp Defence after 3 ... Nf6 4 Nc3 d5 5 exd5.

see diagram 191

Here two main continuations will be considered: **5 ... Nxd5 (16.121)**

and **5 ... Bd6 (16.122).**

Other alternatives for Black:

a) 5 ... Bb4 6 Bc4 (after *6 Bb5+ c6 7 dxc6 0-0!* Black gains good attacking chances) 6 ... 0-0 7 0-0 c6! 8 dxc6 Nxc6 9 d4 Bxc3 10 bxc3 Qc7, with roughly equal chances (Cortlever-Prins, Leiwarden 1940).

b) 5 ... c6 6 d4 Bd6! (after *6 ... Nxd5 7 Nxd5 Qxd5 8 c4 Qe4+ 9 Kf2* White has the advantage, Reti-Grünfeld, Kasau 1918), and now:

7 Qe2+ Qe7 8 Qxe7+ Kxe7, when both 9 Ne5 Nxd5 10 Nxd5+ cxd5 11 Bxf4 f6 12 Nd3 Nc6 13 0-0-0 Bxf4+ 14 Nxf4 Kd6 (Tenenbaum-Estrin, Moscow 1959), and 9 Bc4 Bf5! 10 0-0 Bxc2 11 Ne5 b5! 12 Bb3 Bxb3 13 axb3 b4 14 Ne2 Nxd5 lead to a roughly equal game (Estrin).

7 Be2 Nxd5 8 0-0! (after *8 Nxd5? cxd5 9 0-0 Nc6 10 Ne1 Qc7 11 c3 g5!*, Antoshin-Estrin, Moscow 1953, Black gained a clear advantage, having retained his extra pawn) 8 ... 0-0 9 Nxd5 cxd5 10 Ne5 (Balashov-Sydor, Cienfuegos 1975), and now 10 ... f6! 11 Nd3 g5 would have led to a sharp game with chances for both sides.

16.121

5 ...	Nxd5
6 Nxd5	

Other replies have also been made in tournament practice:

a) 6 Be2 Nxc3 7 bxc3 Bd6 8 d4 0-0 9 0-0 Nc6 10 c4 b6, and Black retains his extra pawn with a good position (Spielmann-Nyholm, Abbazia 1912).

b) 6 Bc4 Nxc3 7 bxc3 Bd6 8 0-0 0-0 9 d4 Bg4 10 Rb1 Nd7, with a solid position for Black, who has retained his pawn (Opocensky-Hromadka, Baden 1914).

c) 6 Bb5+ c6 7 Qe2+ Be6 8 Bc4, and after 8 ... Be7 9 Nxd5 cxd5 10 Bb5+ Nc6 Black's position is preferable (Rubinstein-Tarrasch, Meran 1924).

d) 6 Qe2+, and after 6 ... Be7 7 Qe4 White regains his pawn, with roughly equal chances.

6 ...	Qxd5
7 d4	

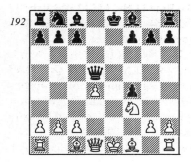

The basic position of the variation in question.

7 ...	Be7!

This subtle move, found by Mieses (1903) and improved by Yates (1922) is the strongest. Other continuations are less promising for Black, for example:

a) 7 ... Bd6 8 c4 Qe6+ (*8 ... Qe4+* leads to advantage for White after *9 Kf2 Bf5 10 c5 Be7 11 Bb5+ c6 12 Bc4*, Schlechter-Mieses, Vienna 1903) 9 Kf2 c5 10 Bd3 Qh6 11 Re1+ Kf8 12 Qe2 Bd7 13 b4!? with a good game for White (Reti-Nyholm, Baden 1914).

b) 7 ... Bg4 8 Bxf4 Nc6 9 Bxc7! Kd7 (also insufficient is *9 ... Bxf3 10 Qxf3 Qxf3 11 gxf3 Rc8 12 Bf4 Nxd4 13 0-0-0!*, with advantage to White, Stoltz-Rellstab, Swinemünde 1932) 10 Bg3 Re8+ 11 Kf2 Kc8 12 c3 h5 13 Qb3 Qf5, and now both **14 Qb5** Qc2 15 Kg1! (Spielmann-Eliskases, Semmering 1937), and **14 Bb5!** Re6 15 Rae1 (Barle-Mariotti, Portoroz 1975) give White a clear advantage.

c) Also after **7 ... g5?** 8 c4 Bb4+ 9 Kf2 Qd8, by continuing 10 c5! c6 11 Bc4 Be6 (if *11 ... 0-0*, then *12 h4! g4 13 Ne5*, with a clear advantage) 12 Bxe6 fxe6 13 Qb3 Na6 14 Qxe6+ Qe7 15 Nxg5 White gains a won position (Provotorov-Svirin, Moscow 1980).

8 c4

8 Bxf4? is of course bad because of 8 ... Qe4+, while the quiet **8 Bd3**

allows Black by 8 ... g5! to retain his pawn with a good position. For example:

a) 9 Qe2 Bf5! 10 Bxf5 Qxf5 11 g4 Qd7! 12 Bd2 Nc6 13 0-0-0 0-0-0 (Rubinstein-Yates, Hastings 1922).

b) 9 c4 Qe6+ 10 Kf2 0-0 11 Re1 Qf6 12 Bc2 Nc6! 13 Qd3 Qh6 14 d5 Bc5+, and in both cases Black gains the advantage.

193

8 ...   Qe4+

8 ... Qd6 is weaker, in view of 9 c5! (Stoltz's recommendation of *9 Qe2* is bad because of *9 ... Bg4! 10 Qe4 Bxf3 11 gxf3 Nc6*, when Black has the advantage) 9 ... Qf6 10 Qd2! g5 11 b4 and 12 Bb2, after which White develops strong pressure along the long diagonal (*E.C.O.*).

8 ... Qa5+!? is interesting, and now:

a) 9 Bd2 Bb4 10 Bd3 Nc6 11 Qe2+, with great complications (Tennebaum—Pavlov, Moscow 1961).

b) 9 Kf2 Nc6 10 Bxf4 Bg4 11 d5 0-0-0 12 Be2 Qb6+ 13 Kf1 Rhe8, with a good game for Black

(McKay-Macles, Nice 1974).

9 Be2!

The best move.

9 Kf2, suggested by Spielmann in his time, affords Black good prospects after 9 ... Bf5, e.g.:

a) 10 c5 Nc6! 11 Bc4 (on *11 Bb5* there follows *11 ... Qd5!*) 11 ... 0-0-0 12 Re1 Qc2+ 13 Qxc2 Bxc2 14 Bxf4 Bf6, and Black's position is preferable (Keres).

b) 10 Qa4+ Nc6 11 Bd2 0-0-0 12 Re1 Qc2 13 Qxc2 Bxc2 14 Bxf4 Rhe8 15 d5. This position is evaluated by *E.C.O.* as 'unclear', but we think that after the obvious 15 ... Bc5+ 16 Kg3 Nd4! Black has a clear advantage.

c) 10 Be2 Nc6 11 Re1 0-0-0 12 Bf1 Qc2 13 Qxc2 Bxc2 14 Bxf4 (Novikov-Borisenko, Leningrad 1956), and now by 14 ... Rhe8! Black could have gained a definite advantage.

9 ...	Nc6
10 0-0	Bf5
11 Re1	0-0-0

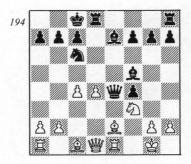

194

This position was reached in Spielmann—Milner-Barry (Margate 1938), which continued **12 Bf1** Qc2 13 Qxc2 Bxc2 14 Bxf4 Rhe8 15 d5 Bc5+ 16 Kh1 Nb4 17 a3, when the game was level.

16.122

5 ...   **Bd6**

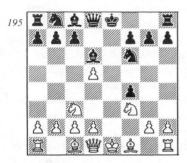

195

6 Bc4

This is considered best.

In Aurbach-Duras (Abbazia 1912) White played the passive **6 Be2**, and after 6 ... 0-0 7 0-0 Nbd7 8 d4 Nb6 9 Ne5 Nbxd5 Black seized the initiative.

Also insufficient is **6 Bb5+** c6 7 dxc6, and now:

a) 7 ... bxc6 8 Bc4 ·(not *8 Qe2+? Kd7!*) 8 ... 0-0 9 0-0 Nbd7 10 d4 Nb6 11 Bd3 Nbd5, with a slight advantage for Black (Lutikov-Bannik, Moscow 1955).

b) 7 ... Nxc6! (more energetic) 8 0-0 0-0 9 d4 Qb6! 10 Kh1 Bg4 11 Bxc6 Qxc6 12 Qd3 Rad8 13 Bd2 g6, and Black's position is clearly better

(Westerinen-Boey, Skopje 1972).

6 Qe2+ Qe7 7 Qxe7+ Kxe7 8 Bc4, which has not yet occurred in tournament practice, deserves consideration.

6 ...   0-0
7 0-0   c6

Examples from practice show that this move is necessary.

Spielmann-Fahrni (Baden 1914) went 7 ... **Nbd7**, but after 8 d4 Nb6 9 Bb3 Bg4 10 Qd3 a5 11 a3 a4 12 Ba2 Bxf3 13 Qxf3 White gained the advantage.

After 7 ... **Bg4**, Heuer-Uusi (Tallinn 1964) continued 8 d4 Nbd7 9 Qd3 Bh5 (*9 ... Nb6 10 Bb3* leads to a position from the previous game) 10 Ng5 Bg6 11 Qh3 h6 12 Ne6!? fxe6 13 dxe6 Kh8 14 exd7 Nxd7, and now White should have continued 15 Bd3!, with the better prospects.

8 d4   **cxd5**

It is interesting to note that, if Black plays here **8 ... Bg4**, then after 9 Qd3 we reach, by transposition, a position which is mentioned back in Jaenisch's opening guide *Novy Analis* (1842). Lange-Metger (Leipzig 1868) then continued 9 ... Re8 10 Ne5! Bxe5 11 dxe5 Nxd5, after which White could have gained a clear advantage by 12 Bxf4! Nxf4 13 Bxf7+.

8 ... b5? 9 Bd3 cxd5 10 Nxb5 Nc6 11 Nxd6 Qxd6 (Bulkovstein-Kupfer, St Petersburg 1903) is dubious, since after 12 Ne5! Nxe5 13 Bxf4! White could have gained a clear advantage.

9 Nxd5   Be6
10 Nxf6+   Qxf6

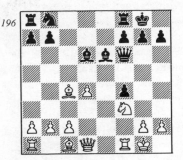

This position was reached in Bronstein-Matanović (Lvov 1962), which after **11 Bxe6** fxe6 12 Ne5 Bxe5 13 dxe5 Qxe5 14 Bxf4 ended in a draw.

E.C.O. recommends **11 Be2!**, preparing the advance of the Q-side pawns, which gives White chances of seizing the initiative.

16.13

5 Bc4

This move, which was recommended formerly by Leonhardt, is better than those considered above. In recent times it has been employed in a number of games by Spassky and Bronstein.

5 ...   Nxd5

5 ... Bd6 6 Nc3 leads to the variation considered above.

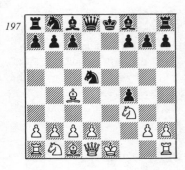

6 0-0

In this position Leonhardt used to continue **6 Bxd5** Qxd5 7 Nc3, which is considered in the chapter on the Bishop's Gambit, section 5.3 (cf. the note to White's 5th move).

6 ...   Be7

Here **6 ... Be6** can be played, often leading merely to a transposition of moves. In Bronstein-Zaitsev (Moscow 1969), White chose 7 Bb3, and after 7 ... Bd6 8 c4 Ne7 9 d4 Ng6 10 c5 Be7 11 Bxe6 fxe6 12 Re1 0-0 13 Rxe6 Keres considers that Black should have played 13 ... Nc6 or 13 ... Qd5, with an equal game. The move in fact chosen, 13 ... Bxc5?, allowed White by 14 Qb3! Bxd4+ 15 Nxd4 Qxd4+ 16 Be3! to gain a spectacular victory.

7 d4

7 Bb3 should also be considered. After **7 Bxd5** Qxd5 8 Nc3 Black does best to reply 8 ... Qd8, while on the immediate **7 Nc3** he should play 7 ... Nb6!

7 ...   Be6

Spassky-Averbakh (Moscow 1955) went 7 ... c6 8 Nc3 0-0 9 Ne5 Be6 10 Bxf4 f6 11 Bxd5 cxd5 12 Nd3, and after 12 ... Bf7? 13 Qg4! Kh8 14 Bxb8! Rxb8 15 Rae1 Re8 16 Ne5! Rf8 17 Nxf7+ Rxf7 18 Qe6 White gained a won position. Black should have played 12 ... Nc6!, with roughly equal chances.

8 Qe2

Less promising is 8 Bxd5 Bxd5 9 Bxf4, which after 9 ... 0-0 10 Nc3 c5! leads to an equal game (Bronstein-Lengyel, Sarajevo 1972).

8 ...   0-0

9 Nc3

In Spassky-Bannik (Rostov 1960) White chose 9 Bb3, but after 9 ... Bf6 (not *9 ... g5 10 c4 Nb6 11 d5*, with advantage to White) 10 c4 Ne3 11 Bxe3 fxe3 12 Qxe3 c5 he did not achieve anything.

9 ...   c6

9 ... Nxc3 10 bxc3 Bxc4 11 Qxc4 Bd6 is weaker, in view of 12 Qb5 b6 13 Ng5! with good prospects for White.

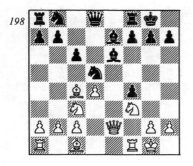

198

The critical position of the variation in question.

Spassky against Pytel (Nice 1974) continued here **10 Nxd5**, and after **10 ... cxd5** 11 Bd3 Nc6 12 Bxf4 Nb4 13 Bb5 a6 14 Ba4 b5 15 Bb3 Nc6 16 c3 b4 17 Rae1 gained the advantage.

Black should have played **10 ... Bxd5** 11 Bxd5 cxd5 12 Bxf4 Nc6, when the chances are roughly equal.

16.14

5 Bb5+

The most interesting continuation.

5 ...   c6

At the present time this move is the most popular.

Less good is **5 ... Bd7** (on *5 ... Nbd7 E.C.O.* recommends *6 c4! a6 7 Bxd7+!* and *8 0-0* with a clear advantage to White), with two possibilities:

a) 6 Bc4 Bd6 (*6 ... Qe7+* is weaker, in view of *7 Be2! Nxd5 8 0-0 Nc6 9 c4 Nb6 10 d4 g5*, Cheremisin-Ivanov, Moscow 1956, *11 Nc3!*, and White gains the advantage) 7 0-0 0-0, with an equal game.

b) 6 Bxd7+! Nbxd7 (after *6 ... Qxd7 7 c4! c6 8 Ne5* White seizes the initiative) 7 0-0 Nxd5 8 c4, followed by 9 Re1+ and 10 Qe2, with the better chances for White.

6 dxc6

see diagram 199

Now Black must choose between two continuations: **6 ... bxc6 (16.141)** and **6 ... Nxc6 (16.142)**.

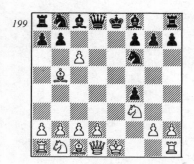

199

16.141

　　6 ...　　　　　　**bxc6**
　　7 **Bc4**

Also good is **7 Be2** Bd6 8 d4 0-0 9 c4 Re8 10 Nc3 Nbd7 (on *10 ... Ng4* White can continue *11 c5 Bc7 12 d5!* or *11 0-0 Ne3 12 Bxe3 Rxe3 13 c5 Bc7 14 d5*, in both cases gaining the advantage) 11 c5! Bc7 12 0-0, when Black is in difficulties.

The move recommended by Thimann, **12 ... Nd5**, gets him nowhere after 13 Nxd5 cxd5 14 Bb5. Lutikov-Kholmov (Moscow 1969) went instead **12 ... Nf8** 13 Ne5! Bxe5 14 dxe5 N6d7 15 b4 a5 16 Ne4 Rxe5 17 Nd6 Rd5, and now by 18 Qa4! White could have secured a clear advantage.

　　7 ...　　　　　　**Nd5**

This continuation first occurred in Bronstein-Botvinnik (Moscow 1952), although it had been prepared by Botvinnik back in 1941 before the Match-Tournament for the title of Absolute USSR Champion.

The alternative **7 ... Bd6** affords White the better chances after 8 Qe2+!, for example:

a) 8 ... Qe7 9 Qxe7+ Kxe7 (or *9 ... Bxe7 10 d4 Nh5 11 0-0 Ba6*, and after *12 Ne5* White gained the advantage, Rabinovich-Cohn, Karlsbad 1911), when there can follow: **10 d4** Bf5 11 Ne5! Bxe5 12 dxe5 Nd5 13 Bxd5 cxd5 14 Nc3 (Nimzowitsch-Schweinburg, 1934), or **10 0-0** Be6 11 Re1 Nbd7 12 d4 Rhe8 13 Bxe6 fxe6 14 Nbd2 h6 15 Nc4 (Bhend-Barcza, Zurich 1959), in both cases with a clear advantage to White.

b) 8 ... Kf8 (recommended by Furman) 9 d4 Bg4 10 0-0 Nbd7 11 Bb3! (an important improvement, since after *11 Nc3* Black gains the better game, according to Zak, by *11 ... Qc7, 12 ... Re8* and *13 ... g5*) 11 ... Qc7 12 Na3 Re8 13 Qd3 g5 14 Nc4! Bxf3 15 Qxf3 Rg8 16 Nxd6 Qxd6 17 c3 Nd5 18 Bd2 N7f6 19 Rae1, with clearly the better game for White (Glazkov-Poromsnyuk, Moscow 1972).

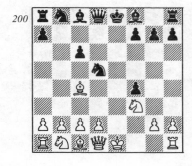

200

8 0-0

Spassky's move.

Bronstein-Botvinnik (Moscow 1952) went **8 d4** Bd6 9 0-0 0-0 10 Nc3 Nxc3 11 bxc3, and after 11 ... Bg4 12 Qd3 Nd7, White, instead of the reckless 13 g3?!, should have continued 13 Bd2 and 14 Rae1, with an equal game.

A year later Lilienthal against Bronstein improved Black's play by 11 ... Nd7, and after 12 Bd3 c5 13 Nd2 cxd4 14 cxd4 Nf6 15 Ne4 Bg4! Black firmly seized the initiative, since on 16 Nxf6+ Qxf6 17 Qxg4 there would have followed 17 ... Qxd4+.

In the diagram position Muchnik's move **8 Nc3** also deserves consideration. There can follow:

a) 8 ... Be6 (on *8 ... Be7, 9 d4!* is good) 9 Bb3 (also possible is *9 Qe2 Be7 10 0-0 0-0 11 d4 Nxc3 12 bxc3 Bxc4 13 Qxc4 Bd6 14 Ne5*, with the initiative for White) 9 ... Bd6 10 Ne4 Bc7 11 Nc5 Bg4 12 Qe2+, and if 12 ... Ne7?, then 13 Bxf7+!, with a clear advantage to White (*E.C.O.*).

b) 8 ... Nxc3 9 dxc3! Bd6 (after *9 ... Qxd1+ 10 Kxd1 Bd6* White seizes the initiative by *11 Re1+*) 10 Qd4 0-0 11 Bxf4 Qe7+ 12 Kd2! Rd8 13 Bd3, with an excellent game for White. Krustaln-Endre (corr. 1970) continued 13 ... c5 14 Bxd6 Rxd6 15 Rae1! Be6 16 Qe4, and Black resigned.

8 ...   **Bd6**

On **8 ... Be6** Zak considers that White should continue 9 Bb3 Bd6 10 c4, after which both **10 ... Nb6** 11 d4 Nxc4 12 Qe2 Ne3 13 Bxe3 fxe3 14 Qxe3, and **10 ... Nf6** 11 d4 0-0 (or *11 ... c5 12 d5* followed by *13 Re1+*) 12 c5 Bxb3 13 Qxb3 Bc7 14 Nc3 give him the better chances.

9 Nc3   **Be6**

After 9 ... Nxc3 White prevents Black from castling by the intermediate check 10 Re1+, and after 10 ... Kf8 11 bxc3 Bg4 12 d4 Nd7 13 Qd3 gains better prospects than in the main variation.

10 Ne4

In Holtzfogt-Tzevin (corr. 1965) White played 10 Nxd5, and after 10 ... cxd5 11 Bb5+ Nd7 12 d4 0-0 he should have continued 13 Bxd7! Bxd7 14 Ne5, with a roughly level game.

10 ...   **Bc7**

The other retreat of the bishop, **10 ... Be7**, is weaker, in view of 11 Bb3 Nd7 12 d4, when there can follow **12 ... N7f6** 13 Neg5 Bg4 14 Qd3 Nd7 15 Bxd5 cxd5 16 Bxf4 (Tal-Winter, radio game 1960), or **12 ... 0-0** 13 Qe2 g5 14 c4 N5b6 15 h4 h6 16 hxg5 hxg5 17 Nfxg5! Bxg5 18 Bxf4 (Spassky-Sakharov, Leningrad 1960), in both cases with a decisive attack for White.

see diagram 201

With material equal, White's position is somewhat freer, and he has good chances of developing an

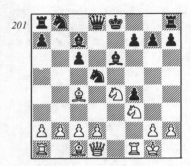

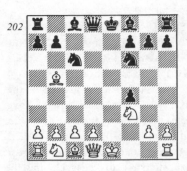

initiative.

In the radio game Tal-Haubt (1960) after **11 Bb3** 0-0 12 d4 Nd7 13 c4 Ne3 14 Bxe3 fxe3 15 Nfg5 Nf6 Black succeeded in neutralizing his opponent's initiative, and a draw was soon agreed.

Also possible, however, is **11 Neg5** 0-0 12 Nxe6 fxe6 13 Qe2 Qf6 14 Re1 Re8 15 Ne5!, with a favourable position for White, whose forces are more harmoniously deployed (Kuznetsov-Zhuravlev, Kalinin 1970).

Therefore the 6 ... bxc6 continuation must be deemed risky for Black.

16.142

6 ...   Nxc6

This move of Grünfeld gives Black more possibilities than 6 ... bxc6.

see diagram 202

7 d4

Orienter-Grünfeld (Vienna 1944), in which this variation first occurred, continued **7 Qe2+** Be7 8 d4 0-0 9 Bxc6 bxc6 10 0-0 Bd6, with a good game for Black.

7 ...   Bd6

7 ... Qa5+ achieves nothing, since after the continuation recommended by Keres, 8 Nc3 Bb4 9 0-0 Bxc3 10 Qe2+ Be6 11 bxc3, White obtains clearly the better chances (Pachman-Vymetal, Prague 1953).

8 Qe2+

After 8 0-0 0-0 9 Na3 (on *9 c3, 9 ... Nd5!* is good, while on *9 Nc3 Qb6!* leads by transposition to a position, favourable to Black, from Westerinen-Boey, considered in section 16.122) 9 ... Bg4 10 Nc4 Bc7 11 Bxc6 bxc6 12 Qd3 Qd5 a roughly equal position is reached (Glazkov-Sinitsin, Moscow 1972).

8 ...   Be6
9 Ng5!

This move was suggested by Glazkov in 1967. Hartston against Spassky (Hastings 1965/66) went 9 Ne5?, when Black sacrificed a pawn by 9 ... 0-0!, and after 10 Bxc6 bxc6 11 Bxf4 Nd5 12 Bg3 f6 13 Nf3 (*13*

Nxc6 is no better, in view of *13 ... Bxg3+ 14 hxg3 Qd6!*) 13 ... Bxg3+ 14 hxg3 Re8 gained a powerful initiative (cf. Game No. 14).

9 ...	0-0
10 Nxe6	fxe6
11 Bxc6	bxc6
12 0-0!	

The most accurate move order. After 12 Qxe6+? Kh8 13 0-0 Black gains a strong attack by 13 ... f3! 14 Rxf3 Re8 (Holtzfogt-Schreiber, corr. 1968/69).

12 ...	Qc7

In Issler-Neutsch (Basel 1970) Black chose 12 ... Nd5 13 Qxe6+ Kh8 14 Nc3 Qc7 (*14 ... Nxc3! 15 bxc3 Qc7* is correct), but after 15 Ne4 Bb4 16 Ng5 h6 17 Qh3 Qe7 18 Nf3 Ne3 19 Ne5 White gained a won position.

13 Qxe6+

13 Nd2 e5 14 dxe5 Bxe5 15 Nf3 Bd6 16 Bd2 Rae8 17 Qc4+ Kh8 18 Rae1 led to an equal game in Gross-Plachetka (Stary Smokovec 1973).

13 ...	Kh8
14 Nd2	Rae8
15 Qh3	

see diagram 203

A double-edged position is reached in which Black has good piece play for the sacrificed pawn.

According to analysis by Thimann, White answers **15 ... Nd5** with 16 Nf3, with good chances of beating off the opponent's attack, both

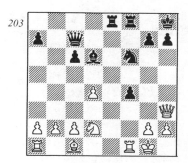

after 16 ... Ne3 17 Bxe3 fxe3 18 Rae1 19 Ng5!, and after 16 ... Rf6 17 Bd2 Rh6 18 Qf5 Ne3 19 Bxe3 fxe3 20 Ne5!

Black does best to continue **15 ... c5**, which after 16 Nc4 Ne4 17 d5 Be5 18 c3 leads to a roughly equal game (Burgi-Parolek, corr 1971). Instead of 18 c3, 18 Nxe5 Qxe5 19 Qd3 is also possible.

The examples given do not, of course, exhaust the possibilities for either side, and the concluding position requires further practical testing.

16.2

4 ...	Bd6
5 d4!	

After other moves Black has little difficulty in attaining a good game, for example:

a) 5 Nc3 Ne7 (Black can also play *5 ... Nf6*, transposing into section 16.122, or *5 ... c6*) 6 d4 0-0 7 Bd3 Nd7 8 0-0, and now:

8 ... h6? 9 Ne4 Nxd5 10 c4 Ne3 11 Bxe3 fxe3 12 c5 Be7 13 Bc2! and 14

Qd3, with a clear advantage for White (cf. Game No. 15, Spassky-Bronstein, Leningrad 1960).

8 ... Ng6 9 Ne4 Nf6 10 Nxd6 Qxd6 11 c4 Bg4, or 8 ... Nf6 9 Ne5 Nexd5 10 Nxd5 Nxd5 11 Bxf4 Nxf4 12 Rxf4 Qg5, which, according to analysis by Spassky, gives Black a roughly equal game.

b) 5 Bc4 Ne7! 6 0-0 0-0 7 d4 Bg4 8 Nc3 c6! 9 dxc6 Nbxc6 10 Nb5 Bb8 11 Be2 a6 12 Na3 Bxf3, with a good game for Black (Smigielsky-Hozler, 1855).

c) 5 Bb5+ c6! 6 dxc6 bxc6 (*6 ... Nxc6 7 d4 Ne7! is also good*) 7 Bc4 (*7 Be2 also deserves consideration*) 7 ... Ne7! 8 0-0 0-0 9 Nc3 Ng6 10 d4, which leads to a double-edged position with roughly equal chances (Smigielsky-Hozler, 1855).

| **5 ...** | **Nf6** |

After 5 ... Ne7 White again plays 6 c4, which after 6 ... b6 7 Bd3 Bg4 8 0-0 Nd7 9 Nc3 gives him the more promising position.

| **6 c4** | **Bg4** |

As long ago as 1853 Urusov recommended answering 6 ... 0-0 with 7 Ne5, gaining the advantage.

| **7 Bd3** | **0-0** |
| **8 0-0** | |

see diagram 204

The resulting position is undoubtedly in favour of White. In Dashevsky-Goloshapov (Moscow 1960) Black incorrectly played **8 ... b6 9 Qc2 c5**, when White should

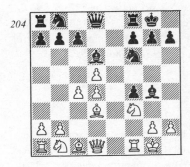

have replied 10 b4!, retaining the advantage.

Game No. 14
Hartston-Spassky
Hastings 1965/66

1 e4 e5 2 f4 exf4 3 Nf3 d5 4 exd5 Nf6 5 Bb5+ c6 6 dxc6 Nxc6

As is shown in the analysis, 6 ... bxc6 is less promising for Black.

7 d4 Bd6 8 Qe2+

Of course, not 8 d5?, in view of the simple 8 ... Nxd5.

8 ... Be6 9 Ne5

In this way White wins a pawn, but comes under a dangerous attack. 9 Ng5 is correct, as shown in the theoretical section.

9 ... 0-0 10 Bxc6 bxc6 11 Bxf4

Of course, not 11 Nxc6 Qb6!

11 ... Nd5 12 Bg3 f6 13 Nf3 Bxg3+ 14 hxg3 Re8

The opening is over. It is clear that for the pawn Black has a powerful

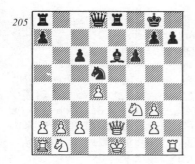

205

initiative. White is seriously behind in development, and has a difficult defensive task.

15 Kf2 Bf5 16 Qc4 Kh8 17 Nc3 Ne3

Black's attack develops unhindered.

18 Qc5 Ng4+ 19 Kg1 Qd7 20 Rf1 Bxc2

Material equality has been re-established, and Black's threats continue to grow.

21 Rh4 Ne3 22 Rc1 g5! 23 Rh6 Bg6 24 Na4 Ng4

Black's pieces have taken up ideal positions; White is helpless.

25 Rh3 Qe6 26 Qc3 Qxa2 27 Nc5 Re3 28 Qd2 Rae8 White resigns.

Game No. 15

Spassky-Bronstein

Leningrad 1960

1 e4 e5 2 f4 exf4 3 Nf3 d5 4 exd5 Bd6

Regarding 4 ... Nf6, see the previous game.

5 Nc3

As is shown in the analysis, the strongest continuation is 5 d4!, and if 5 ... Nf6 or 5 ... Ne7, then 6 c4.

5 ... Ne7

On 5 ... Nf6 White gains a slight advantage by 6 Bc4 0-0 7 0-0 c6 8 d4. In the event of 6 Bb5+ c6 7 dxc6 Nxc6! 8 0-0 0-0 9 d4 Qb6! 10 Kh1 Bg4 Black gains a clearly better position, as is shown by Westerinen-Boey (Skopje 1972).

6 d4 0-0 7 Bd3 Nd7 8 0-0 h6?

A crucial mistake. In this way Black merely weakens the position of his king. As shown by Spassky, he should have played 8 ... Ng6 9 Ne4 Nf6 10 Nxd6 Qxd6 11 c4 Bg4, or 8 ... Nf6 9 Ne5 Nexd5 10 Nxd5 Nxd5 11 Bxf4 Nxf4 12 Rxf4 Qg5, with equal chances.

9 Ne4 Nxd5 10 c4 Ne3 11 Bxe3 fxe3 12 c5 Be7 13 Bc2!

A highly important move, which enables White to build up a strong attack on the enemy king position. The plausible 13 Qe2 Nf6! gives Black adequate play after 14 Qxe3 Nd5, or 14 Nxf6+ Bxf6 15 Qxe3 Re8.

13 ... Re8

Now 13 ... Nf6 no longer works, since by 14 Qd3 White regains his pawn, while retaining an attack.

14 Qd3 e2

see diagram 206

15 Nd6!?

A showy move. Spassky sacrifices a rook and a minor piece, being guided, clearly, by competitive and psychological reasons: the opponent

206

was running very short of time. Simpler and safer was 15 Rf2, which would have consolidated White's advantage without risk.

15 ... Nf8?

The decisive mistake, which gives White the opportunity to carry out a brilliant combination. As shown by Spassky, Black should have played 15 ... Bxd6 16 Qh7+ Kf8 17 cxd6 exf1=Q+ 18 Rxf1 cxd6 19 Qh8+ Ke7 20 Re1+ Ne5 21 Qxg7 Rg8 22 Qxh6 Qb6 23 Kh1 Be6 24 dxe5 d5, with good chances of a successful defence.

16 Nxf7! exf1=Q+ 17 Rxf1 Bf5

On 17 ... Kxf7 White wins brilliantly by 18 Ne5++ Kg8 19 Qh7+!! (nothing is gained by the tempting *19 Rxf8+ Kxf8 20 Qc4*, in view of *20 ... Be6! 21 Qxe6 Qxd4+ 22 Kh1 Qxe5 23 Qxe5 Bf6 24 Qg3 Rad8*, when it is Black who has the initiative) 19 ... Nxh7 20 Bb3+, and mate is inevitable, while after 17 ... Qd5 18 N3e5 Bxc5 he has the decisive 19 Nxh6+! gxh6 (if *19 ... Kh8*, then *20 Rxf8+* and *21 Qh7 mate*) 20 Bb3.

18 Qxf5 Qd7 19 Qf4 Bf6 20 N3e5 Qe7 21 Bb3

Black is now only the exchange up (for a pawn), and his king position is defenceless.

21 ... Bxe5 22 Nxe5+ Kh7

This loses immediately, although after 22 ... Kh8 23 Qf5 g5 24 h4 Kg7 (or *24 ... gxh4 25 Rf4*) 25 hxg5 hxg5 26 Rf3 Black would again have had to admit defeat.

23 Qe4+ Resigns.

Thus the following conclusions may be drawn:

1.   The King's Gambit has recently been enriched by new positional ideas, and has been transformed into a solid opening system.

2.   This ancient gambit emphasizes convincingly the correctness of the tactical approach to the solving of modern opening problems.

3.   If Black plays openly for equality, he risks ending up in an inferior position, whereas if he boldly goes in for double-edged positions he is assured of a good game.

List of Illustrative Games

Index of Main Variations

Bibliography

1. *Novoye Vremya*. Chess section by M.Chigorin in the magazine *Niva*, 1891-1906.
2. C.Bardeleben und J.Mieses *Lehrbuch des Schachspiels*, Leipzig 1894.
3. E.Schmidt *Systematische Anordnung der Schacheröffnungen*, Leipzig 1895.
4. Oskar Cordel *Theorie und Praxis des Schachspiels*, II Band, Potsdam, 1913.
5. Gustaf und Ludvig Collijn *Lärobok i Schack*, Stockholm, 1921.
6. P.R. von Bilguer *Handbuch des Schachspiels* 8.Auflage, Berlin und Leipzig, 1922.
7. Dr.A.Claparede *Die moderne Ablehnung des Königsgambits*, Berlin 1924.
8. *Sovremenny Debyut*, Moscow-Leningrad, 1940.
9. T.D.Harding *Counter-Gambits*, B.C.M., 1973.
10. T.D.Harding *Vienna Opening*, London 1973.
11. R.G.Thimann *King's Gambit*, Nottingham, 1974.
12. A.E.Santasiere *The Vienna Game & Gambit*, Dallas, Texas, 1974.
13. *Encyclopaedia of Chess Openings*, Vol C, Belgrade, 1974.
14. P.Keres *Dreispringerspiel bis Königsgambit*, 5.Auflage, Berlin, 1980.
15. *Shakhmatny Bulletin*, 1955-1980.
16. *Shakhmaty* [*Riga*], 1959-1980.
17. *Informator* Vols 1-28, Belgrade, 1966-1980.
18. H.Harro Dahlgrün *Königsgambit*, Bande 1-4, Hamburg 1977-1980.
19. V.Panov, Y.Estrin *Kurs Debyutov*, 6th edition, Moscow, 1980.